Policymaking in the
Open Economy

EDI Series in Economic Development

EDI Series in Economic Development

Maxwell L. Brown, *Farm Budgets: From Farm Income Analysis to Agricultural Project Analysis.* Johns Hopkins University Press, 1979.

James E. Austin, *Agroindustrial Project Analysis.* 2nd ed. Johns Hopkins University Press, 1992.

William Diamond and V. S. Raghavan, editors, *Aspects of Development Bank Management.* Johns Hopkins University Press, 1982.

J. Price Gittinger, *Economic Analysis of Agricultural Projects.* 2nd ed. Johns Hopkins University Press, 1982.

Gerald M. Meier, editor, *Pricing Policy for Development Management.* Johns Hopkins University Press, 1983.

J. D. Von Pischke, Dale W. Adams, and Gordon Donald, editors, *Rural Financial Markets in Developing Countries.* Johns Hopkins University Press, 1 983.

J. Price Gittinger, *Compounding and Discounting Tables for Project Analysis.* 2nd ed. Johns Hopkins University Press, 1984.

K. C. Sivaramakrishnan and Leslie Green, *Metropolitan Management: The Asian Experience.* Oxford University Press, 1986.

Hans A. Adler, *Economic Appraisal of Transport Projects: A Manual with Case Studies.* Revised and expanded edition. Johns Hopkins University Press, 1987.

Philip H. Coombs and Jacques Hallak, *Cost Analysis in Education: A Tool for Policy and Planning.* Johns Hopkins University Press, 1987.

J. Price Gittinger, Joanne Leslie, and Caroline Hoisington, editors, *Food Policy: Integrating Supply, Distribution, and Consumption.* Johns Hopkins University Press, 1987.

Gabriel J. Roth, *The Private Provision of Public Services.* Oxford University Press, 1987.

Rudiger Dornbusch and F. Leslie C. H. Helmers, editors, *The Open Economy: Tools for Policymakers in Developing Countries.* Oxford University Press, 1988.

Policymaking in the Open Economy

Concepts and Case Studies in Economic Performance

Edited by

Rudiger Dornbusch

Published for the World Bank

Oxford University Press

Oxford University Press

OXFORD NEW YORK TORONTO
DELHI BOMBAY CALCUTTA MADRAS KARACHI
KUALA LUMPUR SINGAPORE HONG KONG TOKYO
NAIROBI DAR ES SALAAM CAPE TOWN
MELBOURNE AUCKLAND
and associated companies in
BERLIN IBADAN

© 1993 The International Bank for Reconstruction
and Development / THE WORLD BANK
1818 H Street, N.W.
Washington, D.C. 20433 U.S.A.

Published by Oxford University Press, Inc.
200 Madison Avenue, New York, N.Y. 10016

Oxford is a registered trademark of Oxford University Press

Manufactured in the United States of America
First printing February 1993

The findings, interpretations, and conclusions expressed in this study
are entirely those of the authors and should not be attributed in any
manner to the World Bank, to its affiliated organizations, or to
members of its Board of Executive Directors or the countries they
represent.

Library of Congress Cataloging-in-Publication Data

Policymaking in the open economy : concepts and case studies in
economic performance / edited by Rudiger Dornbusch.
    p.   cm.—(EDI series in economic development)
    Includes bibliographical references and index.
    ISBN 0–19–520884–6   ISBN 0–19–520985–0 (pbk.)
    1. Economic policy.   2. Monetary policy.   3. Commercial
policy.   4. Fiscal policy.   5. Foreign exchange.   6. Debts,
Public.
I. Dornbusch, Rudiger.   II. Series.
HD87.P63   1993
338.9—dc20   92–33405
                                         CIP

Contents

Preface

THE ECONOMIC DEVELOPMENT INSTITUTE (EDI) was established by the World Bank in 1955 to help mobilize the Bank's knowledge and experience for the purpose of strengthening development decisionmaking in its member countries. The EDI meets this objective by organizing courses and seminars for officials who make or influence development policy and management; by carrying out institution-building activities to help training institutions in member countries strengthen their capacities to make and manage policy, and by publishing training materials on investment and development policy. In addition, the EDI makes these materials available for independent study. In principle, EDI materials are written in nontechnical language so that they will be understandable to interested persons outside the economics profession.

This volume examines several areas of policy that critically influence economic performance: monetary policy, exchange rate policy, financial reform, tax reform, and foreign capital. The conceptual discussions of these topics are complemented by several country case studies that illustrate the effects of various policy options. The book does not offer specific policy prescriptions for every conceivable situation a country might face, but the writers give valuable advice based on their experience. Although intended for use in courses and seminars at the EDI and its partner institutes, the study should also be of interest to government officials and policymakers in the developing world who want to have an overview of the various policy issues. Professional economists may also find it useful.

This collection of essays on economic policy in the open economy follows on and complements *The Open Economy: Tools for Policymakers in Developing Countries,* a volume edited in collaboration with the late Leslie Helmers for the EDI. In 1986 Leslie Helmers took the initiative to organize a group of policy studies that would address economic policy issues faced in developing countries. His untimely death after the first volume was published made it impossible for him to complete the task to which he had brought so much enthusiasm. It is appropriate, therefore, to dedicate this volume to his memory. Special thanks are also due to Beth Anne Wilson for her editing of the volume.

1

Introduction

Rudiger Dornbusch

MILTON FRIEDMAN is fond of observing that there is no such thing as "no policy"; whatever governments do, they are doing something. If they do not print money, that is a policy, and if they print money, that is also a policy. The same goes for all other areas in which government has any involvement: protecting domestic industry by trade restrictions or running an open economy, borrowing abroad or not borrowing, accepting foreign direct investment or not allowing any, and so on.

What governments do affects economic performance. Good policies enhance growth, and poor policies slow it down; very poor policies can set development back by decades. Of course, a country's resources and the international environment in which it trades will have a critical effect on its standard of living. But the extent to which these resources can raise a country's standard of living depends on economic policy.

We cannot look at economic performance over time—as measured by, say, growth in real per capita gross domestic product (GDP)—and infer whether a country has pursued good or bad policies. Consider table 1-1, which shows the growth experience of four countries. Did Zambia do poorly in economic policy and Korea do well? The data can tell us only that Korea experienced a nearly sevenfold increase in per capita income, whereas Zambia is today 20 percent below where it was in 1960. But more often than not, we find that countries which did very poorly not only experienced adverse shocks but also responded poorly in terms of economic policy, whereas countries which did exceptionally well not only escaped unfavorable shocks but also exploited the favorable environment by creating a policy setting conducive to stability and growth. To some extent, case studies can support these claims, but ultimately there is also the need for faith in the belief that good policies pay off, slowly and steadily, and bad policies do not pay and can be dramatically expensive.

Table 1-1. Real Per Capita Income, Selected Countries and Years, 1960–90

(1960 = 100)

Country	1960	1970	1980	1990
India	100	116	127	177[a]
Korea, Rep. of	100	172	320	683
Peru	100	130	145	102
Zambia	100	123	106	80[b]

a. 1989.
b. 1987.
Source: IMF (various issues).

We will argue in this book that policy accounts for much of the difference in economic performance and that this difference is at the discretion of policymakers. But we go further to make the following argument: the poorer a country and the more adverse the conditions it faces in terms of resource availability, export prices, or world market access, the more important it is to implement good policies precisely to minimize the severe costs of an unfavorable environment. Rich countries can afford to waste resources; poor countries cannot. Rich countries may be able to neglect saving and investment (at least for a while); poor countries cannot.

Thus, good economic policy is critical for developing countries. What remains is to define good economic policy. There is no manual of conduct that offers advice for all occasions. But a substantial body of principles is on hand, and case studies can help policymakers analyze what the problem is, what options are available, and which option best meets the need. This book seeks to aid in this process.

The Objectives of Economic Policy

There are three basic objectives of economic policy: prosperity, equity, and the twin objectives of stability and continuity.

The pursuit of prosperity, for better or worse, is the deepest motivation of individual economic behavior. Individuals not only want to survive; they also want to improve their standard of living. Whatever philosophers say about the merit of a society of consumers, individuals do want to increase their material welfare. Governments can advance the standard of living by creating the environment that is most hospitable to developing a country's resources.

Equity is no less important an objective than prosperity, although it is frequently neglected. In some countries, notably in Latin America, income distribution is highly unequal (see table 1-2); the injustice and social discontent that inequality fosters are clearly visible. Economic

Table 1-2. Income Distribution, Selected Countries, 1990

(percent)

Country	Share of top 20 percent of households	Share of bottom 20 percent of households
Brazil	62.6	2.4
India	41.4	8.1
Morocco	39.4	9.8

Source: World Bank (1990).

prosperity must reach all people, and any economic policy must address both equity and prosperity.

Attempts to equalize income distribution often lead to policies that seek to dampen the consequences of shocks for poorer groups. Ironically, these policies may have the opposite effect. An overvalued exchange rate, meant to keep import prices low to help consumers, may ultimately lead to a currency crisis (see, for example, Dornbusch and Edwards 1990).

Equalizing the income distribution of a country is tricky because if it is pursued too vigorously or with poor means, the effort may be mostly frustrated; prosperity might decline without much improvement in equity. But it is also true that a startling lack of equity, quite aside from the moral offense, can invite political instability, which in turn hurts economic performance.

The status of stability and continuity is somewhat subsidiary. For many economists these twin objectives are more a means for achieving prosperity than desirable goals in themselves. For example, low inflation and stability of property rights make for a good business environment and hence for prosperity. But we must take seriously the possibility that people psychologically value stability and continuity per se. Whichever of the two reasons applies, stability and continuity rank among the objectives of policy.

The Economic Policy Environment

The institutional setting in which economic life takes place provides the environment in which policies operate. Its most important characteristics include the presence or absence of property rights, the extent to which these rights are accepted or challenged, and the resources available. The institutional environment also includes provisions that determine the interaction of individuals and the state. At one extreme, the state has extensive discretionary powers to intervene in the economy and dictate in detail people's economic lives. Socialist countries are examples. At the other extreme, the scope for governmental intervention is severely restricted by the country's constitutional limitations, and individual economic freedom is maximized. The United States and Switzerland might be examples of such a system.

Superficially it might appear attractive to have a situation in which the state is entitled to intervene in economic life, dictating who gets what and who does what. Regardless of how powerful government is, however, people will find a way to circumvent the restrictions. If their savings are at hazard, they will keep them abroad; if prices are controlled, goods may not be produced. The best economic system is one in which individual self-interest is the driving force but market outcomes in terms of individual income and wealth are mitigated by policies that enhance equality. The more a government is bound by institutions, the less need there is for individuals to assume a defensive posture against possible governmental action.

The following three rules describe the basic institutional setting for what might be described as a "social market economy."

- The right to own property is acknowledged by the culture and protected by a well-functioning legal system. (Property rights in a broad sense include all forms of contracts entered into by economic agents.)
- Competition—both within and across borders—is accepted as the basic rule in markets. Competition is enforced by allowing entry into all and any markets, by vigorously opposing monopolization, and by opening the economy to world trade. Competition makes the most of resources.
- Equity is a distinct social objective and need not emerge from the operation of competitive markets. The government promotes equity through a tax system that strikes a balance between equity and efficiency and, above all, by investing in education and health, which are key determinants of economic advance.

With these principles in mind, microeconomic and macroeconomic policies focus on creating a favorable climate for economic activity.

Microeconomic Policy

The maintained hypothesis for microeconomic policy is that free markets best maximize the real income a country can derive from its resources.

There are clearly specific instances in which markets fail. The restriction of competition by oligopoly or monopoly is an instance. Market failure also occurs when spillover effects are not priced in the market. In this case, activities that have favorable externalities are not carried forward sufficiently, and activities with negative externalities are maintained at excessive levels.

From the perspective of the open economy, well-conceived microeconomic policies can be especially effective in two areas: trade and foreign investment.

Trade policy determines whether a country is closed—with firms producing for the domestic market, which can be very small, and often at scales that imply very unfavorable cost conditions—or open, in which case more of the country's resources are devoted to producing exports. Trade policies determine not only the level and dispersion of tariffs but also the existence of quotas and licenses and the extent of trade in technology, design, accounting, advertising, transport, and legal services. There is abundant evidence that countries that choose to trade openly perform better.

Foreign direct investment used to be controversial. Today a more informed view is held. In addition to allowing the savings of one country to promote the development of another, foreign direct investment often brings with it technology that cannot be easily bought or rented in the market, superior management that may be in short supply in a developing country, and access to markets in industrial countries.

The smaller the developing country is, the more critical it is to take advantage of scale economies available when doing business with multinationals. Policies that encourage foreign direct investment should not limit the fields in which the rest of the world can invest (why restrict, say, manufacturing to domestic capitalists?). Such policies should provide prompt and efficient procedures for handling new investment, an effective tax system that does not punish foreign investment with double taxation, and a clear set of rules that protect the withdrawal of profits and principal.

These are just two examples of microeconomic policies that affect the use of resources in an open economy. They are discussed here to suggest that countries do make choices about their business environment and that these choices are critical to the effective utilization of resources.

New domestic concerns such as environmental issues and labor standards also have implications for trade policy. International differences in the level of regulation or standards create incentives for "social dumping." Poor countries may become attractive locations for "dirty jobs" and "poor jobs." A country must ask whether it wants to become the world's dumping ground for toxic waste and hazardous production and whether its lack of child labor laws should become the basis for an industrialization strategy. On the surface, the answer is clearly no. But regulation and standards must strike a balance between the severely negative effects of environmental degradation or poor labor standards, on the one hand, and the need to make a living in a very competitive world, on the other. Two more remarks should be added. First, denying that tradeoffs exist is poor economics; a country that sets very high standards must be aware that these regulations have some costs. Environmental degradation that later needs to be cleaned up at great expense may be a very bad idea. Similarly, "cheap" labor may mean high accident rates and poor productivity. Second, we must recognize that lack of regulation is also expensive. Therefore, a serious cost-benefit analysis, both in labor standards and in environmental regulation, involves investment choices.

Macroeconomic Policy

In contrast to the focus on market competition and regulation, the four main goals of macroeconomic policy are controlling inflation, maintaining a stable and competitive real exchange rate, exercising fiscal prudence, and operating efficient capital markets. Some comments on each of these follow.

INFLATION. An environment of high and unstable inflation deters productive economic activity. Capital market horizons shorten, and economic decisionmaking is distorted. Spurious gains and losses related to the vagaries of inflation rather than to effort and productivity become the rule. Inflation at high and variable levels represents a basic malfunctioning of the economy. A primary rule of macroeconomic policy, therefore, is to create a monetary and fiscal environment conducive to price stability. There may be considerations of public finance that favor a *moderate* level of inflation, but given the risk that such a strategy might lead to high and unstable inflation, more than caution is required.

EXCHANGE RATE. A key link between a country and the rest of the world, both in goods and assets markets, is the exchange rate. The profitability of production and investment in a country is based on their costs in dollars in relation to world prices. Poor exchange rate policy risks misrepresenting true opportunities and thus misallocating resources. For example, an exchange rate that is kept competitive to gain access to cheap imports (financed by borrowing abroad) may be reasonable in a period of high and productive investment, but it is certainly not a reasonable strategy when used to support a consumption boom. In fact, as the experience of Latin America in the 1970s shows, once the financing stops, a policy of overborrowing invariably ends in a foreign exchange crisis and a massive devaluation. The crisis, in turn, risks igniting inflationary pressures, and massive devaluation represents a cut in the standard of living that brings difficult political consequences. The lesson is that exchange rate policy is an area in which mistakes must be avoided and that a competitive, stable real exchange rate is the goal.

FISCAL PRUDENCE. In choosing fiscal policy the government must decide on the size of the budget deficit and how it should be financed—through domestic debt, foreign debt, money creation, or a combination of methods.

Here I will make a remark on the microeconomic implications behind deficit policies that affect the structure of the tax system itself, with its incentive effects and equity considerations. A good fiscal system applies cost-benefit analysis to determine the public sector effects of taxes, spending, and production. Today it is widely recognized that a broadly based system with moderate taxation is desirable and that subsidies have become too pervasive. One source of large budget deficits has been government involvement in industry. The current move toward privatization represents a healthy swing of the pendulum. There is a special need to consider privatization when the public sector faces constraints on borrowing and experiences a high marginal cost of fiscal resources. Turning industries such as telecommunications and airlines over to the private sector solves the investment problem and thus avoids bottlenecks.

Next, a key macroeconomic decision concerns the size of the budget deficit and how to finance it. The budget need not be balanced every year, and small deficits clearly do not destroy macroeconomic stability. But the question must be asked: how will the deficit be financed? The existence of capital markets offers a temptation to borrow to the fullest, but ultimately loans must be serviced and even repaid. Moreover, excessive borrowing may end in complete credit rationing, with even emergency loans no longer available.

The alternative to borrowing is printing money. In a growing economy, some money printing is acceptable, but the scope for it is sharply limited. Beyond a certain threshold, money creation becomes inflationary, and not much farther down the road it becomes a possible source of violent inflationary instability. Budget deficits, therefore, are a problem. The trouble is that often policymakers do not recognize the problem until they have used up all available credit and are reduced to printing money.

CAPITAL MARKETS. Because the growth of an economy is often linked to the size of its capital stock, the effect of governmental decisions on investment is key. The only way a country can add to its productive capacity is by investing. Investment may take the form of an expansion in the amount of human capital or of physical capital.

One way or another, it requires resources, and these must come from savers, either domestic or foreign. A well-functioning capital market serves to *mobilize* and *allocate* savings among competing uses. Moderate and stable inflation is a prerequisite for a well-functioning capital market and so is, of course, a vigorous system of property rights. Without well-functioning contracts there can be no financial intermediation.

The Importance of Economic Policy for Performance

The importance of economic policy in advancing or setting back a country's economic performance is brought out by a comparison between Argentina and Spain (table 1-3). During the postwar period Argentina's wealth of human capital and natural resources gave it the head start that enabled it to thrive for decades. Until the 1970s its real product per capita was above Spain's. By the mid-1970s, however, Argentina had fallen back from the stellar position it held at the turn of the century (see Maddison 1989). During the mid-1970s, Spain modernized, opened, kept down inflation, cleaned up public finance, and prepared to join the European Community. Argentina, instead, indulged in cycles of populism, experimented with policies that overvalued the currency, and imprudently liberalized financial markets. As a result, in the 1980s Spain moved sharply ahead, supported by domestic adjustment and a favorable European environment, while Argentina disintegrated to unimaginable extremes—a process that is still under way. Whereas Spain's per capita income grew at an average annual rate of 2.3 percent in the 1980s, Argentina's shrank by 2.9 percent a year (see figure 1-1). Argentina today represents a situation of political and economic distress—possibly pauperization—which is not unlike that of Germany in 1923.

The extent to which differences in performance can be attributed to economic policy remains an open question. More striking than the

Table 1-3. Real Product Per Capita, Selected Countries, 1950–90
(1975 international dollars)

Year	Argentina	Spain
1950	1,877	1,163
1960	2,124	1,737
1970	3,231	2,751
1980	3,209	4,264
1990[a]	2,484	5,561

a. Estimate based on real per capita GDP growth rates.
Source: Summers and Heston (1984).

Figure 1-1. Real Per Capita Income, Argentina and Spain, 1973–89
(1980 = 100)

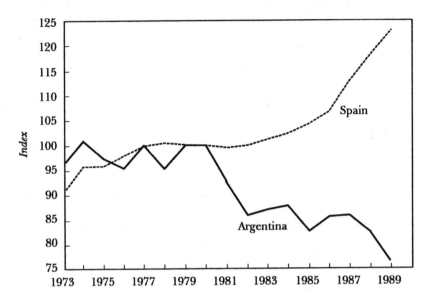

Source: IMF (various issues).

differences in growth between Spain and Argentina are the very different growth experiences of Asia and Latin America. In some way the economic success of Asia must be linked to the fact that countries there saved, invested, innovated, and sought out world markets while maintaining economic stability. And the problems of Latin America reflect the extent to which countries there borrowed, spent, destroyed economic institutions, and neglected the crucial role of trade in raising the standard of living.

Table 1-4. Per Capita GDP Growth, Selected Countries, 1950–87
(annual percentage change)

Region and country	1950–73	1973–87
Asia	3.1	2.6
India	1.6	1.8
Korea, Rep. of	4.1	6.2
Latin America	2.4	0.0
Argentina	2.0	−0.9
Brazil	3.8	2.2

Source: Maddison (1989).

Economic policy is part of the explanation for superior economic performance. History, resources (including human capital), location, the external environment, and luck all have their share. Experience shows, however, that mismanagement can overcome the most favorable conditions and bring a country down and that superior management can greatly improve a country's chances of getting ahead, even when the preconditions are not especially favorable.

About This Book

This volume reviews how policy choices critically influence economic performance. Given the large scope of policies, the work focuses on several key areas.

- *Monetary policy*. In a small, open economy there is not much scope for independent monetary policy. The latitude for noninflationary money creation is limited by growth in the real demand for money. If the central bank overestimates its degree of independence and selects too rapid a path of domestic credit growth, an exchange rate crisis and inflation are inevitable. If money creation and inflation get out of hand, the next question is how best to stabilize (see also Bruno and others 1988).
- *Exchange rate policy*. Policymakers must choose from the full range of possibilities—from floating rates to fixed rates. A fixed rate is too inflexible, given shocks to the real economy or disturbances in the price level. A floating rate may be too unstable except in the rare economies in which fundamentals are never in question. A crawling peg with occasional adjustment of the real exchange rate to accommodate changes in fundamentals may come closest to ensuring external competitiveness without creating opportunities for counterproductive speculation.
- *Financial reform*. The financial sector should function so as to mobilize domestic resources for growth. Effective financial intermediation ensures that household savings are channeled to domestic productive investment rather than to inventories or dollars. What are the requirements for effective financial intermediation, and what challenges arise in the process of financial reform? The debate has focused on the need for positive real interest rates, but that emphasis may well have been overdone. The lesson is that real interest rates should not be consistently negative (see also Polak 1989). Once more, Argentina, as shown in figure 1-2, serves as an example of what is clearly wrong.
- *Protection*. In the 1950s the Economic Commission for Latin America preached import substitution as a way for countries to industrialize and avoid the growth-inhibiting effects of an exter-

Figure 1-2. Real Value of an Investment, Argentina, 1983–90

(January 1983 = 100)

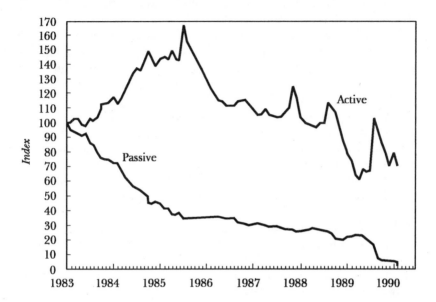

Source: IMF (various issues).

nal constraint. Today, in large measure as a result of the poor experience with import substitution and the closing of economies, the pendulum has swung strongly in the opposite direction. Protection is being questioned radically, and opening the economy is increasingly seen as a key step toward using resources more effectively and attracting foreign capital.

- *Tax reform.* A productive and efficient tax system is the cornerstone for macroeconomic stability. Sound tax policies eliminate the need for inflationary money creation and offer maximum incentives for resources to be allocated without waste. A government does need revenue to supply public goods and services that the market does not supply according to political and social priorities. The principal problem is to design a tax structure that minimizes the resource cost of taxation. Given this criterion, should the tax system be selective, or broadly based? Should rates be differentiated, or uniform? Taxation that is broadly based improves efficiency by lowering marginal rates without sacrificing revenue. Moreover, it enhances the enforcement of tax collection and thus reduces evasion. Theory says that differentiated systems are optimal, but the practitioner urges a broad base and a uniform rate._

- *Foreign capital.* Should a country rely on external resources to supplement domestic saving? And if it does, what form is best— debt or foreign direct investment? In the aftermath of the debt crisis the case for borrowing seems weakened by the apparently negative experience of the 1970s. But that is a misreading of the experience. Two crucial questions must be asked. What form should the borrowing take—debt or equity? And what are the resources used for—to finance budget deficits, consumption, and capital flight, or to finance productive investment? Since the nineteenth century, external capital has been an important instrument for economic development in Africa, Asia, and Latin America. The occasional debt crisis must not detract from the basically positive experience with foreign borrowing.

This book addresses both the conceptual issues involved in these topics and how problems arise in practice. As in the earlier volume (Dornbusch and Helmers 1988), the conceptual approach is complemented by case studies that review country experiences. The main emphasis is on money, capital markets, and exchange rates and on trade and taxes in relation to resource allocation. Two case studies— on Bolivia and Nigeria—round out the discussion.

In the lead essay (chapter 2), Bruno discusses rules for monetary policy in an open economy. He emphasizes that money has two kinds of effects: it influences nominal variables and, specifically, the evolution of prices over time, but it also affects real variables, at least in the short run. This double influence poses a problem because control of inflation, given the real effects of money, becomes costly. Hence, choices must be made. Ultimately, a central bank cannot give a country prosperity simply by printing money; that is an illusion. The best contribution the central bank can make to a country's economic performance is to establish immediately *rules* for the behavior of money and credit and thus to create a stable economic environment. It is not enough to announce that rules are desirable. We need to learn about what kinds of rules are useful in an open economy. We also need to look at some experiences, as Bruno does, to see how monetary policy works out in practice.

In the 1980s many countries undertook financial reform and liberalization. The inspiration for these actions came in part from experiences with highly distorted capital markets that increasingly malfunctioned. Reform was also attributable to the constant efforts of scholars who documented that economic performance is negatively related to financial repression (see McKinnon 1988; Polak 1989; World Bank 1987).

In chapter 3 Cottani and Cavallo discuss financial reform and liberalization from the perspective of Argentina's experience. They describe the link between financial repression and public finance. Governments finance deficits by creating money. To do so without much inflation, they try to repress financial markets. But, as the experience of Uruguay shows, more often than not the attempt is unsuccessful. In fact, negative real interest rates lead to misallocation of credit and to capital flight. The authors clearly recognize that financial repression is a bad idea; interestingly, they give financial liberalization only two cheers, not three.

Chapter 4, by Dornbusch and Reynoso, attempts to qualify what we know about the effects of financial repression. The qualification runs in the following direction: very negative real interest rates and extremely overvalued currencies have a disastrous effect on economic performance because they are an invitation to refrain from saving or to move one's savings offshore. Such a situation must surely be avoided. But the essay also argues that the posited relation between real interest rates and growth does not hold outside the circumstances described above. Empirically, it is simply not the case that countries with higher real interest rates perform better. Moreover, even if there were evidence in support of such a relation, one would still have to ask whether policy should try to raise real interest rates. It may be, of course, that real interest rates are high because the profitability of capital is high, as has been argued by Gelb (1989).

A complement to the discussion of capital markets and real interest rates is offered by Dornbusch and Tellez Kuenzler, who in chapter 5 look at the foreign exchange market. Under conditions of capital mobility, there is a tight link between interest rates within a country and abroad and the expected rate of depreciation. If interest rate differentials fall short of expected depreciation, capital flight is certain. Policies to depress real interest rates will quickly run into trouble in the exchange market. The chapter evaluates various exchange market arrangements toward which countries gravitate as they try to segment the exchange market. These arrangements include multiple exchange rates for commercial transactions and dual rates that separate commercial and financial transactions.

The chapter comes out strongly against multiple rates, not only because they distort trade but also because they involve serious budgetary problems. Dual rates are found to be useful tools provided that the premium of the free rate for capital transactions does not significantly exceed the commercial rate. But by no means are dual rates a panacea that relieves domestic mismanagement of its external consequences.

The discussion of multiple rates has already drawn attention to the costs of resource allocation when prices are distorted from their world levels. The essay by Krugman on trade policy (chapter 6) addresses this issue squarely. The question "Can broad trade restrictions help a country push its economic development further or faster?" is given a sympathetic hearing and then answered with a strong, unwavering No! Neither in theory nor, certainly, in practice is there a case for a small country to adopt protection as a strategy for growth.

The case for trade liberalization—turning away from the accumulated protection of the 1950s, 1960s, and 1970s—has been made by Chile, the Republic of Korea, Mexico, and Turkey. Today these countries are examples of highly successful liberalization. And the success of these countries is encouraging others to turn away from their increasingly negative experiences with protection and to open up. (For further discussion, see Dornbusch 1992.)

Harberger's essay on tax reform (chapter 7) is a masterpiece in political economy. Its central message is that being overly ambitious is counterproductive. Whereas discussion of tax policy typically has concentrated on the presentation of elaborate optimal tax structures, Harberger focuses on how to get results. He concludes, "Tax reform in today's world is . . . more appropriately focused on the giving of robust signals that will improve the private sector's allocation of resources than on the niceties associated with formal, technical optimization." But the statement should not be misconstrued as selling economics short. On the contrary, Harberger, here and in other writings, sets out a strong case for uniform taxation as a way of striking a balance between the administration of taxation and the efficiency of the tax structure.

Two case studies complete this volume. Chapter 8, by Gavin, reviews Nigeria's adjustment to a terms of trade shock. The great merit of the paper is that it links the terms of trade to a wide range of macroeconomic variables and issues. When a country's export prices fall, everything must adjust. And when the government owns the resources—the prices of which have declined—the adjustments have to reach all the way to monetary and fiscal policies. With a favorable shock, there are basically two options: to spend the resources while they last, or to set aside a portion and build up a reserve against less fortunate days. Needless to say, Nigeria failed thoroughly. The resources were dissipated to such an extent that after oil prices declined, adjustment became especially difficult. Worse, handling the transition poorly—that is, late and incompletely—ultimately added to the burden of adjustment.

The case of Bolivia, described by Morales in chapter 9, brings to the fore the link between budget deficits and money creation. When a country runs a deficit, it can finance the excess of spending over taxes by borrowing at home, borrowing abroad, or printing money. If the former two sources of finance have dried up, the third comes on with all its risks. In Bolivia in the mid-1980s that meant hyperinflation. Morales shows how the country gradually drifted in that direction until, in the end, control was lost and money creation translated into explosive inflation. The stabilization is equally interesting. It was uncompromising, harsh, and ultimately successful. Price stability was reestablished, even if growth of per capita income was slow to return.

The essays in this book seek in their diversity to convey a central message: economic policy cannot be intelligently conducted without a healthy dose of economics. There are choices to be made. Economics helps us decide on the objectives and to assess and compare the available instruments or mechanisms. Above all, economic theory and case studies teach us what measures will *not* succeed—money-financed deficits, protection, and financial repression, to name just a few.

In concluding, we present here Harberger's thirteen rules for good economic policy management.[1]

1. Avoid poor technicians in policymaking.
2. Keep budgets under adequate control.
3. Keep inflationary pressures under reasonable control.
4. Take advantage of international trade.
5. Keep in mind that some types and patterns of trade restrictions are far worse than others.
6. When import restrictions become excessive and reducing them is politically impossible, attack them indirectly by increasing export incentives.
7. Make tax systems simple to administer and (as far as possible) neutral and nondistorting.
8. Avoid excessive income tax rates.
9. Avoid excessive use of tax incentives to achieve particular objectives.
10. Use price and wage controls sparingly, if at all.
11. Remember that only rarely can a cogent rationale be found for quotas, licenses, and similar quantitative restrictions.
12. Take a technical rather than ideological view of the problems associated with public sector enterprises.
13. Make the borderlines between public and private sector activity clear and well defined.

Fischer (1987) has argued for adding

14. Don't overvalue the exchange rate.

The reader will want to bear these rules of good management in mind as the issues are addressed in the essays in this book.

Note

1. Some of the precepts are paraphrased to shorten the exposition. See Harberger (1984) for the detailed development.

Selected Bibliography

Bruno, Michael, Guido di-Tella, Rudiger Dornbusch, and Stanley Fischer, eds. 1988. *Inflation Stabilization: The Experience of Israel, Argentina, Brazil, Bolivia, and Mexico.* Cambridge, Mass.: MIT Press.

Dornbusch, Rudiger. 1992. "Trade Liberalization in Developing Countries." *Journal of Economic Perspectives* 6(1):69–85.

Dornbusch, Rudiger, and Sebastian Edwards. 1990. "Macroeconomic Populism." *Journal of Development Economics* 32(3):247–77.

Dornbusch, Rudiger, and F. Leslie C. H. Helmers. 1988. *The Open Economy: Tools for Policymakers in Developing Countries.* EDI Series in Economic Development. New York: Oxford University Press.

Fischer, Stanley. 1987. "Economic Growth and Economic Policy." In Vittorio Corbo, Morris Goldstein, and Mohsin Khan, eds., *Growth-Oriented Adjustment Programs.* Washington, D.C.: International Monetary Fund and World Bank.

Gelb, Alan H. 1989. "Financial Policies, Growth, and Efficiency." Policy, Research, and External Affairs Working Paper 202. World Bank, Financial Policy and Systems Division, Country Economics Department, Washington, D.C.

Harberger, Arnold C. 1984. "Economic Growth and Economic Policy." In Arnold C. Harberger, ed., *World Economic Growth.* San Francisco: Institute for Contemporary Studies.

IMF (International Monetary Fund). Various issues. *International Financial Statistics.* Washington, D.C.

McKinnon, Ronald. 1988. "Financial Liberalization in Retrospect: Interest Rate Policies in LDCs." In Gustav Ranis and T. Paul Schultz, eds., *The State of Development Economics: Progress and Perspectives.* Oxford, U.K.: Basil Blackwell.

Maddison, Angus. 1989. *The World Economy in the 20th Century.* Paris: Organization for Economic Co-operation and Development.

Polak, Jacques J. 1989. *Financial Policies and Development.* Paris: Organization for Economic Co-operation and Development.

Summers, Robert, and Alan Heston. 1984. "Improved International Comparisons of Real Product and Its Composition." *Review of Income and Wealth* 30(2):207–62.

World Bank. 1987. *World Development Report 1987.* New York: Oxford University Press.

———. 1990. *World Development Report 1990.* New York: Oxford University Press.

2

Monetary Policy Rules for a Small, Open Economy

Michael Bruno

MONETARY POLICY CONCERNS the determination and allocation of money and credit in terms of quantity and price, that is, interest rates. The first important distinction in this connection is the difference between the form in which money is issued and measured, namely, in units of nominal domestic currency (pesos, liras, and so on), and the way in which the quantity of goods that the money buys is measured, namely, in real terms (tons, square feet, or GDP in real constant prices). The real economy deals with the production and sale of goods, the quantity of exports and imports, and the employment of labor, where relative prices matter (the real wage, the real exchange rate, and so on). The nominal economy deals with items such as the nominal wage, the nominal exchange rate, and money and credit, whose value will usually be inflated along with the general level of domestic-currency-denominated prices.

Money, and therefore monetary policy, may stabilize or inflate the price level, depending on whether it is contractionary or expansionary. However, because the government may exercise direct and indirect control not only on the nominal aggregate but also on the exchange rate and the wage rate, the link between monetary policy and the price level is complex. The close link between money and the exchange rate suggests that the best way to view exchange rate policy is as part of the larger complex of monetary policy in the open economy.[1]

In addition to affecting nominal magnitudes in the economy, monetary policy may also have real effects, at least from a short-run perspective. The most obvious example in a closed economy is the expansionary role that an increase in money and credit and a reduction of interest rates may have on real output when the economy is in a slump. In an open economy, monetary policy may have added real effects by promoting short-run capital flows in or out of the country. Moreover, especially in less developed financial systems, many instruments of monetary policy exist that may have direct real allocative effects, for example, instruments of credit rationing and credit allocation by specific destinations (such as subsidized export credit). Although effective in reallocating resources, such instruments may undermine the effectiveness of monetary policy in its more conventional stabilizing roles. More generally, monetary policy can have real effects because central banks may be expected to target their varied monetary tools at other objectives, such as employment levels, foreign exchange reserves, or specific industrial objectives.

The degree of independence of monetary policy and of the central bank differs widely from country to country and may change drastically over time in a particular country. The most important element is the degree to which budget requirements and fiscal policy objectives dominate monetary objectives. Monetary institutions and operating rules evolve over time, depending on the development of financial and capital markets.

Monetary policy is usually depicted in macroeconomic textbooks as the way in which a well-advanced, industrial economy controls the money supply. This assumes the existence of separate, and at least minimally independent, fiscal and monetary authorities; the existence of well-developed markets for short-term debt instruments; and a clear definition of the monetary objectives. As economists are increasingly learning, however, even the typical industrial country's financial structure no longer conforms to the standard model. Nevertheless, it is instructive to understand the workings of this model in order to trace the gradual evolution of monetary institutions in a developing economy. We shall also discuss situations in which the underlying institutional structure is much less developed. In this respect, the experiences of some economies that have been or still are in a state of transition are instructive. Our main illustrations will be taken from the Israeli case.

The Basic Monetary Framework

In a typical small, open economy the public will hold an array of financial assets—currency in circulation, demand deposits (in banks), interest-earning time deposits, foreign currency (or foreign-currency-linked deposits), short- and long-term bonds, various forms of long-term savings funds, and so on. People will hold only some of these assets for transaction purposes, and the rest are held as a store of value or as longer-term savings. Monetary policy is usually designed to affect the quantity and price only of financial assets used mainly for transactions. Expansion of the aggregate money supply over and above the level desired (at a given cost) may increase the demand for goods and thus cause inflationary pressure (assuming the economy's output cannot be increased in the short run) or a loss of foreign exchange reserves or both. The choice of a suitable aggregate for the targeting of monetary policy is problematic, because the dividing line between one type of money and another is somewhat arbitrary. For example, short-term government debt may be almost as liquid as bank deposits. Likewise, foreign-exchange-linked deposits may, in some economies, play a very liquid role. For the moment we shall confine ourselves to the narrowest definition of the means of payments (*M*), consisting of currency in circulation (*CU*) and demand deposits in banks (*DD*).[2]

Before discussing how money is supplied in the economy, consider a simplified version of the banking system in terms of the balance sheet of the central bank and the consolidated balance sheet of the commercial banks (figure 2-1). The central bank's assets include the authorities' foreign exchange reserves or its net foreign assets (*NFA*), as well as all the domestic securities that the central bank holds against credit that it hands out, which we shall call central credit (*CC*), to distinguish it from credit that commercial banks give out, which we shall call bank credit (*BC*). For the moment, let us assume that all central credit goes to the government and that all commercial bank credit goes to the private sector. (Later on we shall change these assumptions, in particular to allow for central bank credit to both the private sector and the banks.) On the liability side, the central bank issues all the currency in circulation (*CU*) and holds the reserves owned by the commercial banks (*R*) (which for that reason also appear on the asset side of the balance sheet for the commercial banks). The central bank's two liability items make up the monetary base, or high-powered money (*H*).

Figure 2-1. The Banking System: A Simplified Version

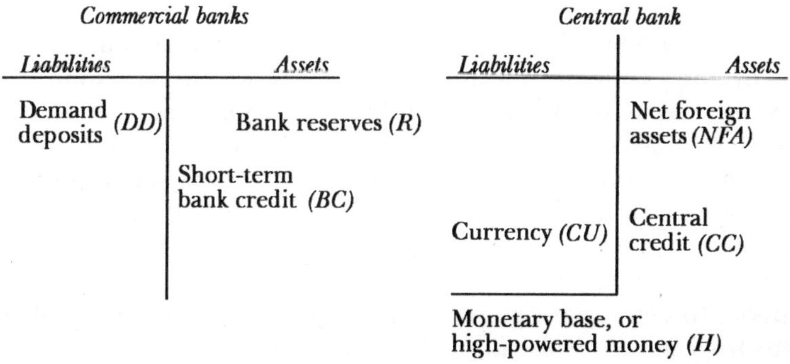

Commercial banks		Central bank	
Liabilities	*Assets*	*Liabilities*	*Assets*
Demand deposits *(DD)*	Bank reserves *(R)*		Net foreign assets *(NFA)*
	Short-term bank credit *(BC)*	Currency *(CU)*	Central credit *(CC)*
		Monetary base, or high-powered money *(H)*	

The commercial banks' liabilities are deposits held by the public, which for the moment we shall assume consist only of demand deposits (*DD*). Against these, the commercial banks hold their reserves (*R*) in the central bank and issue short-term bank credit (*BC*) to the private sector (ignoring other types of credit for the moment).

Simple balance-sheet-equality rules tell us that for the commercial banks we have:

(2-1)   Deposits (*DD*) = Bank reserves (*R*) + Bank credit (*BC*)

whereas for the central bank we get:

(2-2)   Monetary base (*H*) = Bank reserves (*R*) + Currency (*CU*)
$$= \text{Net foreign assets } (NFA) + \text{Central credit } (CC)$$

Remembering our definition of money (*M*) as the sum of currency in circulation (*CU*) and deposits in banks (*DD*) ($M = CU + DD$), and consolidating the balance sheet of the central bank with that of the commercial banks, using equations 2-1 and 2-2, we get the following simple, consolidated, monetary identity of the open economy:

(2-3)   Money or means of payments (*M*) = Total domestic credit (*DC*)
$$+ \text{Net foreign assets } (NFA)$$

where total domestic credit (*DC*) is defined as the total credit issued by the commercial banks (*BC*) plus that issued by the central bank (*CC*), namely:[3]

(2-4) $$M = BC + CC + NFA = DC + NFA$$

Equation 2-4 is an extremely important financial balance equation for consideration of monetary policy in the open economy, and it can be used in a number of ways. What it says first and foremost is that money can be created in several ways: by banks giving credit to the public (providing they are "allowed" to do so), by the central bank giving credit to the government, and by the sale of foreign exchange to the central bank. The last two forms of increase in the quantity of money are ways of expanding the monetary base (*H*) (what is often called the "printing" of money), whereas the first component, credit issued by the commercial banks, is one over which the monetary authorities may have an indirect influence through the exercise of monetary policy on the banks. For example, credit may be controlled by stipulating *r*, which is the ratio of bank reserves to deposits ($r = R/DD$, from which it follows that $BC = [1 - r]DD$). All of the above relationships apply to monetary expansion and obviously apply symmetrically for the contraction of money and credit.

Suppose foreign exchange reserves are to be kept constant. In that case the basic monetary identity, equation 2-4, says that any change (or stabilization) of money depends entirely on an equivalent change (or stabilization) of total domestic credit (to the private and public sectors).[4] Likewise, if foreign exchange reserves change (because of, say, a deficit or surplus in the current account) the only way to keep the quantity of money constant is by changing total credit in the opposite direction (and in an equivalent amount) to that of the foreign exchange inflow or outflow. If a change is denoted by delta (Δ), we have $\Delta M = 0$, which leads to $\Delta DC = -\Delta NFA$. This is called full sterilization of foreign exchange flows.

Now we can immediately see the dual role that monetary policy can, in principle, play in the open economy. It may affect or stabilize domestic prices, or it may be used to stabilize the balance of payments by mechanisms that will be discussed later.

Let us go one step back and consider how the domestic sources of increase in the money supply operate under the assumption of no change in the country's net foreign asset position (that is, keeping *NFA* constant so that $DC = M$), as would be the case in a closed economy.

The simplest form of monetary expansion is one in which the government borrows from the central bank to finance fiscal expenditure. In that case the central bank increases its credit to the government (*CC* on the asset side of the central bank balance sheet) and "prints" money, that is, it increases the monetary base *(H)*. The way this could take place in practice is for the government to pay for its additional expenses with cash (an increase in *CC*) or by writing checks that the public deposits in banks (thus increasing *DD*). The latter also automatically increases commercial bank reserves in the central bank *(R)*. At this point both high-powered money *(H)* and money *(M)* increase by the same amount. If, however, the monetary authorities operate under a rule that requires a fixed reserve ratio and the government payment is not in pure cash, there is scope for additional monetary expansion because banks can now issue additional bank credit *(BC)* up to the amount that will return *r*, the ratio of reserves to bank deposits, to its initial level.[5]

So far, we have shown that an increase in fiscal expenditure leads to a monetary expansion that is either of the same magnitude (if done in pure cash that the public is willing to keep holding) or bigger (if causing an increase in *r* and *DD*), providing the banks now avail themselves of the opportunity to lend more to the public. In either case, we can say that the monetary authorities are fully accommodating to the fiscal expansion by not exercising any independent monetary policy.

How can the monetary authorities neutralize the effect of the fiscal expansion on the money supply? They can do so by increasing the required reserve ratio (*r*) so that *M* (and *BC*) are constant. Thus the authorities can exercise monetary policy by changing the reserve ratio either up (for monetary contraction) or down (for monetary expansion). Other tools will be discussed below.

So far, we have ignored the effect of the initial fiscal expansion on the economy. If the economy is in a state of underemployment, the increase in demand (by the government) may also activate unemployed factors of production and bring about an increase in real income and product. In that case, the authorities would not need to exercise monetary restraint. If, however, real output cannot grow and the monetary authorities want to avoid the inflationary consequences of an increase in demand that cannot be matched by higher real output, money and credit must be reduced appropriately.

Alternatively, the government could achieve the fiscal expansion not by borrowing from the central bank, but by borrowing from the public, that is, by selling bonds. Selling more bonds entails reducing their price (raising the interest rate on the new bonds), which will also raise interest rates elsewhere in the economy. When interest rates rise in the process of inducing people to buy more bonds, people will want to hold less money because the opportunity costs of holding it will have increased. In this case, the economy will exhibit less inflationary pressure, and less of a monetary contraction will be required to avoid the price increase. The higher interest rates will in any case show in less investment in inventories and other physical assets. Fiscal expansion will have crowded out investment.

Suppose, however, the government insists on financing the fiscal expansion by borrowing from the central bank. The central bank itself could carry out a neutralizing operation through open market operations—that is, by selling government bonds that it holds in its portfolio, thus directly reducing bank reserves, money, and credit and raising interest rates in the economy. A similar effect is obtained when commercial banks borrow from the central bank (so as to increase their reserves). The central bank gives access to funds at a discount window. The central bank effectively reduces the money supply when the discount rate offered at the window is raised.[6] The banks then reduce their borrowings from the central bank (and thus the money base falls) and raise interest rates to their own borrowers.

So far, we have conducted the analysis as if we were in a completely closed economy. What is the meaning of our initial working assumption that net foreign assets (*NFA* in the central bank balance sheet) are kept constant? It means that the central bank avoids extra buying or selling of foreign exchange on a net basis, whereas some of the operations that we have described above could otherwise cause such net changes. For example, fiscal expansion may cause increased demand for imports, or higher interest rates may induce capital inflows. The first effect might cause downward pressure on exchange reserves (and a depreciating effect on the exchange rate), whereas the reverse would be true for capital inflows, when they are feasible.

The assumed constancy in *NFA* can be maintained only if the exchange rate is allowed to float. But a floating exchange rate policy is highly problematic for a small, open economy, especially if its wage and price system is not fully flexible. Pressure on the exchange rate (namely, forces making for devaluation), especially when resources in the export and import substitute industries are fully employed, will cause a cost-push effect on prices and wages. But reverse forces for an appreciation will harm exports (and import substitutes) and will not have a symmetrical downward pressure on prices (and wages) because of their downward rigidity. For this reason, we shall confine ourselves to the case of pegged or crawling exchange rate regimes. In this case we can no longer assume the automatic constancy of *NFA*.

Suppose now that we are in an open economy with a fixed exchange rate. The effect of monetary expansion or contraction is no longer confined to the link with prices (or output) that has already been described. An upward pressure on domestic prices implies pressure for real depreciation (at a given nominal rate), a rise in the current account deficit, and a reserve outflow (*NFA* falls), which in itself has a contractionary effect on the money supply (consider the central bank balance sheet). A rise in domestic interest rates, however, may induce more borrowing from abroad, if allowed, causing a capital inflow that will have an expansionary effect on the domestic money supply. Expansion will be avoided only when foreign capital flows are under strict controls.

To sum up, in an open economy operating under a fixed exchange rate, monetary policy affects not only domestic prices but also foreign exchange reserves. When there is a tendency for a reserve fall (because of a deficit in the current account or capital flight), a monetary contraction, although having a depressing effect on output (and a possibly disinflating effect on prices), may at the same time protect foreign exchange reserves from such a fall. Likewise, changes in foreign exchange reserves coming from the balance of payments will have a direct effect on the domestic money supply and may thus require countervailing pressure from the exercise of monetary policy. Finally, the effectiveness of monetary policy in an open economy under a fixed-exchange-rate regime depends on the degree of substitution between domestic and foreign assets and liabilities. When there are no foreign exchange controls at all, any domestic monetary intervention may be completely neutralized by an opposite effect coming from a capital inflow or outflow. The domestic interest rate will be equal to the foreign interest rate (with allowance for expectations of a devaluation and some risk factor), and monetary policy will be ineffective. At the other extreme, when there are no capital inflows at all, there will be complete sterilization.

Most real-life cases lie somewhere in between. Even with fairly strict foreign exchange controls, there is room for capital inflows or out-flows through the current account (holding back repatriation of export proceeds, incorrect invoicing of import costs, and so on), thus causing partial substitution between domestic and foreign assets. As the economy develops and gradually opens up its capital account, the degree of substitution rises, and the independence of monetary policy becomes more questionable unless the exchange rate is not kept strictly fixed (that is, if some small-scale floating within a band is allowed).

So far, we have conducted our analysis within an economy that has reasonably well-developed financial institutions, where government debt is fairly widely held, and where financial transactions (including lending and borrowing operations) are done within fairly competitive markets to which there is more or less general access. In most coun-tries that are considered here, this is not the case. When financial markets are segmented or thin, the exercise of conventional monetary tools is fraught with difficulties. Monetary contraction may cause excessive increases in interest rates in some markets rather than others, and if credit is rationed, the contractionary effects on eco-nomic activity may far outweigh the possible deflationary effects on prices. Likewise, the speed of adjustment to monetary policy, whether contractionary or expansionary, may be very slow. It is thus important to look at the operation of a variety of monetary tools under imperfect financial markets, inflationary budget policies, cartelized banking sys-tems, and so on, before coming back to the operation of monetary policy under more reformed systems.

Monetary Policy under Fiscal Excess and Fiscal Reform

The kinds of problems that imperfect markets and institutions may cause for the operation of monetary policy, especially under inflation-ary conditions, are best discussed using actual country examples. We shall use examples and episodes from the Israeli experience.[7]

In Israel, as in many other cases, the central bank's traditional role as the main monetary policy authority in charge of price stability was often dominated by other tasks, such as maintaining full employment or promoting investment and growth (especially in the export sector). Until 1985 a large and persistent government budget deficit had severely limited the Bank of Israel's ability to exercise independent monetary control. In addition, the bank had to cope with a highly concentrated and oligopolistic banking system.

A major limitation imposed on monetary policy in a period of high government deficits is the absence of restrictions on central bank credit to the government. In Israel that absence made for a highly accommodative monetary policy during the period of high inflation from the early 1970s to 1985. In 1985 the government introduced new banking legislation, and by 1987 such credit was limited to small bridging loans within the fiscal year.

In the face of large and persistent budget deficits the authorities tend to use monetary tools to prevent the crowding out of preferred sectors of production, such as agriculture or exporting industries. This is done by providing such preferred users with cheap, restricted credit. While alleviating demands from these sectors, the introduction of directed credit narrows the monetary and free credit base on which conventional monetary policy can operate. It also causes wide spreads among various rates of interest.

A major monetary tool used in Israel until quite recently is required reserve ratios. The required reserve ratio against various deposits in local currency was close to 50 percent during 1977–87, which is quite high when compared with ratios in industrial economies. Banks financing directed credit were granted exemptions from such requirements, thus reducing the net reserve requirement by 10 percent or more. The actual reserves held for most of the period were below these requirements despite the high fines that had to be paid and the interest rates paid on the discount window (by which some of these deficiencies were bridged). This made for a highly volatile money multiplier. In addition, formal changes in reserve requirements in Israel had to get government approval, a cumbersome and slow process.

An example of a financial innovation that increased monetary accommodation during the high-inflation period in Israel was the introduction in 1977 of foreign-exchange-linked domestic accounts (Patam accounts). The required reserve ratio on such accounts varied between 80 and 100 percent. When exchange rate policy follows a crawling peg for balance of payments reasons, such accounts can divert some of the demand for pure foreign currency assets, thus leaving the central bank with greater foreign exchange reserves. Such deposits, however, tend to be a highly liquid asset whose value rises automatically with inflation, thus making monetary control much less effective. During 1984, at the height of inflation, these Patam accounts formed 65 percent of all short-term assets held by the nonfinancial private sector. With the July 1985 reform, their liquidity was reduced (allowing new entry only for a minimum deposit period of one year), and their share in total short-term assets fell to 25 percent by 1987. Obviously the existence of such indexed deposits seriously hampered the macroeconomic policy response during the oil price and exchange rate shocks.

During much of the period, the Bank of Israel used bank credit as its intermediate monetary target rather than some measure of the quantity of money. This is understandable, given the need to control speculative waves during times of expected devaluation, when the public tends to reduce domestic currency deposits and moves to foreign exchange or foreign-exchange-linked assets. Stabilization of domestic credit rather than a monetary aggregate helps to reduce the demand for foreign exchange assets by raising domestic interest rates. Moreover, banks have greater control over credit than over their deposits. Finally, the difficulty of controlling credit expansion by any other monetary tool (such as reserve requirements) has often led to the application of credit ceilings to individual banks. Whereas this may be an effective tool for a short-term monetary contraction, with time it may distort the allocation and price of credit throughout the economy.

Our final example—of an action to be avoided—is the use of central bank intervention to support the price of government-indexed bonds in an attempt to reduce the cost of government borrowing. Such intervention weakens the central bank's control over the monetary base and the quantity of money. Suppose the government wants to sell a certain quantity of bonds over and above actual demand, which has fallen. To prevent a fall in the price of bonds (that is, a rise in their yield), the central bank buys up the excess (increases the monetary base) independent of whether economic conditions justify such monetary expansion. Israel abandoned this policy of interest rate pegging after the financial crisis of 1983. The more general question of whether the nominal interest rate rather than the quantity of money or credit should be a target of monetary policy is discussed later.

Until the 1985 reform, monetary policy was on the whole highly accommodative to inflationary shocks. The government tried to affect interest rates, either directly for specific kinds of preferred credits or indirectly for free credit, by setting the interest rate on the loans the central bank extended to the commercial banks. During some periods the government tried to control quantities directly by means of credit ceilings. Such a highly segmented system inevitably leads to wide differences between short- and long-term interest rates as well as among the short rates charged to different users of credit. These differences in turn cause considerable distortions in the allocation of money and capital throughout the economy. In addition, direct control of a large segment of credit implies that the conventional role of monetary policy in stabilizing prices and the balance of payments is confined to a relatively narrow part of the credit market. Limiting the stabilizing power of monetary policy allows large fluctuations in both quantities and interest rates in that market. Under these adverse conditions the stabilizing role of monetary policy is hampered further, because the excessively high marginal interest rates that result invoke public criticism and exert pressure on the central bank to reduce rates and thus become even more accommodative.

The July 1985 stabilization program enabled the government to initiate reforms in the operation of monetary policy, starting with reforms that substantially reduced the budget deficit. (The reduction in itself loosened the pressure on monetary policy to be accommodative.) An outward manifestation of reform is new legislation that no longer allows direct government borrowing from the central bank except for a temporary loan that does not exceed 1.6 percent of the annual budget and that must be repaid by the end of the fiscal year.[8] The only loophole that remains is the government's ability to borrow abroad and sell the proceeds to the central bank. The stabilization of bond prices has also been terminated. Although a substantial portion of directed credit to exporters remains, it is now financed by bank borrowing on international markets, with interest rates charged close to international rates. Note that this method of financing still subsidizes borrowers in the export sector as long as domestic interest rates remain high.

Another element in the reform of monetary policy has been a shift from rate fixing and ceilings to the control of monetary aggregates to unify interest rates for short-term credit across the economy. The greater flexibility in the money market results from a new, simplified structure of central bank loans to the commercial banks; more of these loans are now sold by open auction rather than at predetermined prices. Likewise, there has been a return to the widespread use of short-term government bills (those that mature in one to twelve months) sold by auction and which the central bank can at times repurchase before the date of maturity. Other advances have been a gradual reduction of reserve requirements on demand deposits to about 20 percent and unification of reserve requirements across different types of fixed-term deposits.

The balancing of the government budget also implies that the government no longer expands its long-term, net, indexed debt and that an increasing portion of its existing debt, which is recycled, has become tradable on the secondary market, thus facilitating open market operations by the central bank.

All these changes, which would not have been possible had large budget deficits continued, permitted gradual loosening of the rather rigid monetary system and unification of interest rates. Quite a few problems remain, however. As long as domestic inflation is higher than inflation in the countries of Israel's main trading partners—by 1988 Israel's annual inflation rate was still 16 percent, whereas it was some 3 to 5 percent in the trading partners' countries—ceilings on foreign credit cannot be reduced. An attempt to introduce a flexible capital import tax instead has failed because it could only be applied to a very narrow tax base. As a result, differences remain among different types of external and domestic credit.

Another problem is the wide spread that persists between the interest rate that banks pay on time deposits and the rates that they charge on their credit to the public. This spread is caused by the highly concentrated nature of the Israeli banking system, which is conducive to oligopolistic practices. Another contributing factor is that the government still controls the quantity and price of a large portion of the banks' borrowing and lending operations. Bank profits from regulated lending are very low, thus motivating the banks to compensate themselves on the "free" portion of the market, where they charge excessive margins. The authorities hope to alleviate this problem through further reform of the financial system, which would include the gradual abolition of directed credit, further reduction of the government's role in the capital market, and an increase in the degree of competition in the banking system.

Monetary Targets and Tools under Normal Conditions

The previous section covered some of the structural problems that limit the effectiveness and independence of monetary policy when government deficits are high, or there is a need to achieve multiple objectives, or both of these conditions exist. Let us now return to some of the issues that have to be considered under more normal circumstances, assuming the existence of a relatively well-functioning money market and a reasonably balanced government budget.

Monetary policy is only one of a set of instruments (such as fiscal policy and incomes policy) that authorities use to achieve multiple objectives for employment and growth, current account balance, and price stability. We shall now assume that other instruments take care of employment, growth, and current account objectives, so that the main task of monetary policy (including exchange rate policy) is to achieve stability in prices and the balance of payments. In principle, the tools at the disposal of the monetary authorities are transactions in domestic assets that they hold or create, transactions in foreign assets (buying or selling *NFA*), and administrative measures in either of these fields (for example, fixing domestic credit ceilings or handling foreign exchange controls).

One important choice is selection of a key anchor for the price system. Is it primarily the exchange rate or is it some monetary aggregate? In a small, open economy the relationship between the general price level and the exchange rate is considerably tighter than between money and prices, primarily because import prices play a large role in the input-output system. Any increase in the cost of imports (say, through a devaluation) quickly feeds into the general price level, which is further enhanced when there is also some formal linkage between another important cost element, wages, and the price level. For this reason there is an advantage in anchoring the price level primarily to the exchange rate and using incomes policy to keep a wage level that is consistent, given the nominal exchange rate, with the required real exchange rates determining international competitiveness and the current account. What this means, however, is that an important potential tool of monetary policy—transactions in foreign assets—is subjugated to the pegging (or stabilization) of the exchange rate. In other words, the central bank buys and sells foreign exchange at a predetermined price and thus loses control over *NFA* in its balance sheet. But in that case, transactions in domestic assets, which affect domestic interest rates, must be conducted in a manner that supports the exchange rate and sustains a reasonable level of *NFA*. If, for example, the monetary authority is tempted to maintain too low an interest rate when the public expects a devaluation, capital will flow out of the country, the exchange rate will have to be adjusted, and its credibility as an anchor will be lost.

As the balance of payments fluctuates more under a pegged-exchange-rate regime, the government must hold larger foreign exchange reserves than it would otherwise need. Another consequence of the choice of a pegged-exchange-rate regime is the stronger bias in favor of keeping foreign exchange controls. Such controls may be required anyway as long as the internal reform processes have not been completed (see Bruno 1988), but the controls will introduce other distortions in the economy. On balance, however, the choice of the exchange rate as a key anchor for the price system and the use of monetary policy to support it have considerable advantages.[9]

The next issue that comes up in the practical planning of monetary policy is the choice of the monetary aggregate that is most suitable as an intermediate target for policy. The choice of that target may differ from one country to another and within one country over time. An important first step is to choose the monetary aggregate that represents transactions demand for money and that bears a relatively stable demand relationship with respect to nominal income or product. The aggregate used in Israel, for example, is an M_3 figure, comprising ordinary means of payment (M_1) and time deposits, in both domestic currency and foreign-exchange-denominated terms (Patam accounts). Assuming a relatively stable relationship with respect to nominal income, the planned growth rate of the chosen nominal aggregate over any period of time should then approximately equal the sum of the growth rates of the targeted price level and of real income (or product). Considering the basic monetary identity for the open economy ($M = DC + NFA$), the authorities could then use a domestic credit (DC) aggregate as their intermediate target, given a specified level of expected reserves (NFA). Using the Israeli example again, having chosen a definition of M_3 and a planned level of reserves based on the expected figures for the current account and long-run capital flow, the difference—the net domestic credit (NDC)—is then targeted.[10]

What would be the implication of holding onto a DC or an NDC target? Suppose the current account deficit increases unexpectedly, leading to a fall in NFA in the hands of the central bank. If the authorities attempt to keep to a predetermined NDC target, the money supply will fall (remember that $M = (N)DC + NFA$, thus $\Delta M = \Delta NFA$ in this case). The public, which continues to demand a given quantity of money for transaction purposes, will then have to sell bonds, thereby driving down their price, that is, raising the interest rate. This in itself may activate a capital inflow and will attenuate the fall in reserves. In addition the rise in the interest rate will slow down domestic demand, cause a real depreciation (if prices are flexible downward), reduce the current account deficit, and thus bring about an upward correction in foreign exchange reserves (NFA). A similar analysis applies to the opposite case of an unexpected increase in the current account surplus leading to a rise in NFA.

The example above shows that using an M aggregate as a target instead of $(N)DC$ is an inferior procedure if the objective is to stabilize foreign exchange reserves. The relative disadvantage of keeping M stable is particularly clear when a devaluation is expected, leading to a reduction in M and a fall in reserves. Expanding M in this case (that is, following an accommodative policy) will keep interest rates low, causing reserves to fall further and threatening the stability of the exchange rate. The strict prevention of change in NFA, however, will cause greater fluctuations in the interest rate than will the stabilization of NDC.

Should policymakers be indifferent to changes that may take place in the interest rate? Too strict a maintenance of credit limits may at times cause such steep increases in the interest rate that the fall in real production may outweigh the possible gain in short-term stability. Obviously, this is a problem of weighing one bad outcome against another. In practice, even if monetary policy follows certain quantitative targets, policymakers should consider its implication for interest rates. By contrast, an inadvisable move would be to go to the other extreme of adhering to strict interest rate targets (which was a policy followed in Israel, for example, during much of the high-inflation period). Adhering to strict interest rate targets has the great disadvantage of releasing control over the quantity of money and credit and thus of giving up the stability of monetary targets. An intermediate course to follow is to set a narrow band for the quantitative targets and also keep some maximum and minimum interest rate constraints in mind (these should not be published, however). Strict adherence to quantitative targets may not work simply because the transaction demand for money tends to be unstable. Financial innovation and other unforeseen disturbances keep the velocity of money (the ratio of nominal income to the stock of money) from being constant. This outcome has been borne out by the recent experience of several advanced industrialized countries.

The planning of monetary policy can be conducted on an annual basis and on a quarterly and monthly basis, right down to a weekly correction. Annual targeting should be consistent with the annual planned government budget. Quarterly adjustments have to be made in view of changes that take place either in actual fiscal balances or in the output, price level, and balance of payments data. Monthly and weekly financial programming would usually concentrate on the analysis of the major components of the monetary base, or high-powered money (H). These components include two factors that can be taken as exogenous to monetary policy in the very short run, namely, government net injections of liquidity and net sales of foreign exchange. A third component of the monetary base is that which the central bank itself plans to inject into the banking system, either through a monetary loan (or a "discount window," for which the interest rate and fine structure can be varied at will) or through the sale and purchase of government short- and long-term securities. By making assumptions about various monetary multipliers (for example, required reserve ratios) one can then try to compute the implied changes both in monetary aggregates and in interest rates that the banking system is likely to charge. The shorter the planning period, however, the more unstable are the multipliers and the more attention is given only to the movements in the monetary base.

Monetary Policy in Practice: Some Recent Israeli Examples

The functioning and role of monetary policy is illustrated by examining the Israeli economy, starting with the July 1985 stabilization program.

The stabilization program ended a twelve-year period of deep crisis: two- and (later) three-digit inflation, recurrent balance of payments problems, and very low growth. At the center of the program was a cut in the government budget deficit from 12 to 15 percent of GDP to a virtual budget balance and a freeze on the exchange rate (after an initial devaluation of 20 percent), on credit, and on prices, on condition that the trade unions agree to a temporary wage freeze. Eventually the program also included an agreement on wage policy. The program imposed a series of supplementary measures on the financial and capital markets, including abolition of the liquid foreign-exchange-linked accounts (Patam accounts). As figure 2-2 shows, the monthly inflation rate dropped dramatically from 15 to 25 percent to some 1 to 1.5 percent and was still at that level at the end of 1988. We will now consider the monetary component of the policy package as well as the program's immediate aftermath (for additional details see Bruno and Piterman 1988, on which some of the following discussion is based).

Apart from the removal of the initial source of inflation—the government budget deficit—an important part of such a stabilization plan is the determination of one or more nominal anchors and secur-

Figure 2-2. Interest Rates and Inflation, Israel, 1984–88

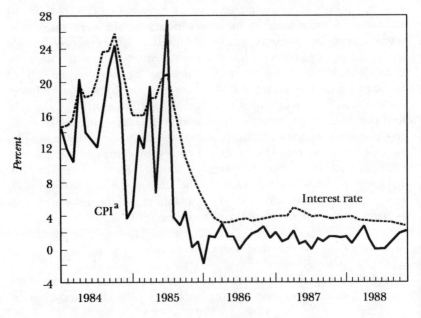

Note: The interest rate is the effective cost of overdraft facilities in local currency.

a. Consumer price index.

Source: Bank of Israel data.

ing them through social agreements and appropriate policy measures. The main anchors chosen were a combination of the exchange rate and the wage rate (plus a temporary price freeze), with monetary policy as an auxiliary anchor. Under sharp disinflation, the demand for both ordinary means of payment (M_1) and also for the more general aggregate of domestic-currency-denominated unindexed assets (M_2) is bound to increase quite rapidly, and using any of these as nominal anchors would be a mistake (this was apparently done at the early stages of the Argentine Austral Plan). Figure 2-3 shows that both M_1 and M_2 rose from mid-1985 to almost the end of 1988, whereas Patam deposits, represented by the difference between the M_3 and M_2 curves, declined. For the stabilization program, the authorities preferred to rely on the overall volume of bank credit. Control over the level of credit, however, was indirect (in the preceding years the Bank of Israel had controlled the price of credit rather than its quantity). A proposal to set credit ceilings for each individual bank was not

Figure 2-3. Nonindexed Financial Assets and Resident Foreign Currency Deposits (Patam Accounts), Israel, 1984–88

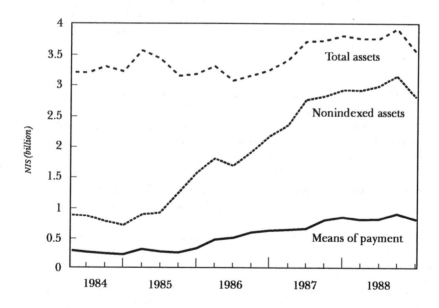

Note: At December 1984 prices; monthly average for quarters. Resident foreign currency deposits (Patam accounts) are represented by the difference between the total and the nonindexed assets.

a. A billion is 1,000 million.

Source: Bank of Israel data.

adopted at the time; instead, the Bank of Israel used the interest rate charged on the monetary loans to the commercial banks as an indirect means of trying to achieve an overall credit restraint target on the commercial banks. This target was defined as the level of credit that accommodated the initial price shock minus a cut of 10 percent.

Fiscal and incomes policies were aimed chiefly at an initial reduction of private disposable income. The public tends to offset such policy by borrowing, especially if it perceives the policy as temporary. The steep decline in the expected return to foreign currency (after the exchange rate freeze) was anticipated to lead to higher capital inflows. Also, a sharp improvement of bank liquidity was expected as indexed bonds and the Patam deposits (on which the reserve requirement was 100 percent) were converted into domestic currency deposits, which had lower reserve requirements.

To prevent credit expansion under these circumstances, the Bank of Israel raised reserve requirements on domestic currency deposits and maintained an extraordinarily high interest rate on its discount window loans. The quantitative target on credit was indeed achieved, but at a cost of steep real interest rates, which, in annual terms, reached an average of 168 percent on overdraft facilities during the first six months after the program's initiation. That nominal interest rates were reduced only slowly in the first few months partly reflected the monetary authorities' initial lack of trust in the speed of success of the sharp disinflation strategy (see figure 2-2: the upper curve represents the nominal interest rate on overdraft facilities and the vertical height between the two curves gives some measure of the ex post monthly real rate).

These high real interest rates caused undue hardship to the business sector. Whereas high real interest rates are necessary in the course of sharp disinflation, they probably need not be that high. In any case, the nominal (and real) interest rate was gradually lowered during the second half of 1985 and until March 1986, even though credit increased in excess of the target. By that time a boom in demand and a deterioration of the private sector's current account, together with a rapid increase in credit, caused the Bank of Israel to raise the prime rate by 3 percent a year.

In retrospect the choice of commercial bank credit as the target of monetary policy at the time of rapid disinflation may have been inappropriate. As argued above, with a fixed-exchange-rate regime, the authorities must pay more attention to the total domestic sources of monetary expansion: credit to the government and to the public from both the central bank and the commercial banks. Thus a concept like net domestic credit (*NDC*), which was introduced in 1987, could have been employed. Figure 2-4 shows the curve for M_3 and for the *NDC* that is derivable from it after the subtraction of foreign exchange reserves (this is measured by the height difference of the two upper curves). The bottom curve gives the part of the *NDC* that goes to the private sector, and the difference in height between the two *NDC* curves is the part that goes to the government. As the figure shows, the latter contracted dramatically (along with the cut in the budget deficit).

In January 1987 a 10 percent corrective devaluation was carried out as well as a new agreement between workers and employers to waive part of the cost of living adjustment. Apprehensive about impending price increases after the devaluation (forecasts of a renewed outbreak of inflation were widespread), the Bank of Israel raised nominal interest rates on monetary loans and the interest rate on commercial bank deposits with the central bank by 1 percentage point a month, announcing that these raises would be temporary. Afterward, it turned out that price increases were much lower than feared and that real

Figure 2-4. Money Supply, Net Domestic Credit, and Net Domestic Credit to the Private Sector, Excluding Treasury Bills, Israel, 1984–88

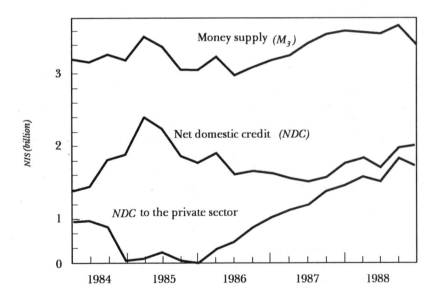

Note: At December 1984 prices; end-of-month balances; M_3 = Cash + Demand + Time deposits + Resident foreign currency deposits (Patam accounts).
NDC = M_3 — Foreign exchange reserves.

Source: Bank of Israel data.

interest rates rose again substantially (see figure 2-2 for the first half of 1987).

The devaluation was successful in increasing export profitability, but it upset the equilibrium in the asset market. During the months following the devaluation there was a capital inflow of about $1 billion[11] (see the increasing gap between the two top curves in figure 2-4 after the beginning of 1987). This capital inflow began primarily as a result of the sharp decline in the cost of foreign currency credit after the devaluation, when the public realized that another devaluation was not imminent. This inflow might have caused monetary expansion, additional demand pull, pressure on domestic prices, and a rapid real appreciation. On the one hand, the policy of absorbing liquidity prevented a rapid choking off of capital imports (because of the higher domestic interest rates), but on the other hand, it helped to restrain domestic demand and moderate the price increases following the devaluation. This moderation was highly valuable in reinforcing the public's expectations that price stability would be maintained. Interest rates were reduced again after a few months, and domestic credit was allowed to increase.

In the second half of 1987, when domestic demand slackened off, the time was ripe for a sustained reduction in nominal (and real) interest rates, a process that was continued through most of 1988 as the economy went into a deepening recession. The tools used were gradual increases in the quantity of monetary loans and reductions in their cost and, in August 1988, a direct intervention by the Bank of Israel with the managers of the top commercial banks: the Bank of Israel called upon them to contract their high interest rate spreads and cut their lending rates by an additional 5 annual percentage points (on top of the 6 percent cut in the preceding six months).[12]

The operation would have been successful had the hoped-for accompanying correction in the exchange rate been made. But because of the impending election and the subsequent long deliberations over the formation of a new government, neither this correction nor a negotiated agreement between the trade unions and the employers' association could take place. Expectations of an impending devaluation intensified, and from July 1988 until the end of November 1988, some $2 billion in private capital flowed out. Monetary policy largely accommodated this outflow and allowed only a small increase in domestic interest rates for fear that too high an interest rate hike would deepen the recession and would be difficult to reverse quickly (given the oligopolistic structure of the banking system), once the expected exchange rate correction was carried out successfully. After another correction of the exchange rate in December 1988 and January 1989, the same amount of foreign exchange flowed back in, and the process of sharp reductions in interest rates was resumed.

We have thus considered a few examples of monetary policy in action. Obviously, well-specified rules are one thing and practice is often another, but the main underlying principles are closely linked to our earlier general discussion. Conditions in different countries and in one country over time vary; therefore, monetary policy rules cannot be applied equally well under all circumstances. In the end, there is nothing better than one's own mistakes to learn from, unless one can also learn from others' mistakes.

Notes

1. The wage rate is, under some circumstances, at least as important a nominal anchor for the price level as is money or the exchange rate. For policy, however, the wage rate is usually considered under a separate heading: wage or incomes policy.

2. This is usually termed M_1, whereas M_2 includes short-term government debt. M_3 may also include such items as foreign-exchange-linked indexed deposits.

3. From the definition of M and from equations 2-1 and 2-2, we get $M = DD + CU = (R + BC) + (H - R) = BC + H = BC + (CC + NFA)$.

4. In that case, the situation is the same as it would be in a closed economy; the term NFA does not appear, and we simply get $M = BC + CC = DC$.

5. If all the initial injection of money (ΔH) is done through r and not CC, the increase in credit will be $\Delta H(1 - r)/r$. In this way, there will be monetary expansion by the amount $\Delta M = \Delta H/r$, which is the monetary multipler effect. The formula will be a bit more complicated if individuals now also wish to readjust their cash holdings in relation to their bank deposits, but this relatively minor point can be ignored here.

6. Note that we have now extended the role of CC in the balance sheet of the central bank to include credit to the banks.

7. A recent, detailed study of monetary policy and institutions in Israel (on which some of the discussion is based) is given in Cukierman and Sokoler (1988). For a good account of similar developments and problems in Italy, see Padoa-Schioppa (1987).

8. Italy introduced a similar reform in 1981. This was the discontinuation of the commitment of the Bank of Italy to act as residual buyer at treasury bill auctions. It was termed the "divorce" (see Padoa-Schioppa 1987).

9. With time, as reforms of internal financial, capital, and labor markets are sufficiently advanced, there may be a case for more equal sharing of the anchoring job between the exchange rate and the monetary aggregates. This can be achieved by making the exchange rate more flexible, for example, making it move within a specified band. Such flexibility might reduce the fluctuations of NFA and give greater autonomy to monetary policy.

10. The NDC is a net number because one has to subtract from private and public bank credit that part of the banking sector's liabilities that consist of bank deposits not included in the definition of M_3 as well as the net foreign liabilities of the commercial banks. These items are not included in our simplistic balance sheet representation, but can in practice be quite sizable.

11. Throughout this book, a billion is 1,000 million. All dollar amounts are U.S. dollars and are current, unless otherwise specified.

12. This action illustrates one important tool of monetary policy that has so far not been mentioned, namely, "moral suasion." Direct talks with bankers or the governor of the central bank "raising his or her eyebrows" in public can at times be quite effective tools provided they are used rarely.

Selected Bibliography

Bruno, Michael. 1988. "Opening Up: Liberalization and Stabilization." In Rudiger Dornbusch and F. Leslie C. H. Helmers, eds., *The Open Economy: Tools for Policymakers in Developing Countries*. New York: Oxford University Press.

Bruno, Michael, and Sylvia Piterman. 1988. "Israel's Stabilization: A Two-Year Review." In Michael Bruno, Guido di-Tella, Rudiger Dornbusch, and Stanley Fischer, eds., *Inflation Stabilization: The Experience of Israel, Argentina, Brazil, Bolivia, and Mexico*. Cambridge, Mass.: MIT Press.

Cukierman, A., and M. Sokoler. 1988. *Monetary Policy and Institutions in Israel: Past, Present, and Future*. Discussion Paper Series 88.05. Jerusalem: Bank of Israel, Research Department.

Padoa-Schioppa, Tommaso. 1987. "Reshaping Monetary Policy." In Rudiger Dornbusch, Stanley Fischer, and J. Bossons, eds., *Macroeconomics and Finance: Essays in Honor of Franco Modigliani*. Cambridge, Mass.: MIT Press.

3

Financial Reform and Liberalization

Joaquin Cottani and Domingo Cavallo

DESPITE A SLIGHT TREND toward liberalization during recent years, the financial systems of most developing countries have been and continue to be excessively regulated. In this chapter, we argue that deregulation of the financial system, although necessary for encouraging increased levels of investment and improvements in resource allocation, can be successful only in countries that have achieved a high degree of fiscal discipline, low inflation, and macroeconomic stability.

We first discuss financial repression. The literature has focused on two aspects of this phenomenon: the need to collect seigniorage as a common cause of financial repression, and the effects of financial repression on saving, investment, and growth. Next, we use evidence from past reforms to analyze difficulties that may arise when liberalization of domestic financial markets is imposed upon macroeconomically unstable economies. Finally, we deal with the problems of external liberalization and dollarization.

Financial Repression: The Traditional Approach

Unnecessary regulation of the financial system is not exclusive to developing countries. It has also occurred in industrial countries, such as Japan and, to a lesser extent, the United States. No perfect empirical correlation exists between economic success and financial liberty in developing countries. Nor is it possible to demonstrate that the economic stagnation of some developing countries can be primarily attributed to institutional imperfections in the financial market.

On the one hand, Taiwan and the Republic of Korea, two of the most successful exporters in East Asia, have highly regulated financial systems and banks that, to a great extent, depend on the state. On the other hand, the financial reforms of the late 1970s undertaken by Argentina, Chile, and Uruguay not only failed to improve economic performance in terms of saving, investment, and investment efficiency but also caused an actual banking crisis that endangered the stability of their financial systems. To understand the effects of financial policies on economic development, one must distinguish conceptually between regulation, restriction, and repression of financial activities.

Financial Regulation, Restriction, and Repression

Prudential regulation is always necessary in financial markets. Banks act not only as intermediaries between savers and investors (brokers in the strict sense) but also as participants in money creation by offering deposits. The close relationship of deposits to real output, employment, and the rate of inflation creates a significant externality. Therefore, by regulating the credit market, monetary authorities try to maintain the solvency of deposit institutions, thereby assuring the stability of the monetary system. The authorities establish rules concerning bank capital and requirements for the relationship between debt and capital or between deposits and reserves. They supervise risk taking by controlling the quality of loans and requiring set-asides when loan quality deteriorates.

Prudential regulation that the New Deal legislation established was to require financial institutions to insure their deposits with institutions such as the Federal Deposit Insurance Corporation and the Federal Savings and Loan Insurance Corporation. Although some observers originally saw obligatory low-cost insurance as a perverse mechanism that would encourage destabilizing conduct by the banks, experience has shown that the combination of insurance and strict supervision to avoid situations characterized by moral hazard[1] was an undeniable success in the degree to which it prevented massive bankruptcies in the financial sector.

As in other markets, however, regulation of financial activity can occasionally become excessive—that is, costly in terms of efficiency and welfare. For example, in the United States, the fear of bank runs and financial panics after the crash of 1929 led to the establishment of maximum limits on interest rates that commercial banks and savings and loan associations could pay their depositors. Although this action prevented some of these institutions from financing very risky projects by attracting deposits through high interest rates, the cost of this policy was an occasionally serious degree of financial disintermediation,[2] especially during 1973–74 and 1978–80, when market interest rates were substantially above the limits that the banks were permitted to offer.

Outside the United States, in Korea and Taiwan, for example, strict government controls on credit were the result of state efforts to promote growth, especially of exports, rather than to stabilize the banking industry. Credit was controlled primarily through loan subsidies for selected activities.

In other economies, such as those of Latin America, financial restriction has had a deeper fiscal root. Fiscal deficits were financed by monetary emission. As a result, governments had to perfect the use of financial instruments to collect the inflation tax. A requirement for high levels of reserves and obligatory bank holdings of public debt instruments formed part of a group of measures that were designed to extract seigniorage from the private demand for financial assets.

Financial restriction becomes financial repression when regulations that limit competition in the financial sector are combined with high and growing inflation.[3] Therefore, the difference between a regime that is merely restrictive and one that is repressive depends less on the quality of the measures (for example, institutional limits on interest rates) than on the effect that the measures exert on real variables, such as the real rate of interest or the real demand for money, that depend on the level of inflation.

The majority of economies that function under restrictive regimes are similar in their institutional organization of the financial market, but notable differences exist in their economic performance. Some economies, for example, Korea and Taiwan, have sustained moderate inflation rates, avoided fiscal excesses, and maintained realistic real exchange rates. Regulated real interest rates in these economies have been generally positive or moderately negative. In other economies, such as Argentina, Chile, and Uruguay, the opposite has occurred (see table 3-1). The phenomenon of financial repression, the most immediate symptom of which is demonetization—that is, a drastic fall in the real demand for money relative to GNP—is closely related to the level and the trajectory of the inflation rate.

Seigniorage as a Source of Financial Repression

Seigniorage is generally defined as the amount of resources the government obtains from the issuance of fiat money. Thus, if m is the ratio of money to GNP and μ is the rate at which money is printed, the seigniorage (s) "collected" as a proportion of national income is the product of the two. Expressed as an equation, $s = \mu m$.

In the long run, seigniorage equals the inflation tax plus the increase in money supply needed to meet the requirements associated with economic growth. Letting g represent GNP growth and π represent the rate of inflation, $s = (g + \pi)m$ defines seigniorage, whereas $t = \pi m$ defines the inflation tax. Needless to say, these two measures are equal in the long run when $g = 0$, that is, when the economy is not growing.

Table 3-1. Real Interest Rates on Short-Term Deposits, Selected Countries, 1967–76
(percent)

Economy	1967	1968	1969	1970	1971	1972	1973	1974	1975	1976
Argentina	−16.7	−6.9	0.3	−4.8	−17.1	−25.8	−27.3	−7.0	−58.2	−73.3
	(29.6)	(16.0)	(7.7)	(13.5)	(24.8)	(58.4)	(61.3)	(23.4)	(182.7)	(443.8)
Chile	−14.9	−18.3	−20.3	−22.7	−13.4	−41.9	−77.3	−64.0	—	—
	(21.1)	(26.1)	(29.3)	(33.3)	(19.0)	(77.3)	(354.5)	(504.5)	(374.7)	(211.9)
Korea, Rep. of	7.0	8.5	8.5	6.3	5.9	0.2	−1.9	−2.5	−4.0	−4.1
	(14.7)	(14.8)	(13.6)	(14.6)	(11.5)	(14.5)	(12.4)	(25.9)	(22.1)	(16.3)
Taiwan	5.4	3.1	3.5	6.3	6.0	2.9	−5.0	−14.5	9.3	5.8
	(4.4)	(6.6)	(6.2)	(3.4)	(3.0)	(5.7)	(13.9)	(28.0)	(2.3)	(5.4)
Uruguay	−44.0	−52.9	−11.3	−9.9	−14.2	−39.9	−45.2	−37.6	−35.0	0.3
	(89.3)	(124.9)	(19.5)	(17.6)	(23.6)	(76.5)	(97.0)	(77.2)	(81.6)	(50.6)

—Not available.

Note: All figures in parentheses are rates of inflation; others are real interest rates.

Source: Galbis (1979) for Argentina, Chile, and Uruguay; Fry (1985) for Korea and Taiwan.

In the short run, however, μ may be different from π, even if $g = 0$, because of inflationary rigidities or unemployment.

In most developing countries, governments extract seigniorage not only by means of unsupported monetary emission but also by paying artificially low or zero interest rates on the public debt, including commercial banks' deposits at the central bank. To prevent the cost of high reserve requirements from being transformed into an overly heavy burden on the banks and the borrowers, governments set deposit and loan rates at lower-than-market rates.

The need to extract seigniorage also forces the government to resort to measures that broaden the base on which it collects the inflation tax or to measures that at least avoid erosion of the base. To accomplish this, the demand for financial assets that substitute for currency, public bonds, and deposits is systematically reduced by taxes and increased transaction costs.[4] This happens in the case of the stocks and bonds of private corporations and in the case of external assets and liabilities. Thus, financial restriction is complemented by measures that inhibit the development of the capital market and cause the economy to be financially closed in relation to foreign markets.

Why does the government need to resort to seigniorage? The answer is, simply, to finance fiscal deficits or to transfer resources among various economic sectors. The first of these motives is obvious. If fiscal expenditures are greater than income, and other sources of financing do not exist, the only remaining resource is monetary emission. As long as the rate at which the monetary base expands does not exceed the growth in real money demand, inflation does not appear as a long-run phenomenon. When the opposite occurs, the monetary authorities collect the inflation tax from the holders of base money (that is, banks) and from private individuals. The real payers of the inflation tax are private individuals because the banks will introduce a larger spread between the interest rates for loans and savings. Because the government limits the interest rate on loans, the weight of the greater spread will fall on the savings rate, which frequently becomes negative in real terms.

The second motive, to act as a redistributor of resources, is also simple to explain. By means of the commercial or development banking systems, the central bank apportions funds for specific ends by printing money. As a result, it collects the inflation tax from savers and holders of money to subsidize chosen sectors. The subsidization scheme is complemented by interest rate controls on commercial bank loans and deposits. Of course, another alternative exists: explicitly subsidizing chosen sectors without controlling interest rates and incorporating the subsidies as part of the fiscal deficit. But, for various reasons—antidumping laws, a reticence to show high deficits, and so on—developing countries have rarely used this strategy.

As McKinnon and Mathieson (1981) demonstrate, if the government's only objective is to maximize seigniorage collection for a given rate of monetary expansion, the best way to attain this is to allow the interest rate to be determined freely and use the reserve coefficient as the only control variable. Doing so permits the tax on reserves to be transferred to borrowers and savers in proportions that depend on the elasticities of loans and deposits. At the same time, it avoids the imposition of the tax exclusively on savers, which occurs when the loan rate is controlled.[5] As argued later, however, freeing interest rates on loans in a context of macroeconomic instability can lead to prohibitively high real interest rates and moral hazard complications.

The Effects of Financial Repression

As already mentioned, the syndrome of financial repression results from the interaction between two kinds of measures: those that severely restrict financial competition and those that cause a high and variable rate of inflation. The effects of financial repression on saving and investment are well known. First, the flow of saving falls when the real return on deposits diminishes. Second, low real interest rates for loans attract projects of low profitability and low risk and ration or eliminate more productive (and riskier) investments. This happens because banks cannot establish varying interest rates in accordance with the degree of risk. Therefore, they try to minimize risk by choosing only safe projects.[6]

To improve seigniorage collection while taxing deposit or money holdings, the government must be able to establish effective restrictions on the demand for nonmonetary assets. When inflation is high, however, the demand for assets that hedge against inflation increases. Thus, if there are ceilings on interest rates, a higher rate of inflation decreases the real rate of interest on loans and deposits, thereby generating a process of financial disintermediation that is a characteristic of repressive regimes. This translates into a lower level of deposits and a smaller supply of bank loans as people try to invest in assets that provide a better level of protection against inflation, such as assets denominated in a foreign currency. The rate of inflation is also affected because, with a lower monetary base, the rate of monetary expansion needed to finance the same fiscal deficit becomes greater.

During periods of financial repression, private businesses not only find themselves with decreased access to bank credit but also find themselves less capable of self-financing, because high inflation makes accumulating enough savings to maintain a stable real value more difficult. Under these conditions, private investment decreases, and, when the cost of credit decreases too much, the quality of investment often deteriorates.

Usually, firms with low access to bank credit must resort to informal or curb markers. Thus, an unregulated credit market appears that competes with the regulated financial system, thereby giving rise to market segmentation. The interest rates in the unregulated market may be high in real terms because the benefits of financial intermediation are lost. Examples of benefits that could be lost would be (a) accommodating lenders of high liquidity preference with borrowers who desire longer terms, (b) reducing the risk of default by means of portfolio diversification, (c) taking advantage of economies of scale in portfolio management, and (d) decreasing information costs by means of specialization (Gurley and Shaw 1960; Tobin 1963). Although many governments have tried to suppress informal markets in an attempt to avoid losing control over credit and to avoid a fall in the volume of deposits, this has rarely been effective. Draconian laws do not work well in the face of economic incentives.

Moreover, many countries have relaxed their regulations to combat the threat that savings not intermediated by domestic banks could be invested abroad. Thus, the appearance of nonbank intermediaries that are subject to less regulatory control has been allowed. Generally, these intermediaries can establish interest rates and have more freedom than banks do to decide to whom to lend. As a counterpart, official guarantees are not offered to the same extent as those given to the regulated institutions.

The characteristics described above—credit market segmentation, disintermediation in the regulated segment, scarcity of savings and investments, and low capital productivity—identify financially repressed economies. Will these problems disappear if, as proposed by the theorists, liberalization is undertaken? Regrettably, the available empirical evidence is inconclusive. Although those countries that have liberalized have witnessed a rapid reorientation of savings flows to the deregulated sector, the effect on total saving has been less noticeable.

McKinnon's (1973) and Shaw's (1973) emphasis on the response of saving to liberalization has led to an intense theoretical discussion and numerous empirical studies. According to McKinnon, bank deposits are the principal vehicle by which businesses in developing countries accumulate funds for future investment (this is the hypothesis of complementarity between money and capital). Therefore, if the real return on deposits is negative, both saving and investment are reduced. In accordance with this mechanism, lumpy investment outlays depend on previously accumulated savings by the same investment units, because a well-developed capital market does not exist.

Shaw, however, emphasizes the role of banks as intermediaries between savers and investors. When deposits decrease, the banks' ability to offer loans deteriorates and businesses invest less. To attract a greater volume of deposits, the real interest rate must increase. In this case, the mechanism for investment financing also implies an increase in domestic deposits, as Shaw postulates that assets in banks are the only assets to which savers have access in countries of low per capita income.

Using a combined time-series and cross-sectional study of eighteen developing countries, Giovannini (1985) shows that there is little empirical support for the assumption that the elasticity of saving with respect to the real interest rate is positive and high. His results coincide with those of Leff and Sato (1980), who examined the effect of changes in the inflation rate on personal saving. In addition, analyses of individual countries whose financial reforms are well known, such as Argentina, Chile, Korea, and Uruguay, reach similar conclusions (Giovannini 1985; de Melo and Tybout 1986; Barandiaran 1987).

Some relevant data for these four countries are shown in table 3-2. Financial liberalization episodes occurred almost simultaneously in Argentina, Chile, and Uruguay in the late 1970s. Korea's financial reform took place in 1967 at a time when interest rate ceilings were increased. Liberalization was partially reversed in Argentina in 1982 and in Korea in 1973. Some deregulation of financial markets is currently under way in Korea, but its effects cannot be evaluated as yet. Despite the debt and financial crisis that hit Chile and Uruguay, these countries managed to keep positive real interest rates and moderate inflation after 1981, thus avoiding the reversal of financial liberalization that took place in Argentina.

Financial deepening (increased financial intermediation) occurred in Argentina, Chile, and Uruguay as a result of liberalization. This is illustrated by an increase in savings and time deposits (the difference between M_2/Y and M_1/Y in table 3-2). Curiously, the same phenomenon also took place in Korea despite higher inflation and a shift toward greater financial restrictions in 1973. In Chile and Argentina, failure to reduce inflation quickly may explain why monetization did not occur immediately after financial liberalization reforms were introduced in the 1970s. In Chile, however, the situation changed completely when inflation rates went down in 1982.

Investment behavior has been more ambiguous. In Korea financial restrictions did not prevent the rate of investment from increasing after 1973, but the Chilean liberalization reform was not accompanied by an increase in investment. Of the three Latin American countries, only Uruguay experienced a significant increase in the rate of capital formation in passing from one period (repression) to the other (liber-

Table 3-2. Economic Indicators, Selected Countries and Periods

Country and period[a]	Real interest rate[b] (1)	Inflation rate (2)	M_1/Y[c] (3)	M_2/Y[c] (4)	Invest-ment[d] (5)	Foreign savings[e] (6)	Public savings[f] (7)	Private savings Total[g] (8)	Inflation tax[h] (9)	Net[i] (10)	Fiscal deficit[j] (11)	ICOR[k] (12)	Real exchange rate index[l] (13)	Growth rate (14)
Argentina														
1967–76	−23.7	87.3	14.4	20.8	21.3	0.3	−2.7	23.7	6.4	17.3	4.0	8.5	100	2.5
1977–81	−4.8	143.2	9.0	18.2	23.3	0.4	−2.2	25.1	6.7	18.4	4.0	29.1	80	0.8
1982–84	−20.3	379.6	4.8	16.8	15.7	3.6	−7.0	19.1	7.8	11.3	8.3	78.5	141	0.2
Chile														
1967–74	−34.1	182.8	9.0	15.5	17.9	1.7	−1.2	17.4	6.4	11.0	4.5	11.2	100	1.6
1975–81 L	10.5	115.4	4.9	13.9	17.1	6.2	3.4	7.5	2.7	4.8	−1.8	4.0	196	4.3
1982–83 L	13.2	18.6	6.1	27.0	10.5	7.5	−0.4	3.4	1.4	2.0	1.8	1.4	225	7.4
Korea, Rep. of														
1966–72 L	6.1	12.5	8.2	23.2	24.6	5.8	−0.7	19.5	1.5	18.0	1.1	2.2	100	11.2
1973–80	−2.3	17.4	10.1	28.3	29.3	5.0	−0.4	24.5	1.6	22.9	1.6	3.4	100	8.5
1981–83 L	−3.7	10.6	9.2	32.7	28.4	4.1	−1.1	25.4	0.9	24.5	2.5	3.6	101	8.0
Uruguay														
1967–75	−28.2	67.3	11.7	17.7	11.9	0.9	−2.1	13.1	4.9	8.2	2.8	6.0	100	2.0
1976–81 L	−6.4	52.9	9.2	26.1	16.0	4.0	1.1	10.9	3.0	7.9	1.0	4.0	83	4.0
1982–83 L	13.2	34.1	8.3	46.0	12.2	1.8	−4.6	15.0	2.6	12.4	6.5	−1.6	64	−7.6

a. "L" indicates a period when financial liberalization occurred.

b. Ex post thirty-day deposits, calculated as $(i - \pi)/(1 + \pi)$, where π is actual inflation based on the consumer price index.

c. M_1 = Money; M_2 = Money + Quasi money; Y = Nominal GDP.

d. Total gross investment as a percentage of GDP at constant prices.

e. Current account balance of payments deficit as a percentage of GDP.

f. Consolidated government savings as a percentage of GDP.

g. Column 5 − Column 6 − Column 7.

h. Estimated as $\Delta M_1 - g(M_1/Y)$, where ΔM_1 is the absolute increase in M_1, and g is the rate of growth in real GDP.

i. Column 8 − Column 9.

j. Percentage of GDP.

k. Incremental capital-output ratio (Column 5 / Column 14).

l. Trade-weighted multilateral real exchange rate.

Source: IMF (various issues). Data sources for *i* are Galbis (1979); Fry (1985); FIEL (various issues); Hanna (1986); and de Melo and Tybout (1986).

alization). In Argentina the higher rate of investment during 1977–81 is mostly explained by the behavior of public investment. In Chile monetary contraction and a deep recession at the beginning of the liberalization period explain why investment did not increase during 1975–81.

Since 1982 the debt crisis has been taking its toll in South America, where investment rates have fallen quite dramatically. Current account imbalances increased in Argentina and Chile as a result of higher interest payments. Because in Argentina and Uruguay the government owes most of the external debt, avoiding a decrease in public saving has been impossible, despite fiscal adjustments. Chile, where fiscal discipline has been the rule since the mid-1970s, is an exception to the experience of other South American countries.

Table 3-2 also shows savings estimates corrected to account for the effect of the inflation tax. This correction is necessary because accumulating nominal money balances in order to catch up with inflation does not represent an increase in real wealth. Despite this adjustment, the results do not support a positive relationship between financial liberalization and personal saving. This conclusion is consistent with the idea that liquidity constraints affect consumption in developing countries where credit markets are underdeveloped; liberalizing liquidity constraints produces a higher credit supply, which allows increases in consumption instead of encouraging saving.

By contrast, the incremental capital-output ratio has fallen in all countries that underwent liberalization reforms except Argentina, where government intervention in investment decisions was haphazard during and after the liberalization episode.

If one accepts that the interest elasticity of savings is low, the effects of liberalization on financial intermediation are a consequence of portfolio reshuffling from other assets to deposits and not a result of postponing consumption. This conclusion does not, however, preclude increases in investment, because if more funds are intermediated within the banking system, the restriction on domestic credit is reduced and more firms have access to a greater quantity of loanable funds. Whether this has been the case in actual liberalization experiences is still open to debate.

Problems with Domestic Financial Liberalization

The 1970s literature on financial repression and liberalization emphasized certain aspects of the problem while ignoring others. Among the aspects ignored were those related to market imperfections unique to the credit market. The question is whether a credit market can be liberalized in the same manner as other markets. The failed liberalization attempts during the last decade in Latin America have necessitated reconsideration of this question. The result is a new analytical framework that includes problems of imperfect information and moral hazard that characterize bank lending activities. The work of Stiglitz and Weiss (1981), Díaz-Alejandro (1985), Cho (1986), and McKinnon (1986) has contributed to the design of this framework.

Credit Allocation in Markets with Imperfect Information

One of the most generalized statements made about financial repression is that institutional limits on interest rates ration credit and allocate it inefficiently. A liberalization of interest rates, however, does not necessarily imply either that all possible borrowers will receive credit or that the most productive projects will receive financing. The representation of the credit market by means of conventional supply and demand curves is a useful, albeit deceptive, point of departure.

It is simplistic to believe that interest rate ceilings behave like maximum prices and that when ceilings are removed, excess demand for credit will be totally eliminated. Although the demand for credit is a decreasing function of its cost, the supply does not grow indefinitely with the rate of interest. Strictly speaking, each bank increases loans while the expected revenue from the loans increases, but at high interest rates expected revenue could fall.

Stiglitz and Weiss (1981) suggest that this possibility is the result of combining two effects. First, the incentive effect causes borrowers to assume more risky projects when the cost of credit increases. Second, an adverse selection of loan portfolios occurs when the banks' most reliable clients are discouraged by high interest rates and are replaced by less solvent debtors who, because of a lack of perfect information, are indistinguishable from the others.

Let q be the probability of default, namely, the probability that borrowers do not pay back their debts upon maturity. Then the banks' expected revenue equals the capitalized amount of the loans times the probability of nondefault. Because q increases with L, the real interest rate charged on loans, the behavior of R^e, that is, the expected revenue of banks, is as depicted in figure 3-1.[7] At relatively low levels of r_L, an increase in the real interest rate raises banks' expected revenues. Because of a rising risk of default, however, a higher r_L^* is followed by a less-than-proportional increase in R^e. When the interest rate reaches r_L, expected revenue attains a maximum level. Then it starts to fall, because new increases in the interest rate are insufficient to compensate for revenue losses that result from the borrowers' insolvency.

In this manner, if the rate that equalizes supply and demand in the credit market is greater than the rate that maximizes expected bank

Figure 3-1. Credit Rationing in Markets with Imperfect Information

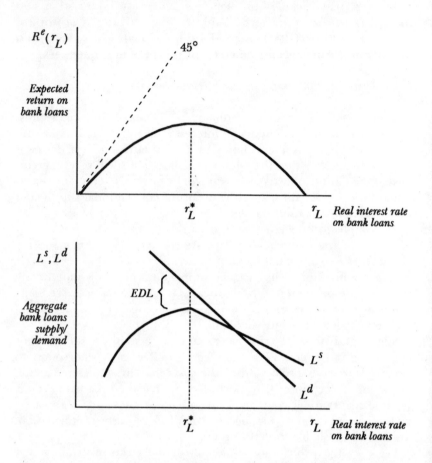

revenue, banks will voluntarily ration credit. The situation appears in the lower panel of figure 3-1, where L^s is the supply of loans and L^d is the demand. r^*_L is the equilibrium interest rate that is compatible with the maximization of expected revenue, and *EDL* is the excess of demand for loans that prevails in equilibrium.

The foregoing analysis has shown that banks ration credit even if interest rates are fully liberalized. Figure 3-2 aids in the analysis of credit allocation. Three expected revenue curves appear that correspond to three different groups of borrowers. The most productive borrowers are those of group 3, and the least productive those of group 1. This means that the investment projects undertaken by the borrowers in group 3 have the highest expected returns, and the proj-

Figure 3-2. Allocation of Bank Credit among Different Groups of Borrowers

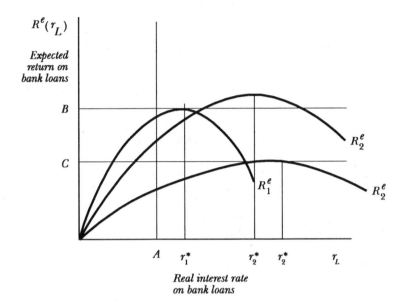

Real interest rate on bank loans

ects undertaken by group 1 borrowers have the lowest expected returns. Note that higher productivity is generally associated with higher uncertainty about project returns.

Although the different groups of borrowers can be distinguished by the expected productivity of their projects, those within each group are observationally equivalent. Given the available information, banks cannot know which of the debtors within a single group are more or less solvent. Therefore, banks charge all borrowers in the same group the same interest rate.

Banks bear some of the uncertainty about investment returns. To be sure, the nature of the loan contract is such that banks will share the losses if the returns on the projects are low and cause investors to default on their loans. But if the opposite occurs, banks will not participate in the benefits, because the interest rate on the loans is fixed and is not contingent upon the projects' results.

Because the variability of the returns of the pool of borrowers increases in passing from group 1 to group 3, the banks' expected profit at each interest rate level decreases.[8] In this context, if there is a ceiling on the real interest rate for loans (*OA* in figure 3-2), and if the supply of loanable funds is scarce, some borrowers from group 1, the group of least productivity, will be the only ones to receive credit.

In establishing loan priorities, banks do not consider the criterion of investment productivity; they consider their expected revenues. In a free market (without restrictions on interest rates), the maximum expected revenue is obtained by lending, in order of priority, to group 2, group 1, and group 3. Although this is better than financial repression, the resulting allocation of credit is not optimal, because it leaves the investors of greatest productivity on the fringe. For example, if competition among banks determines a deposit rate of interest *OB*, loans will be provided to all of the investors in group 2, some in group 1, and none in group 3 (Stiglitz and Weiss 1981). On this basis, Cho (1986) has stated that interest rate liberalization in an economy in which all capital is exclusively intermediated by banks does not guarantee an efficient allocation of capital. For efficiency to occur, a well-developed stock market must also exist.

The adverse selection and incentive effects that characterize loan financing in the presence of imperfect information are related to the noncontingent nature of bank loans, which allows successful investors to keep any profits that are left and failed investors to transfer their losses to the banks. Financing by means of stocks is free of these problems, however, because stockholders share in a firm's progress regardless of its state of health. Therefore, in an efficient capital market, stocks channel very risky and highly productive projects, and banks are left with the financing of investments that are more secure and provide lower expected revenues.

A second-best policy for the case in which a well-developed stock market does not exist is to force banks to lend to sectors that would otherwise be rationed. To accomplish this, the average cost of bank liabilities (deposits plus rediscounts) must not be greater than *OC* (figure 3-2). This type of intervention has been common in many countries. Incidentally, a similar justification led to the creation of development banks in Latin America in the 1930s and 1940s (Díaz-Alejandro 1985). Implementation problems can, however, lead to a vicious circle. To liberalize successfully, a well-organized stock market must exist, but this cannot be developed as long as the largest firms (those expected to stimulate a stock market) continue to have preferential and generally subsidized access to bank credit.

The difficulties associated with the creation of a long-term capital market are well known in developing countries. Nevertheless, Korea's recent experience of combining gradual liberalization of the traditional financial sector with a more active development of the corporate stock and bond market is promising (Barandiaran 1987).

Macroeconomic Instability and Moral Hazard

Díaz-Alejandro (1985) and McKinnon (1986) have formulated an argument that is used to explain the phenomena of high real interest rates, insolvency, and massive bank interventions which characterized the financial reform programs of Argentina, Chile, and Uruguay during the late 1970s. The authors emphasize the problem of moral hazard that exists when, because changing domestic policies and external shocks cause macroeconomic instability, the yields of a large number of investments are found to be mutually and positively correlated. Even when bank liabilities are not formally insured, they are implicitly insured because, as already mentioned, the banks' intermediary function cannot be separated from their role in money creation, at least in a system of proportional reserve requirements.

Macroeconomic instability aggravates the problem of moral hazard because it leads to a positive correlation among bank failures. In other words, the occurrence of one failure is not independent of the occurrence of others. Thus, if a bank failure takes place in the framework of a crisis, the monetary authorities will find sanctioning the bank's imprudence more difficult. The implicit insurance and the reluctance of the authorities to be accommodating provide banks with a strong incentive to lend at very high interest rates.

To avoid this outcome, various institutional solutions have been proposed that move from greater restrictions on financial activities to nearly complete laissez faire. We will examine some of these proposals.

CONTROLS ON INTEREST RATES. McKinnon (1986), in a significant departure from his original position on the issue, suggests controls on interest rates, but only in cases of moral hazard. To be more specific, ceilings on interest rates are justified when, to prevent further interventions, the monetary authorities impose a lower and more secure interest rate than the banks are willing to charge. According to McKinnon, the authorities' failure to recognize the need to limit interest rates was partially responsible for the financial collapses in the Southern Cone of Latin America. The challenge is to set a rate of interest that solves the moral hazard problem without incurring the inefficiencies discussed earlier.

GREATER SUPERVISION OF BANKS. Although, as de Juan (1986) indicates, poor bank administration is an essential ingredient in all crises, in cases of high economic instability, distinguishing between good and bad administrators becomes difficult. This works in favor of bad management. Banks need more supervision when economic conditions are unusual, given the greater incentives for risky conduct. The need for supervision arises because of the system of proportional reserve requirements, with government guarantees on loans. Supervision must be accompanied by regulations that are stricter than those applied in more stable economies in order to prevent, among other things, the concentration of the loan portfolio in the hands of a few clients, excessive exchange rate risk, and a mismatch of terms to maturity between savings and loan operations. The regulatory entity must be more active and be composed of competent, honest, well-paid officials. The authorities should maintain free interest rates only if they are able to make a more objective evaluation than a bank can about the risk associated with a loan portfolio. For supervision to be successful, bank information must be available.

DEPOSIT INSURANCE. Allowing depositors to cover the risk of bank insolvency or failure by acquiring insurance, instead of relying on implicit or explicit protection by the central bank, is an alternative that is compatible with the functioning of a market economy. In this case, the depositors assume the risk but can opt to transfer it to the insurer in exchange for the associated fees. The problem is whether this type of insurance could be offered at a reasonable price.

In a small economy in which external revenues are highly concentrated in relatively few activities, deposit insurance practically becomes national revenue insurance (Rosende 1986). In other words, if fluctuations in international prices affect real domestic output in a manner that is magnified by effects on the prices of assets and domestic credit, insuring deposits assumes insuring the economy against fluctuations in current account balances. Under these conditions, complete insurance coverage lacks viability, especially if the instability coming from outside is combined with erratic domestic policies.

SEPARATING THE CREDIT MARKET FROM THE MONEY MARKET (SIMONS'S PROPOSAL). Accepting a fixed rate of exchange between bank debt and the unit of account while the price of other assets depends on market conditions creates a serious externality when the economy is not sufficiently stable. Financial crises cause the prices of assets to suffer and force the state to apportion the losses within the society by means of taxes, debt, or inflation. With the onset of the crisis of the 1980s in Latin America, some authors (Fernández 1983; Rosende 1986) revived an old proposal by Simons (1936). The proposal was to separate the credit market from the money market to avoid compromising monetary stability when there was a deterioration in the quality of loans.

The core of the proposal is the distinction between the banks' monetary function as safe places to keep money and their intermediary function as sources of investment funds. To comply with the first function, all deposits would be subject to 100 percent reserve requirements and provide rent to the bank, not the depositor. In the case of the second function, the banks would act as mutual fund administrators or investment trusts. They would sell shares to investors, who could choose from a selection of various mutual funds and face the same risk that they would if investing in the stock market.

The internalization of risk on the part of savers would cause a greater level of investment in information and reduce supervision to a minimum. When the prices of shares change, profits and losses would be distributed instantly, without government intervention. These are the advantages. The disadvantage is that in a very uncertain or unstable environment, fluctuations in the prices of shares would promote a great degree of disintermediation by encouraging a demand for safer assets, such as foreign currency.

As we have seen, designing an institutional regime for the financial sector that works better than traditional regimes in times of economic instability is not easy. To be viable, a proposal like the one by Simons requires prudent management of monetary and fiscal policy that encourages predictable economic and political outcomes. But if this occurs, the problems of the traditional financial system, given adequate regulation and supervision, are less noticeable.

Problems with External Liberalization and Dollarization

The debt crisis has delayed the restoration of normal economic and financial conditions in world markets. In some developing countries, overborrowing was partly the result of a premature opening of the capital account, when macroeconomic conditions were unstable and international liquidity was strong, that is, after the 1974 and 1979 oil shocks. Three Latin American countries known for their tight controls on capital mobility chose to abandon them. Uruguay did so in 1974 before liberalizing the domestic financial system. Argentina liberalized the capital account at the time of its 1977 financial reforms, and Chile liberalized in 1979, five years after deregulation and privatization began in the domestic financial system.

The international response to financial liberalization in these three countries was high. In Argentina high real interest rates attracted capital inflows from abroad that compromised monetary stability. This forced the government to set some restrictions, which it later abandoned. As shown in figure 3-3, however, most capital inflows were the result of public borrowing to finance high fiscal deficits. From 1976 the exchange rate system was characterized by a uniform rate coupled with unrestricted currency convertibility. Capital inflows caused the real exchange rate to appreciate significantly. After the public lost its confidence in the government's ability to sustain its exchange rate policies, capital flight occurred and the public debt increased.

In Uruguay the government encouraged dollarization by allowing banks and *financieras* (nonbank financial institutions in Latin America) to offer dollar-denominated deposits to domestic and foreign investors (see table 3-3). Initially, dollarization halted the outflow of financial capital that had been taking place since the beginning of the 1970s by allowing more financial intermediation to occur in the domestic market. After a few years, however, dollarization became a source of great instability. At first, instability was the result of disturbances originating in Argentina, a neighbor that transmitted the fluctuations associated with its changing economic and political conditions. Then, by exposing the Uruguayan financial system to undue exchange rate risk, dollarization postponed necessary adjustments of the exchange rate. When the government finally intervened, Uruguayans had to face high fiscal costs to bail out depositors, protect the solvency of financial institutions, and reestablish monetary confidence.

Chile underwent a similar experience, but not as a result of a dollarization of bank deposits. Since 1979 Chilean banks had been allowed

Figure 3-3. Capital Inflows, Argentina, 1976–81

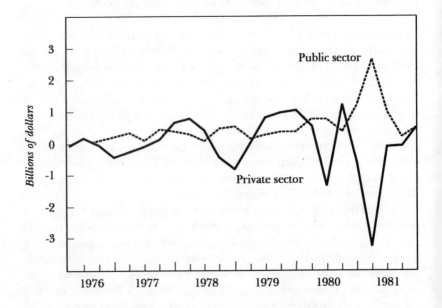

Source: Central Bank of Argentina data.

Table 3-3. Dollarization in the Banking System, Uruguay, 1973–83

Year	Dollar deposits/ total deposits	Nonresident deposits/ total dollar deposits	Resident dollar deposits/ peso deposits	Resident deposits in U.S. banks (millions of dollars)	Resident deposits in U.S. banks/ dollar deposits in UBS[a]
1973	0.24	0	0.30	147	2.81
1974	0.27	0	0.36	164	3.53
1975	0.37	0	0.58	172	1.81
1976	0.48	1.0	0.90	245	1.60
1977	0.57	1.0	1.31	243	0.81
1978	0.54	4.1	1.10	231	0.58
1979	0.49	6.4	0.90	202	0.27
1980	0.45	6.0	0.76	254	0.24
1981	0.49	7.9	0.88	367	0.26
1982	0.75	8.5	2.77	759	0.43
1983	0.67	9.3	2.75	1,222	0.85

Note: All figures are end-of-year values. Dollar deposits are expressed in pesos, using the end-of-year financial exchange rate (buyer).

a. UBS = Uruguay banking system.

Source: de Melo and Tybout (1986).

to borrow abroad without restrictions, which increased their exposure to exchange rate risk (see figure 3-4). Fluctuations in the real exchange rate—first appreciation, then depreciation—were responsible for the collapse of many bank and nonbank intermediaries.

Mexico and Venezuela also allowed an open capital account and unrestricted currency convertibility. Like Argentina, these two countries ended up with high public indebtedness combined with private capital flight. In both cases, the main reason was exchange rate overvaluation caused by unsustainable capital inflows.

These experiences and several hypothetical examples may illustrate the problems related to free capital mobility in developing countries. Opening the capital account reduces the demand for domestic money and, hence, the government's ability to collect the inflation tax. When the fiscal deficit is high, the government is forced to borrow abroad. If, alternatively, the deficit is financed by issuing domestic bonds, domestic interest rates may increase and induce private capital inflows. In both cases, external debt increases and, unless fiscal discipline is restored, may rise unsustainably as in the case of Argentina in 1979–80.

Even if the fiscal deficit is corrected and domestic financial markets are liberalized, as in Chile, financial openness can provoke an initial overshooting of capital inflows that appreciates the real exchange rate above its long-run equilibrium level. This creates dynamic problems as the temporary increase in the stock of reserves results in a squeeze

Figure 3-4. Average Dollar Funding as a Share of Liquid Liabilities, by Type of Bank, Chile, 1978–84

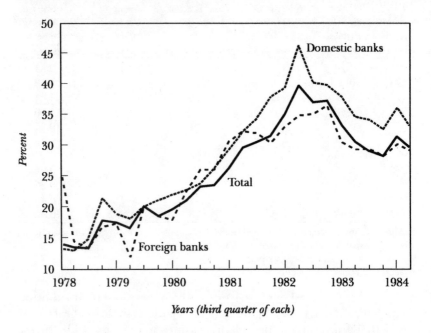

Years (third quarter of each)

Source: Hanna (1986).

on the prices of tradables. Thus, several authors have suggested that financial liberalization should be gradual and take place after implementing other reforms, such as trade liberalization, the sustainability of which depends on a low and stable real exchange rate (Edwards 1984).

On grounds of efficiency, one can also distinguish many situations in which unrestricted capital mobility leads to external overborrowing. Assume, for example, that international lenders perceive the risk of default by an individual debtor as an increasing function of the overall debt in that debtor's country. In this case, even small countries will face an upward sloping supply curve for external funds. The negative externality that results in this case, a difference between the average and the marginal cost of credit, justifies imposing an optimal tax on capital imports (Harberger 1976). Another externality appears when foreign creditors do not distinguish properly between official and private domestic debtors and feel implicitly covered by official guarantees even if the loan recipient is not a public institution. Thus, if private borrowers default on their debts, governments will have to bail them out or face indiscriminate increases in country risk premiums or reduced credit. This occurred in many countries in 1982–83. Lack of attention to this problem helped to increase debt in Latin America during the 1970s.

Other arguments against laissez faire in capital account transactions are those based on the theory of second best (Lipsey and Lancaster 1956–57). Economists know that the liberalization of one market may not be the best choice if distortions exist in other markets. For example, if a tariff protects local goods and services, financial openness will allow capital accumulation to proceed in the domestic economy up to a point at which the world real interest rate equals the distorted (by the tariff) value of marginal product. This, in turn, means higher capital accumulation (and external indebtedness) than is socially desirable, because the domestic value of importable goods exceeds the international value.

The lessons of the 1970s are most apt in a situation of high international liquidity. Doubts exist, however, about the convenience (and relevance) of limiting capital inflows under the world financial market's present conditions. This market is characterized, if anything, by a lack of credit, especially for indebted countries. Once a country has decided to open its capital account, the mobility of loans depends on the attitude of foreign lenders. If they perceive a high political risk associated with lending to a given country, they will ration credit or withhold it entirely. The same holds true for foreign investment. A more important question concerns what can be done about capital outflows. On this issue, Southern Cone policies provide interesting examples. Unrestricted currency convertibility at exchange rates that are set in advance does not seem to be viable under conditions of chronic instability. It may facilitate capital flight, in which case relying on a dual-exchange-rate system (pegged for real transactions and floating for the capital account) to check capital outflows is better, although this does not prevent leakages of foreign reserves through illegal transactions (Dornbusch 1985).

The differences among exchange rate systems become less important in the long run: all systems must converge to a relatively uniform exchange rate that is adjusted according to the difference between domestic and world inflation. Under high and persistent domestic inflation, foreign assets are a hedge against losses in real wealth. Establishing efficient controls on capital flight is difficult. Because of high substitutability between domestic and foreign assets, the real yield on local bank deposits cannot be low or negative in real terms. This rules out taxation of depositors as a means of extracting seigniorage and shifts the incidence of high spreads of the real interest rate onto loans where substitutability with foreign credit is much lower. With high domestic interest rates, financial repression disappears, but banks face a greater risk of insolvency.

The existence of domestic debt, private or public, indexed in dollars or another strong currency, is a two-edged sword in countries lacking economic or political stability. The higher the exchange rate risk, the more acceptable this type of debt is to investors. Nevertheless, debtors' financial positions are seriously compromised when the actual rate of devaluation exceeds the expected rate, unless their current and future incomes are denominated in dollars.

Often, the government itself, under budgetary pressures, is the main issuer of dollar-linked debt. In doing so, the authorities myopically engage in a game of perverse consequences for the economy. When the country accumulates reserves, the government allows the exchange rate to appreciate, thus lowering the fiscal impact of its own debt service. This appreciation also encourages private borrowers to offer dollar-denominated debt or deposits. If external problems appear, the government postpones exchange rate adjustment because of its own exchange rate exposure and that of the private sector. When it finally devalues, the government faces both its own losses and those of domestic private banks. The result is higher inflation, fueled by monetary expansion, and less economic stability.

Conclusion

Does a clear relationship exist between financial policies and growth? This question does not have a simple answer. In theory, the move from a repressed to a freer financial environment should place the economy on a higher real growth path. In practice, however, this has not always been the case. Although the empirical evidence does not fully contradict the expectations of financial liberalization advocates, the theory on which they base their expectations needs some adjustment.

To begin with, the empirical evidence is that private savings are not sensitive to changes in real interest rates or inflation. A higher real interest rate may, however, exert a positive effect on investment if it contributes to freeing liquidity constraints. The latter may occur if the shift in wealth composition from foreign assets to domestic bank deposits enhances, through greater credit availability, firms' investment possibilities.

At any rate, a lack of interest response by private savings places a heavier burden on other sources of savings. If access to foreign credit is limited, long-run increases in investment can take place only when fiscal conditions are improved. But even if fiscal rigidities and foreign constraints inhibit a permanent increase in investment levels, financial liberalization might increase investment efficiency (on this, the empirical evidence is more supportive).

Financial reform is consistent not only with better resource allocation but also with more efficient seigniorage collection. Freeing interest rates in a context of macroeconomic instability, however, usually leads to prohibitively high real interest rates and moral hazard complications. The success of a financial reform depends very much on its timing.

Some economists argue that domestic financial liberalization should precede liberalization of the capital account of the balance of payments (see, for example, McKinnon 1982). They believe that if macroeconomic instability persists, the government should maintain restrictions on borrowing and currency convertibility; otherwise, destabilizing capital inflows or outflows such as those experienced by Argentina, Chile, and Uruguay in the late 1970s may occur. This conclusion has lost some of its relevance, however, because international financial conditions have changed so significantly, especially in relation to the highly indebted developing countries. Destabilizing capital inflows are less likely to occur now that voluntary lending to indebted countries has been reduced to almost zero. Moreover, these countries are having a difficult time attracting direct foreign investment or inducing repatriation of wealth by domestic residents. Under these conditions, the governments fear that strict controls on capital outflows may discourage potential investors and reduce capital inflows.

Because lack of fiscal discipline is one of the main reasons for financial repression, most financially repressed economies have ample room for fiscal adjustment. Significant amounts of private investment can be "crowded in" in many countries if governments manage to reduce unnecessary current expenditures. Greater fiscal discipline is necessary for financial liberalization policies to succeed. Moderate inflation rates and greater control of the budget explain why policy interventions did not result in serious financial repression in Taiwan and Korea. They also explain why financial liberalization was not reversed in Chile amid the problems the banking system faced in 1982, when the central bank intervened in several banks and *financieras*.

Unfortunately, macroeconomic stability does not fully depend on domestic policies. Real depreciation and interest payments on foreign debt have also aggravated budget deficits. For financial reform to be successful, there must be a solution to the debt problem afflicting developing countries as well as an increase in foreign lending and investment.

Notes

1. The moral hazard problem arises because banks have less incentive to be careful about lending when they are fully insured than when they are not.
2. Financial disintermediation occurs when the amount of savings channeled through the commercial banking system is reduced.
3. McKinnon (1973) and Shaw (1973) introduced the term "financial repression." The distinction between financial restriction and repression was employed by Fry (1982).
4. Transaction costs are the costs of converting money into other assets and vice versa.
5. In accordance with a well-known principle of tax collection—to collect more—it is advisable to apply the greater weight of a tax where the elasticity of demand is low. If loans are not very elastic to real interest rates, part of the weight should be transferred to borrowers.
6. This does not, however, discard the possibility that the banks can avoid the limit on the loan rate by demanding compensatory balances or offering loans and other services to depositors to make their deposits more attractive.
7. Mathematically, the function represented in figure 3-1 is $R^e = R^e(r_L) = (1 + r_L)(1 - q)$, where $q = q(r_L)$ and $q' > 0$. This relationship assumes that there is no collateral for bank loans, but the results do not change qualitatively if loans are partially collateralized.
8. Thus, for low values of r_L, R^e_3 lies below R^e_2, which in turn lies below R^e_1.

Selected Bibliography

Barandiaran, Edgardo. 1987. "Financial Liberalization in LDCs: A Review of Experiences." World Bank, Economics and Finance Division, Washington, D.C.

Cho, Yoon Je. 1986. "Inefficiencies from Financial Liberalization in the Absence of Well-Functioning Equity Markets." *Journal of Money, Credit, and Banking* 18(2):191–99.

de Juan, Aristbulo. 1986. "From Good Bankers to Bad Bankers." World Bank, Country Economics Department, Washington, D.C.

de Melo, Jaime, and James Tybout. 1986. "The Effects of Financial Liberalization on Savings and Investment in Uruguay." *Economic Development and Cultural Change* 34(3):607–40.

Díaz-Alejandro, Carlos. 1985. "Good-bye Financial Repression, Hello Financial Crash." *Journal of Development Economics* 19(1–2):1–24.

Dornbusch, Rudiger. 1985. *Special Exchange Rates for Capital Account Transactions.* Working Paper 1659. Cambridge, Mass.: National Bureau of Economic Research.

Edwards, Sebastian. 1984. *The Order of Liberalization of the External Sector in Developing Countries.* Essays in International Finance 156. Princeton, N.J.: Princeton University Press.

Fernández, Roque. 1983. "La crisis financiera argentina." *Desarrollo Económico* 89(June):79–97.

FIEL (Fundación de Investigaciones Económicas Latinoamericanas). Various issues. *Indicadores de coyuntura.* Buenos Aires.

Fry, Maxwell. 1982. "Models of Financially Repressed Developing Economies." *World Development* 10(9):731–50.

————. 1985. "Financial Structure, Monetary Policy, and Economic Growth in Hong Kong, Singapore, Taiwan, and South Korea, 1960–1983." In Vittorio Corbo, Anne O. Krueger, and Fernando Ossa, eds., *Export-Oriented Development Strategies*. Boulder, Colo.: Westview Press.

Galbis, Vicente. 1979. "Inflation and Interest Rate Policies in Latin America, 1967–1976." IMF *Staff Paper* 256(2 June):334–66.

Giovannini, Alberto. 1985. "Saving and the Real Interest Rate in LDCs." *Journal of Development Economics* 18(2–3 August):197–217.

Gurley, John, and Edward Shaw. 1960. *Money in a Theory of Finance*. Washington, D.C.: Brookings Institution.

Hanna, Donald. 1986. "The Chilean Financial System, 1974–1982: The Regulatory Role in Financial Collapse." Harvard University, Department of Economics, Cambridge, Mass.

Harberger, Arnold. 1976. "On Country Risk and the Social Cost of Foreign Borrowing by Developing Countries." University of Chicago, Department of Economics.

IMF (International Monetary Fund). Various issues. *International Financial Statistics*. Washington, D.C.

Jaffee, Dwight M., and Joseph E. Stiglitz. 1990. "Credit Rationing." In Benjamin M. Friedman and Frank H. Hahn, eds., *Handbook of Monetary Economics*. Vol. 2. Amsterdam: North-Holland.

Leff, Nathaniel, and Kazuo Sato. 1980. "Macroeconomic Adjustment in Developing Countries, Instability, Short-Run Growth, and External Dependency." *Review of Economics and Statistics* 62(2 May):170–79.

Lipsey, Richard, and Kelvin Lancaster. 1956–57. "The General Theory of Second Best." *Review of Economic Studies* 24(63):11–32.

McKinnon, Ronald. 1973. *Money and Capital in Economic Development*. Washington, D.C.: Brookings Institution.

————. 1982. "The Order of Economic Liberalization: Lessons from Chile and Argentina." In Karl Brunner and Allan H. Meltzer, eds., *Economic Policy in a World of Change*. Amsterdam: North-Holland.

————. 1986. "Financial Liberalization in Retrospect: Interest Rate Policies in LDCs." Working Paper. Stanford University, Department of Economics, Stanford, Calif.

McKinnon, Ronald, and Donald Mathieson. 1981. *How to Manage a Repressed Economy*. Essays in International Finance 145. Princeton, N.J.: Princeton University Press.

Rosende, Francisco. 1986. "Institucionalidad financiera y estabilidad económica." *Cuadernos de Economía* 23(68):77–99.

Shaw, Edward. 1973. *Financial Deepening in Economic Development*. New York: Oxford University Press.

Simons, Henry. 1936. "Rules versus Authority in Monetary Policy." *Journal of Political Economy* 44(February-December):1–30.

Stiglitz, Joseph, and Andrew Weiss. 1981. "Credit Rationing in Markets with Imperfect Information." *American Economic Review* 71(3 June):393–410.

Tobin, James. 1963. "Commercial Banks as Creators of Money." In Deane Carson, ed., *Banking and Monetary Studies*. Homewood, Ill.: Richard D. Irwin.

4

Financial Factors in Economic Development

Rudiger Dornbusch and Alejandro Reynoso

FINANCIAL FACTORS have been assigned strategic importance in economic development. But different factors have been isolated for different regions. In Asia the role of an unrepressed financial market in mobilizing savings and allocating investments is emphasized. In Latin America the emphasis is on the role of inflationary finance—the scope for using deficits to enhance growth and, increasingly, the connection between high and unstable inflation and poor economic performance. This chapter reviews and contrasts the two approaches. Our analysis concludes that the evidence does not support vigorous claims for the benefits of financial liberalization. Equally, however, we note that the scope for inflationary finance is small and the risks are larger than commonly accepted.

Growth in per capita income derives from the accumulation of physical capital and more efficient use of resources. Efficient use of resources is supported not only by the application of superior techniques but also by policies and institutions. Financial factors influence economic development by affecting the extent to which savings become available and the intermediation of these savings to investment opportunities that bring the highest return.

Economic history is rife with allusions to joint-stock companies as a decisive innovation in the implementation of capitalist production and distribution. Alex Gerschenkron and subsequently other authors have stressed the importance of finance. The Stanford School of John Gurley, Edward Shaw, and Ronald McKinnon has emphasized finance as a determinant of successful economic development, but although their views have become dogma, little evidence exists to support their pervasive claim. The Republic of Korea in the 1963–82 period experienced an average growth rate of output per capita of 4.8 percent—1.6 percent from capital accumulation and 3.2 percent from more efficient resource use. No growth-accounting exercise is available that would show us how much of this growth can be attributed to a favorable financial environment. The role of financial factors thus remains largely speculative.

We argue here that financial factors are important, but probably only when financial instability becomes a dominant force in the economy. In this respect financial factors, like the foreign trade regime, probably do not make much difference to the level of per capita GDP unless there is considerable distortion. This view is supported by Denison's "guesstimate" (1985) that the cost of all trade restrictions in the United States in 1957 was no more than 1.5 percent of the level of gross national product (GNP). By implication, the impact on the growth rate was almost negligible. Of course, an extra 1.5 percent of GNP is well worth having, but in most cases it would be misplaced emphasis to put the trade regime or finance on a par with capital accumulation, technology, scale economies, or education.

Although we believe that there is no significant difference in economic performance when a stable real interest rate is -1 percent instead of $+2$ percent, the financial regime can become a dominant determinant of performance when it deteriorates significantly. Argentina, for example, is sliding back as inflation and finance are increasingly dominating the economy, and the same is true of Peru.

When hyperinflation takes over and foreign exchange crises disrupt the price system and shorten the economic horizon to a week or a month, normal economic development is suspended. Moreover, capital flight, which is difficult to reverse, puts saving outside the home economy. Attention should focus on these extreme cases and explore in greater depth the thresholds at which financial factors become significant, or even dominant, and the particular channels through which this occurs. This argument leads to a discussion of the limits of deficit finance, the risks of overexposure to external debt service, and variations in the ability of different countries to adjust rapidly and smoothly to changes in financial resources. Superior growth performance, in this perspective, may reflect adaptability rather than financial deepening.

This point is best illustrated by comparing Asia and Latin America in the period 1960–80 and in the 1980s (table 4-1).

Finance does matter for the mobilization of resources, but this ordinarily accounts for little in changing growth rates. The more important fact is macroeconomic: poor finance leads to inflation and external bottlenecks, which in turn bring about restrictive macroeconomic policies that slow down growth and investment. A protracted period of poor macroeconomic policy in turn casts a shadow over the future, because it slows down or diverts abroad the supply of capital and the incentives to invest and innovate in the home economy.

Table 4-1. Economic Performance in Asia and Latin America, 1960–80 and 1980–87

(average annual percent)

Period and region	Inflation	Per capita growth	Investment/GDP	Financial deepening[a]
1960–80				
Asia	8.2	2.6	20.4	70.4
Latin America	27.6	3.3	21.5	25.8
1980–87				
Asia	6.0	3.0	26.5	44.9
Latin America	102.3	−0.9	20.2	−8.3

a. Financial deepening is measured by the cumulative percentage change in the ratio of M_2 to GDP. In the 1980s the change refers to 1980–86.
Source: IMF (various issues).

The Financial Repression Paradigm

Financial repression is a major impediment to economic development. If growth is to come from investment, then three conditions must be met; namely, firms (or the government) must be willing to invest, savings must be available, and these savings must be channeled to those who plan to invest and who face the most attractive investment opportunities. The financial structure and institutions can support or disrupt this process. A repressed system, especially in conjunction with high and unstable inflation, is said to interfere in a number of ways with development (see especially McKinnon 1973, Lanyi and Saracoglu 1983, and Fry 1988 for a discussion and references).

- *Savings vehicles are underdeveloped or the return on savings is negative and unstable, or both.* There are two immediate consequences. First, the low and possibly negative real return on savings depresses the savings rate. Second, any money that is saved tends to go into self-finance, relatively unproductive assets (primarily inflation hedges), or foreign exchange.
- *Financial intermediaries that collect savings do not allocate these savings efficiently among competing uses.* Because interest rates on loans are regulated, rationing occurs, which reduces the productivity of investment.
- *Firms are discouraged from investing, because poor financial policies reduce the returns or make them excessively unstable.* In particular, unstable inflation, price controls, and overvaluation of foreign exchange add to the risks of doing business and, as a result, depress investment in productive assets. Beyond depressing investment, an unstable financial business environment and the

rationing implicit in a repressed system also induce the socially wasteful use of resources for rent seeking (see Krueger 1974). This is the case because financial repression creates a ready environment in which firms can secure large transfers from the public sector.

A good morality tale is a story of sin and redemption. Korea, as we shall now see, shifted from repressed financial markets to financial reform, a shift that coincided with and was perhaps instrumental in bringing about a dramatic change in economic development.

The Korean Example

Korea experienced low growth and increasing financial instability after the Korean War. In 1963–64 its performance deteriorated further. Sharply higher inflation, in conjunction with a ceiling on interest rates, reduced real asset returns. The ratio of M_2 to GDP declined by almost 5 percentage points. John Gurley, Hugh Patrick, and Edward Shaw studied the situation and noted:

> Adequate mobilization of capital in Korea will require a major overhaul of the financial system. While financial reform is crucial to achieve the Korean objective of stable growth, our judgment is that tax reform will have to shoulder an even larger burden than financial reform to raise the ratio of domestic saving to national income within the coming few years. The financial system will need recuperation from past repression and abuse. This is no excuse for delay in financial reform. Indeed it only makes more necessary the need for financial reform now. (Reproduced in Cole and Park 1983, pp. 298–303.)

Under the heading "Prerequisites for Financial Reform and Development," they proposed the following:

- Persuade savers that they will not be taxed by inflation.
- Maintain the equilibrium value of the foreign exchange rate of the won; do not allow it to become overvalued again.
- Release domestic interest rates on deposits so that savers are induced to save, and in a financial form, and so that funds can be allocated to investment on a more rational basis.

On the basis of their recommendations, the government of Korea introduced extensive fiscal, financial, and external-balance reforms. As shown in table 4-2, saving, investment, financial deepening, and growth all improved dramatically. The shift toward positive real deposit rates probably deserves much of the credit.

Table 4-2. Financial Indicators, Korea, 1960–74
(average annual percent)

Category	1960–64	1965–69	1970–74
Real curb loan rate	31.1	44.4	28.2
Real deposit rate	−0.7	14.3	3.6
M_2/GDP	12.3	21.2	35.0
National savings rate	4.9	12.9	17.4
Gross fixed investment/GDP	12.2	21.4	22.6
Taxes/GDP	9.3	12.0	13.8
Growth	5.5	10.0	9.2

Source: Cole and Park (1983); Bank of Korea data.

Are There Lessons to Be Learned?

That Korean economic performance improved sharply after 1965 is beyond question. The discussion remains open, however, as to whether financial reform was the chief or essential agent of change (see Cole and Park 1983). Skepticism focuses on the fact that high real deposit rates, to some extent at least, only moved resources from the curb market to the banking system. That resource allocation was improved as a result, or that saving increased in response to the higher yield on bank deposits, has not been shown.

People are still debating the efficiency of the investment selection made by Korea's banking system in the 1970s, so whether the shift toward organized financial markets represented a clear improvement rather than only a redirection of savings flows is not clear. The large-scale investment in heavy and chemical industries in the 1970s was certainly facilitated by the mobilization of resources in the formal financial system. These investments were supported by credit subsidies and are now widely recognized as mistaken because of their low productivity. If this view is correct, financial deepening, which mobilized the resources for this mistake, must have had negative aspects. In addition, Korea's increased saving is a reflection of the government's fiscal correction, real depreciation that promoted export growth, and guarantee programs on foreign borrowing that encouraged capital inflows.

The immediate question is what lessons to draw from the financial repression paradigm and the specific example of Korea. Should financial policy focus on generating significantly positive real returns on deposits, thus seeking to generate high rates of growth in the real size of the banking system? Are growth, financial deepening, positive real interest rates, and the productivity of investment tightly correlated in historical and cross-sectional experience? The answers are clearly no. Paying positive real interest rates on deposits is not a universal panacea for growth, as some of the literature on financial repression might lead one to believe. Only when financial instability becomes large and persistent do the connections between financial reform and growth performance become tight.

Some Key Relations Reconsidered

The financial repression paradigm in some ways seems like supply-side economics—a kernel of truth and a vast exaggeration. Let us examine briefly the theoretical propositions and empirical evidence developed in support of the financial repression paradigm (see Fry 1988 for a review of the literature).

Proposition 1: Positive real deposit rates raise the savings rate. It is well known from the theory of saving that the offsetting income and substitution effects of increased interest rates imply that their net impact on saving must be ambiguous. Within a framework of target saving, increases in real interest rates reduce the effort to accumulate the necessary savings. It is therefore surprising to find so strong a belief that higher interest rates mobilize increased saving. In the U.S. case, with the best data and innumerable attempts to document signs of the effect, confirmation of this belief has eluded virtually all studies. Evidence from other industrial countries points in the same direction: no discernible net effect.

In the case of developing countries, the lack of data and their very poor quality make establishing the facts much harder. Fry (1988) reports a cross-sectional time-series regression of fourteen Asian countries in which the real deposit rate is a significant, although quantitatively unimportant, determinant of saving. Depending on the estimate, an increase of 10 to 25 percentage points in the real deposit rate is needed to raise the national savings rate by 1 percentage point! Giovannini (1985), by contrast, does not find a significant relationship between saving and real interest rates for Asian countries. Reynoso (1988) finds evidence for a Laffer curve, with no significant effects when changes in the real interest rate are around zero.

In some case studies, major stabilization programs do, however, appear to affect the savings rate. Some ready explanations exist. First, during a financial crisis saving is channeled into foreign assets through misinvoicing of trade. Accordingly, in these cases national account data easily underestimate true saving. Second, stabilization is associated with fiscal reform, which directly raises the national savings rate. Third, durable purchases are recorded as consumption. Therefore, in a period of financial instability, a shift into durables—

and following stabilization, a sharp reduction in durable purchases—
has the appearance of a dramatic increase in saving. In fact, however,
true consumption (measured by nondurables and the services of
durables) need not have changed much.

Proposition 2: Financial deepening and growth are positively related. We
already saw in table 4-1 that the correlation between growth and
financial deepening as measured by the change in the M_2/GDP ratios
is not tight. Figure 4-1 shows a cross-section of countries; it is apparent that by judicious choice of sample any partial correlation can be
generated.

A first and important point is that financial deepening need not
correspond to the M_2/GDP ratio. Deposits in nonbank institutions are
an important outlet for financial saving and so is the money market.
Between 1970 and 1987, the M_2/GDP ratio in Korea was practically
stagnant (41.3 percent compared with 39.1 percent), but the M_3/GDP
ratio doubled from 46.0 to 94.4 percent. The focus on M_2/GDP ratios

**Figure 4-1. Financial Deepening and Economic Growth,
Cross-Section of Countries, 1965–85**

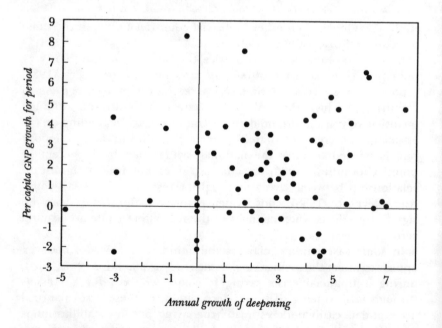

Note: Deepening is the ratio of quasi money to GNP.

Source: IMF (various years).

misrepresents the picture. Brazil has a market for financial assets that is, of course, not part of the narrow money supply. The shift to high inflation is reflected in a decline of M_2 in relation to GDP (from 19.4 to 12.9 percent during 1975–87), whereas a comprehensive measure of money, including the financial market, shows growth from 37.5 to 47.5 percent. The point of these examples is that differences in financial structure create an obstacle to any simple analysis of the relationship between financial development and economic growth.

Proposition 3: Increases in real deposit rates raise investment. The theory here is difficult to pin down. The only immediate link to economic growth is the potential one discussed above: higher real interest rates for deposits raise saving and hence the equilibrium rate of investment. An additional link, suggested by McKinnon (1973), involves the complementarity of money and capital: because investment projects are lumpy, investors must accumulate their investment balances in the form of deposits until the required principal is reached. The more attractive the return on deposits, the more willing investors are to engage in the accumulation process.

We have seen that there is virtually no evidence that higher interest rates mobilize increased saving (and hence investment). As for the additional possible link, it is difficult to see how this view is very different from one that looks in a straightforward way at the effect of real interest rates on saving. After all, the economic choice is between consumption and saving. Econometric models that introduce the savings or investment rate into the equation for real money demand to test this theory are peculiar at best.

Proposition 4: Increases in real deposit rates promote growth. Once again, the immediate link to growth is that higher real interest rates raise domestic saving and hence increase the available supply of resources for investment, a proposition we have already questioned.

Two additional links can be considered. The first deals with external resources: eliminating ceilings on active and passive interest rates can bring about an inflow (or reflow) of external savings. Whereas large firms always have the possibility of borrowing abroad, this is not the case for smaller economic units. The removal of ceilings allows the domestic financial system to draw in resources that would not otherwise be available. We distinguish here between the rechanneling of domestic savings from informal to formal financial markets and the net availability of external savings. The latter have a more difficult task finding their way to finance domestic investment through informal markets. Accordingly, financial reform can potentially raise external finance.

The second link comes through the quality of investments. Experts often argue that a repressed financial system allocates savings inefficiently, because rationing leads to the financing of investments that are below average in quality. This argument is suspect because economic agents have powerful incentives to merge with banks to seize the underpriced savings; they would not have an incentive to invest inefficiently. Indeed, much of the growth of informal markets reflects the laundering, for improved efficiency, of credits obtained from the repressed financial system.

A Test for Linkage

Economists have tested the effect of increased real interest rates on the efficiency of investments by relating the incremental capital-output ratio to real deposit rates. Even though these relationships have been established frequently (see Fry 1988), what they reflect is not clear. Consider the neoclassical growth model. We can write the growth rate of per capita income, y, as:

$$(4\text{-}1) \qquad\qquad y = \alpha(\beta/\phi - n)$$

where α is the distributive share of capital, β is the share of investment in income, ϕ is the capital-output ratio, and n is the growth rate of the labor force.

Which factor is influenced by financial repression, and how long does it take for financial repression to affect the parameter? If the capital-output ratio is raised, the average investment has been less efficient and the impact on growth could be significant. Let $\alpha = 0.7$, $\beta = 0.2$, and $n = 0.025$. If $\phi = 2$, the growth rate is 5.3 percent; if $\phi = 3$, the growth rate is 2.9 percent. Thus, the productivity of the capital stock does make a large difference. This is not the right guide, however, to the benefits of financial liberalization. A more efficient allocation of investments has only an extremely gradual effect on the average capital-output ratio, taking decades rather than a year or two. Moreover, the cumulative change may fall very much short of our example.

To discern a growth effect, it is preferable to focus directly on financial stability. For a cross-section of forty-one countries, we used averages for the period 1965–85 to compare growth of per capita income with the investment rate and the rate of inflation. Specifically, we were interested in the effect of high inflation on growth. The equation we used was

$$y = -1.67 + 0.0005Y + 0.15K - 0.016p \qquad R^2 = 0.30$$
$$ (-1.41) \quad (1.35) \qquad (2.33) \quad (-1.80)$$

where y is the per capita growth rate, Y is the level of per capita income in 1965, K is the cumulative change in the capital-labor ratio, and p is an inflation dummy applied to inflation rates in excess of 20 percent. The regression supported the view that high inflation interferes with growth.

So far we have asked whether a liberalized financial system provides more opportunity than a repressed one to mobilize resources for growth or to allocate them more efficiently. We have concluded that the empirical support for liberalization is episodic. Let us now consider the alternative perspective on financial factors in economic development, namely, the role of inflation and deficit finance.

Budget Deficits and Inflation

The discussion of inflation and its link to development finance in developing countries raises several questions. Why is inflation in Asia moderate, whereas in Latin America it is, at best, chronic and often acute? What are the disturbances and practices that set off an inflation process? What factors make inflation beyond a certain threshold an accelerating process? The experience of Latin America is one of inflation rates accelerating to 1,000 and more percent, even though the government deficits that are being financed are not much larger than those in Asia. Thus identifying the source of inflation differentials is important to obtaining a better understanding of the limits of inflationary finance and of the disturbances and institutions that make these limits especially tight.

Inflation represents the interaction of four factors:

- Deficit finance (which governs growth of the money supply)
- Financial institutions (which determine the demand for money)
- Shocks to the budget
- The ability to react to these shocks by corrective fiscal measures

The combination of these four factors may imply moderate and stable inflation, or it may imply near hyperinflation. Which of the two—low or extreme inflation—is, of course, critical for economic development. As we shall argue, high and unstable inflation leads to a drying up of resources available for development. This is because asset holders are unwilling to accumulate domestic claims, and firms are not prepared to accumulate productive assets in the inflating country.

Inflation Policy

Developing countries in Asia differ from those in Latin America in two major respects: their fiscal and inflation performance and their distribution of income. In Latin America deficits and inflation are chronic, whereas in Asia deficits tend to be limited to the governments' ability to finance them in a noninflationary manner. The relatively equal income distribution in Asia contrasts sharply with the extreme inequality in Latin America. The difference in income distribution in the two continents influences the ability to achieve rapid adjustment of fiscal and real exchange rate positions when these are needed to avoid bottlenecks. This may not be the only reason for the differential ability to adjust, but it is certainly an important one.

It must be emphasized that differences in performance are not merely a reflection of dissimilarities in fiscal discipline. Korea, for example, ran large fiscal deficits and experienced external shocks and debt service problems as recently as 1981. In this respect, its problems were no different from, say, Brazil's. The difference lies primarily in the adjustment to the shock. In one case the adjustment was startlingly rapid; in the other, the consequences of hyperinflation are still being acted out.

Consider a simple model of the adjustment problem. We want to sketch a model of the extent to which a government offsets or dampens an inflationary shock. Let the government minimize a loss function, L:

$$(4\text{-}2) \qquad L = (\pi - \pi^*)^2 + \lambda A^2/2$$

where π denotes the actual rate of inflation, π^* denotes the historical rate, λ is the marginal political cost of adjustment, and A is the adjustment effort. The actual inflation is the historical rate plus the shock (Δ) less the impact of the adjustment effort on inflation, or:

$$(4\text{-}3) \qquad \pi = \pi^* + \Delta - \phi A/2, \text{ where } \phi \text{ is a constant.}$$

Then the inflation rate under the optimal adjustment effort will be

$$(4\text{-}4) \qquad \pi = \pi^* + \alpha\Delta; \alpha = \lambda/(\lambda + \phi^2/2).$$

We are interested in the coefficient α, which would differ across countries. The higher the marginal political cost of adjustment (λ) and the less effective adjustment is in dampening the inflationary impact of shocks (that is, the smaller the ϕ), the less adjustment effort will be supplied and therefore the higher the rate of inflation will be. This will tend to raise the inflation rate over time (π^* will increase), and thus different countries' inflation performance will drift apart over time. The main task now is to identify the shocks and the channels through which they exert inflationary consequences.

Characteristics of the Inflation Process

A high-inflation process has two characteristics. The first is that money creation finances a significant part of the budget deficit. The second is that indexation arrangements link current inflation to past inflation.

MONEY CREATION. In the tradition of Mundell (1971), the budget deficit is a fraction g of real income, and the demand for high-powered money is a linear and increasing function of inflation. A fraction β of the deficit is financed by creating money. This gives us a relationship between the growth rate of high-powered money (μ) and the budget deficit:

$$(4\text{-}5) \qquad \mu = \beta g \,(\rho + \eta\pi)$$

where ρ and η are parameters of the velocity equation. In steady state, with a growth rate of output y and a unitary income elasticity, we obtain an inflation rate equal to:

$$(4\text{-}6) \qquad \pi = (\beta\rho g - y)/(1 - \beta\Delta g).$$

The model makes three basic points. First, the link between inflation and the budget deficit financed by money creation is highly nonlinear. A minor increase in the deficit, when the deficit is high, raises in a major way the inflation rate required to finance the budget.

Second, the financial structure affects the inflationary impact of money-financed deficits. The more sophisticated the financial structure, the higher the coefficients ρ and η are and, accordingly, the higher the inflation associated with a given deficit is. Put another way, inflationary finance thrives on a repressed financial system. We return to this point in the context of financial liberalization below.

Third, growth dampens the inflationary impact of deficit finance. A percentage point decline in the growth of income raises inflation by a multiple that is higher when the deficit is higher and velocity is more responsive to inflation. A major downward shift in real income growth can therefore be an important contributing factor to increased inflation.

Tables 4-3, 4-4, and 4-5 show the revenue from money creation obtained in Asia and Latin America.

INDEXATION ARRANGEMENTS. With indexation the adjustment of relative prices becomes difficult. When wage indexation is adjusted at given intervals, the easiest means of cutting real wages is to allow inflation to accelerate. In this manner, over the indexation period, the real wage is eroded and hence its real value declines. But indexation

Table 4-3. Seigniorage, Growth, and Inflation in Asia and Latin America, 1960–86

(average annual percent)

Period	Seigniorage[a] Asia	Seigniorage[a] Latin America	Growth Asia	Growth Latin America	Inflation Asia	Inflation Latin America
1960–78	1.4	3.2	5.9	6.1	7.9	28.4
1979–86	1.5	4.5	4.9	2.5	9.3	116.6

a. The change in high-powered money as a percentage of GDP.

Note: Figures in each category are income-weighted averages for six countries (listed by continent in table 4-7).

Source: Fischer (1982), updated by the authors.

arrangements accelerate inflation when the periodicity of adjustments shortens. When an inflationary shock—say, a devaluation or the removal of subsidies—reduces real wages beyond a threshold, the response is often to shorten the indexation interval. For a given average real wage, a cut in the interval to half doubles the rate of inflation.

This shortening of adjustment intervals is an important driving force of accelerating inflation. Adjustment periods decline from annual to half-yearly to quarterly to monthly, and then the entire economy converges on the dollar. As every lagging agent in the econ-

Table 4-4. Economic Performance, Selected Countries in Asia and Latin America, 1960–87

(average annual percent)

Period and country	Inflation	Growth	Investment/GDP	NICA[a]/GDP
1960–80				
India	7.0	1.2	22.4	−1.3
Korea, Rep. of	14.3	6.3	23.4	−8.0
Philippines	9.7	2.8	22.9	−2.2
Argentina	78.9	1.7	17.6	−0.1
Brazil	40.3	5.4	22.7	−1.8
Mexico	9.5	3.3	21.3	−1.0
1980–87				
India	9.4	3.1	24.4	−3.5
Korea, Rep. of	8.9	7.1	29.4	−0.9
Philippines	16.1	−2.1	22.1	−0.7
Argentina	279.3	−2.5	14.2	3.5
Brazil	153.3	0.4	18.7	3.8
Mexico	69.5	−1.4	20.2	5.5

a. The noninterest current account measured by net exports (excluding factor payments) in the national accounts.

Source: IMF (various issues).

Table 4-5. Seigniorage, Growth, and Inflation in Selected Countries in Asia and Latin America, 1960–86

(average annual percent)

Country	1960–78 Growth	1960–78 Inflation	1960–78 Seigniorage[a]	1979–86 Growth	1979–86 Inflation	1979–86 Seigniorage[a]
India	3.8	6.8	1.0	4.1	9.1	1.9
Korea, Rep. of	9.3	13.8	2.2	6.8	10.8	0.5
Malaysia	7.8	3.2	1.2	5.5	4.3	1.2
Pakistan	3.7	7.6	1.4	6.7	7.5	2.0
Philippines	5.7	8.4	0.8	1.2	17.9	1.1
Singapore	9.2	3.8	2.5	6.5	3.4	1.7
Argentina	3.3	57.2	6.2	−0.5	282.3	11.1
Brazil	8.3	36.5	3.2	4.2	131.3	2.4
Mexico	6.6	8.0	1.6	2.7	55.3	5.4
Peru	4.6	15.2	2.6	0.8	91.0	8.4
Uruguay	1.9	51.7	4.8	0.5	54.4	4.8
Venezuela	5.6	3.3	1.1	−0.2	12.6	1.2

a. The change in high-powered money as a percentage of GDP.
Source: Fischer (1982), updated by the authors.

omy shortens its lags to try to catch up with the average inflation rate, the average explodes.

The nonlinearity of the inflation to the budget (reflecting the endogeneity of the financial structure) and the shortening of indexation periodicity are channels through which inflation can accelerate once it reaches high levels. Intensifying the budget effect on inflation is the endogeneity of real tax revenue. Because the tax structure is less than fully indexed, high inflation erodes the real value of government revenues. This, in turn, increases the need for money creation to finance the deficit. Attempts to index taxation and speed up collection can help to dampen this process but have virtually no chance of offsetting the impact of a 200 percent inflation.

The endogeneity of tax revenue is altogether inconsequential at rates of inflation of 20 or even 30 percent, but each becomes decisive at 100 or 200 percent. This helps to explain why so many countries in Latin America have recently moved to extreme rates of inflation. It remains to identify what disturbances initiate the process and why high inflation tends to become so unstable and explosive.

Factors and Practices That Cause High Inflation

Apart from an obvious lack of fiscal discipline, three factors have caused major inflation. Their importance is enhanced by their tendency to occur together.

DEBT SERVICE SHOCK. In the 1970s many developing countries borrowed heavily and as a result accumulated debt service burdens. In the early 1980s the debt shock halted the flow of lending. This interrupted the policy of paying interest on old loans by borrowing new money and automatically rolling over the principal. Debtor countries had to start making transfers abroad. In the budget the automatic financing of debt service by foreign loans was replaced by the need to finance at least part of the debt service domestically. Changes in taxes and current spending were unpopular; thus most of the adjustment took the form of either cutting public sector investment or financing the deficit domestically. To the extent that the deficits were financed by money creation (to avoid crowding out or bankruptcies associated with high interest rates), high inflation was the outcome. In many countries where some inflationary finance had been the rule, financing the deficit by creating extra money proved an express lane to extreme inflation. Bolivia is a case in point, as is Argentina.

Over and above the problem of making external transfers from the budget, a debt service shock has a secondary burden. The real depreciation that is required to generate a trade surplus will raise the real value of external debt service in terms of the tax base. Thus for a country that has a debt service of 6 percent of GDP, a 20 percent real depreciation increases the debt service burden by 1.2 percent. The point is simply that a dollar of interest payment now costs more tax dollars. Thus depreciation occurs (except in cases where the government is a net earner of foreign exchange).

FINANCIAL LIBERALIZATION. An immediate reaction to accelerating inflation is agitation in the financial sector for liberalization. Financial repression worsens the social costs of inflation. Allowing banks to offer interest-bearing liabilities permits the financial system to perform its intermediation task and thus minimize the costs of living with inflation. But liberalizing the financial system may imply reducing the government's revenue from money creation, which in turn means increasing the rate of inflation even more. Not liberalizing may entail costs, specifically, the possibility of capital flight, but the alternative of liberalization may also be perilous.

The link between financial liberalization and inflation has been modeled in equation 4-1. Financial liberalization offers asset holders interest-bearing returns; nonbank financial institutions (*financieras* in Latin America) are allowed to offer checkable interest-bearing liabilities (the "overnight") and use the proceeds to hold short-term commercial paper or government debt. Accordingly, financial disintermediation occurs as deposit resources shift from traditional intermediaries (the banking system) to the money market. The demand for the monetary base is reduced because banks lose deposits. A reduction in the demand for the real monetary base raises the rate of inflation consistent with financing a given budget deficit. Thus financial liberalization raises the inflation rate unless there is an accompanying reduction in the budget deficit. Hierro (1988) has documented the quantitative importance of this effect. Of course, if liberalization also involves bankruptcies of financial institutions, as is often the case, the financing requirements also increase.

Thus there is a tradeoff between financial liberalization and seigniorage; a period of fiscal crisis may not be the right time to introduce financial liberalization. Of course, that choice may not really exist: if a country fails to liberalize the financial market by offering interest-bearing domestic assets, the result is capital flight or dollarization, with the same or worse consequences for inflation and intermediation.

EXCHANGE LOSSES AND QUASI-FISCAL DEFICITS. A third major source of accelerated inflation is the widening in fiscal deficits resulting from exchange losses on exchange rate guarantees or exchange rate operations, usually of the central bank, but also from the interaction of inflation and financial subsidies. Attempts to take advantage of secondary-market discounts on the country's external debt by buybacks or debt-equity swaps add another important source of increased financing requirements (see Blejer and Chu 1988). In some cases in Latin America the increased financing requirements resulting from these operations amounted to several percent of GDP.

In 1982–87 Argentina's quasi-fiscal deficit averaged 1.7 percent of GDP. Much of this deficit stemmed from exchange rate guarantees given by the government in 1982. Demands for repayments of these debts were hastened by the expectation of further depreciation. Exchange rate guarantees, rather than high interest rates, seemed the cheaper way at the time; in retrospect, they were the source of a massive increase in inflation.

Peru's quasi-fiscal deficit in 1985–87 averaged 2.1 percent of GDP (in addition to the regular deficit in the budget). Part of the quasi-fiscal deficit arose from large credit subsidies implicit in credits conceded at low interest rates. But the major part arose from multiple exchange rates with massive discrepancies between buying and selling rates for foreign exchange. Quasi-fiscal deficits, because of their sheer size and because they are financed by printing money that nobody wants to hold, are extremely inflationary. In addition, they are an obvious misallocation of resources.

The Effects of Deficits and of High and Unstable Inflation

Large budget deficits and their financing by high and unstable inflation have major effects on economic development. First, and most obvious, the appropriation of resources by the government reduces resources available to the private sector. If the public sector uses resources to finance investment, and if crowding out because of the inflation tax displaces primarily private consumption, this appropriation might well be conducive to development. Mundell (1971) has already questioned the connection between the reallocation of resources and inflation in the discussion of inflation taxation for growth.

The Latin American experience of the 1980s highlights the narrow limits to inflationary finance and the dramatic costs when inflationary finance goes wrong. These remaining costs arise primarily from capital flight and the misallocation of resources as a result of uncertainty.

Capital Flight and Dollarization

Financial repression and high inflation together create an atmosphere in which asset holders seek protection by holding dollar-denominated assets, if possible, or shifting their assets abroad. The timing of a wave of capital flight may well be linked to an obvious overvaluation of the exchange rate as, for example, in Argentina in 1979–80 or in Mexico at the end of the six-year presidential terms, as shown in figure 4-2. Even without such a trigger, a history of large negative returns on assets produces capital flight. Figure 4-3 shows the cumulative performance of a deposit in Argentina (translated at the official exchange rate) in relation to a U.S. deposit and makes the same comparison for Mexico. Clearly, Argentina does not offer a favorable long-run financial return, and the same has been true for Mexico during the past decade. Steady capital flight is the inevitable result.

A recent estimate shows the extraordinary size of capital flight from Latin America: from 1975–85 the cumulative capital flight from Africa is estimated at $28.5 billion, from Asia $18.3 billion, and from the western hemisphere $106.6 billion (Deppler and Williamson 1987). To judge the size of capital flight, note that total Latin American debt in 1987 equaled $300 billion.

Allowing the banking system to offer dollar-denominated (or dollar-indexed) deposits provides an alternative to the actual shift of assets abroad. Available data on the dollarization process in Mexico and Peru give us insight into the dynamics. The shift into dollar deposits is not a once-and-for-all process triggered by a dramatic event. On the contrary, the shift can be approximated by a traditional portfolio choice model based on relative rates of return and dynamics that are repre-

Figure 4-2. Real Exchange Rate, Mexico, 1970–88
(1980–82 = 100)

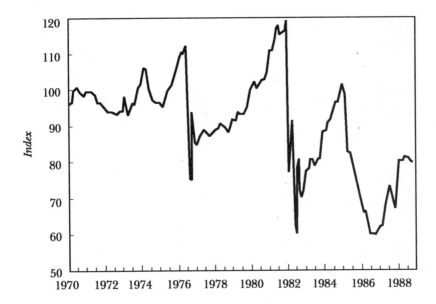

Source: Morgan Guaranty data.

Figure 4-3. Cumulative Return on a Bank Deposit in Mexico and Argentina in Relation to a U.S. Deposit, 1960–87
(deposit = 1.00)

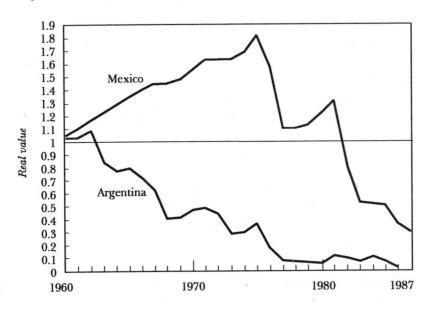

Source: IMF (various issues).

sented by the logistic process. This point is illustrated in figure 4-4, which shows the evolution of dollar deposits as a share of total deposits in Peru (for a further discussion see Dornbusch and Reynoso 1988).

Dollarization is not an instant reaction to the slightest policy mistake. On the contrary, there is substantial inertia in asset holdings. But once people learn to shift their assets into safer, dollar-denominated deposits, bringing about a reversal is difficult. A return to moderate rates of inflation is not rapidly rewarded by a complete reflow into local currency assets.

When dollar deposits are not available and when economic and political instability is pervasive, the response is a shift into foreign currency assets in the form of currency or to real and financial assets located abroad. For example, in Peru, where access to new dollar deposits was eliminated, the large divergence between inflation and depreciation on the one hand and the return to deposits on the other made capital flight irresistible; the depreciation rate averaged 57 percent percent per quarter in 1987, whereas the deposit rate averaged only 5.4 percent! No reliable estimates of foreign holdings of U.S. currency exist, but

Figure 4-4. The Process of Dollarization in Peru, 1976–85
(percentage of total quasi money)

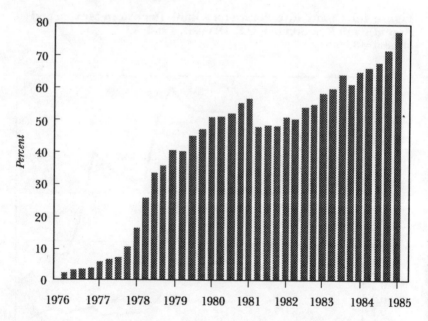

Source: Central Bank of Peru data.

some indication of foreign deposits in the banks of industrial countries is available. Table 4-6 shows the large size of dollar holdings in countries that have experienced financial instability.

Table 4-4 illustrates an interesting difference between Argentina and Brazil. Brazilian capital flight, until recently, was relatively moderate because the domestic financial market was allowed to adapt. The existence of a relatively indexed short-term money market prevented the massive flight of capital that occurred in other Latin American countries. But even in Brazil a form of capital flight was apparent in the shortening of maturities in financial markets to the point where today the entire public debt has a one-day maturity. The next step, increasingly apparent, is flight from the overnight market to the dollar.

Governments that face the risk of capital flight must make a strategic decision: Should they contain the flight by high interest rates on domestic assets? Should they create dollar-linked domestic assets (for example, Mex-dollars)? Or should they continue financial repression and attempt, even with little success, to contain capital flight by controls? A number of considerations bear on the choice of policy, most obviously, whether controls could actually stop capital flight—an issue that is viewed with almost uniform skepticism. Of course, if capital flight can be prevented, the country does not need to acquire external capital, which would require a trade surplus, and thus more resources remain available for domestic absorption. In this sense, domestic dollarization is preferable, and even high interest rates might be, but they carry their own risks. Both create an easily accessible domestic substitute for assets that yield seigniorage, and in this way they increase the inflationary effect of a given deficit.

Moreover, a rise in interest rates would enlarge the domestic deficit and thus aggravate financing requirements. The strategic question, then, is whether the reduction in seigniorage is lower with capital flight

Table 4-6. Cross-Border Bank Deposits, Selected Countries, 1987
(dollars)

Country	Average per capita holdings
Argentina	277
Brazil	85
Egypt	65
Korea, Rep. of	14
Mexico	225
Peru	89
Philippines	24
Venezuela	745

Source: IMF (various issues).

or with domestic dollarization. The answer presumably is that capital flight involves large transaction costs which could prevent some capital loss; therefore, a country may be better off accepting capital flight than instituting dollarization. Furthermore, domestic dollar deposits also create the risk that if a major depreciation is required at some point, the banking system is likely to suffer, which may lead to a tendency to over-value the exchange rate. Mexico's experience with domestic dollar deposits illustrates these considerations.

Brazil's experience illustrates another point: high interest rates are not a good substitute for fiscal correction. High interest rates on a debt in local currency (or indexing of the domestic debt to goods or foreign exchange) can postpone the consequences of a continuing, large budget deficit but cannot make them disappear. The steady accumulation of domestic debt, and the shortening of maturities to what is virtually a spot market, creates a situation in which eventually the entire public debt is matched by interest-bearing, checkable deposits. Seigniorage has all but vanished, and the precariousness of the public debt is an invitation to a funding crisis, which arises when the government cannot roll over the debt.

The Misallocation of Resources

High and unstable inflation also has a major cost in terms of resource allocation. The inflation-induced distortion of the economy is not limited to the printing of new menus every day or month. The uncertainty about inflation and the policy reactions to accelerating inflation are major sources of distortions.

When there is high and unstable inflation, productive factors are devoted to exploiting financial (and hence, by definition, zero-sum) opportunities rather than to innovating in production and trade. Firms' planning horizons shrink, and the possible introduction of controls to slow down the accelerating inflation forces economic agents into a defensive posture, in which investment in productive assets in the corporate sector becomes overly risky. Firms increasingly hold paper assets, and individuals overaccumulate foreign assets or consumer durables. The uncertainty that causes firms to hold paper assets rather than to invest in real resources translates into trade surpluses that finance capital flight or premature debt reduction.

Conclusion

Our discussion of the financing of economic development has emphasized three sources:

- External resources that can be tapped by a favorable investment climate or direct borrowing in the world capital market
- Liberalization of financially repressed systems to enhance private saving
- Development financed by public sector deficits

We have argued that evidence on the beneficial effects of removing financial repression remains open to challenge: the evidence is episodic except when asset returns are significantly negative. The scope for deficit finance as an engine of economic development is extremely limited and extraordinarily hazardous. When overdone, inflationary finance acquires its own dynamics, which can set back the development effort by a decade or more.

Latin America today provides a striking example of the risks of budget deficits and of earlier excessive reliance on external finance. But to conclude from this experience that financial liberalization would have promoted high growth is a mistake. On the contrary, financial liberalization (including the promotion of capital flight at the official exchange rate) in the face of a poor fiscal position continues to be a major factor in accelerating inflation and instability. Argentina is an example of a country altogether destroyed by excessive inflation, which has put an end to net investment and has led households to shift their assets abroad. Brazil is on that same path, and only Mexico has narrowly avoided it.

Following a decade of financial instability, mobilizing resources for growth in Latin America is, of course, extremely difficult. The path that will return the region to rapid, long-run growth is awesomely orthodox: realistic exchange rates, balanced budgets, and a favorable investment climate. Economists in the heterodox mode (and their progressive friends) might easily reject this advice, arguing that the working poor cannot be made to bear the burden of a decade of mistakes, but the evidence suggests that without an early return to orthodoxy they will bear an even larger burden because capital is mobile, whereas labor is not.[1]

Appendix. The Mexican Financial System: From Financial Repression to a Money Market

In Mexico in the late 1950s and the 1960s, a very regulated and specialized financial system supported an impressive record of growth and price stability. By contrast, Mexico in the 1970s and 1980s faced the serious consequences of inflationary finance, large deficits, and a policy of inflexible nominal interest rates. Rapid disintermediation, mostly reflected in capital flight, reduced the financial system's ability to promote macroeconomic stability, productive investment, and growth.

The foundations of the Mexican financial system date back to 1924. In that year the Banco de México was created as the institution in charge of regulating the circulation of currency, foreign exchange transactions, and the rate of interest, and it was the only bank with the privilege of issuing paper money. During the 1920s and 1930s, commercial banks played a very small role. Instead, a number of specialized national institutions were established in an effort to facilitate the movement of loanable funds to sectors for which the market did not provide credit. The General Law of Credit Institutions and Auxiliary Organizations of 1941 set the new rules that would prevail, with only minor changes, for almost forty years. This law defined the financial entities that would be allowed to operate and their sphere of action. Commercial (deposit and savings) banks were permitted to issue sight and short-term deposits denominated in pesos and in dollars and to make only short-term loans. *Financieras* were to capture long-term savings and to offer intermediate long-term credits. Some other institutions, such as insurance and mortgage companies, were subject to regulations similar to those governing *financieras*. The Banco de México set deposit rates, which would remain fixed for long intervals. Under this scheme, there was no money market, and the stock market remained insignificant. Open market operations were not possible, and the central government received its domestic financing from the reserve requirements imposed on banks and *financieras* by the Banco de México.

Between 1940 and 1960 the combination of inflation and low, fixed, nominal interest rates was reflected in slow financial deepening, dollarization (see table 4-7), and capital flight. Inflation averaged 11.9 percent in the 1940s and 7.8 percent in the 1950s, while checking accounts did not pay any interest, and the rate on time deposits stayed

Table 4-7. Mexican Economic Performance and Financial Deepening, 1940–55 through 1980–87

(percent)

Period	GDP[a]	Inflation[a]	Deepening[b]	I/Y[a,c]
1940–55	5.7	11.6	24.3	12.0
1955–70	6.5	4.6	45.8	17.5
1970–80	6.5	17.9	45.6	22.7
1980–87	−0.2	81.1	41.9	20.1

a. Annual average for period.
b. Liabilities of the financial sector/GDP (end of the period).
c. I/Y is the economy's investment ratio.
Source: Banco de México (various years).

below 3 percent during the two decades. Low resource capturing and high reserve requirements limited the availability of financial savings for private use.

In the 1940s, deposit banks were by far the most important credit institutions, while *financieras* took more than a decade to consolidate (see table 4-8). In the meantime, active movement of funds within the system was used to finance long-term projects. For example, funds were channeled from commercial banks to private *financieras*, often by way of fiduciary institutions, and from there either to ultimate borrowers or to national credit institutions.

From 1960 to 1971 financial deepening accelerated noticeably. Total resources captured by commercial banks and *financieras* increased at an average annual rate of 17.1 percent, whereas nominal income grew at only 10 percent. The financial system's total liabilities reached 45 percent of GDP by the end of the period. The combination of moderately positive real interest rates and inflation and exchange rate stability contributed to the consolidation of the system. The average rate of inflation was 3.5 percent per year, the exchange rate remained fixed at 12.5 pesos per dollar, and the interest rate on time deposits paid a constant 4.5 percent in nominal terms.

A central characteristic of this period was fiscal discipline. The budget deficit was kept low, and an increasing proportion of public spending went to capital formation. The combination of fast deepening and small deficits considerably reduced the need for inflation finance and external borrowing.

The expansion of the Echeverría and López Portillo governments (1971–82) put an end to fifteen years of price and exchange rate stability (see Cardoso and Levy 1988; Dornbusch 1988). Inflation came back without any adjustment in the financial structure. It averaged 15.4 percent a year between 1972 and 1976 and 23.4 percent a year from 1977 to 1981, while the interest rates on time deposits remained at 4.5 percent and the return on *financiera* bonds never increased above 13 percent. As a result, dollarization and capital flight reappeared in full force and financial deepening stopped. The banking sector was the

Table 4-8. Structure of the Mexican Financial System, 1940–80

(percentage of total liabilities to the nonfinancial sector)

Institution	1940	1950	1960	1970	1980
Deposit banks	82.9	62.9	46.9	37.5	35.8
Savings banks	0.4	8.0	11.8	16.3	19.6
Financieras	0.0	14.1	30.9	39.4	43.1
Mortgages	9.9	7.4	7.2	5.6	1.4
Others	6.8	7.6	3.2	1.2	0.9

Source: Banco de México (various years).

most seriously affected. Banking liabilities, which had come to represent 34 percent of GDP in 1971, fell to little more than 25 percent of GDP in 1981.

The combination of rapid growth, disintermediation, and incomplete financial markets biased banks, private enterprises, and the government toward borrowing abroad. Between 1970 and 1982, external liabilities expressed as a fraction of total indebtedness of the private and public sector jumped from 12 to 21 percent and from 56 to 75 percent, respectively.

After the devaluation of 1976 the government realized that reform of the financial system was necessary. Some changes were introduced in the last months of 1977, but the experience of 1981 and 1982 proved them inadequate. The first innovation came in October 1977 with the creation of the petrobono, a government bond whose value was indexed to the dollar value of a certain quantity of oil. In January 1978 the government issued the first Certificates of the Federal Treasury (CETES), which gave the government direct access to the money market and, for the first time, provided the central bank with an instrument that enabled it to perform open market operations. At first CETES were offered to the public at a fixed discount rate because of the authorities' reluctance to allow the market to determine interest rates. The first move toward an instrument with freely determined returns did not occur until October 1982, when the auctions of CETES began. By the end of 1982, CETES and petrobonos represented less than 3.5 percent of M_5.

After the 1982 crisis, Mexico faced the burden of a large external debt, a lack of foreign credit resources, and insufficient domestic savings. A drastic change in the way the markets operated became imperative. President de la Madrid (1982–88) promoted major reforms to the Central Bank Law, the General Law of Insurance Companies, and the Stock Market Law. As a result of these reforms the operations and instruments of the banking system were diversified and the Banco de México ceased to act as an intermediary between the federal government and financial institutions. Most important, the reforms gave rise to a more complete and active money market, as most regulations on the issue and trading of nonbanking financial instruments were relaxed.

So far, the flexibility of the new scheme has proved effective in promoting financial intermediation, slowing down capital flight, and accommodating the borrowing needs of the public sector. The Mexican experience of the 1980s demonstrates that if inflation control is not perfect, it is essential to create a domestic money market, at least at the wholesale level. Without the provision of a money market, capital flight becomes a major policy concern.

Note

1. Some observers note that the labor-capital distinction describes the choices for fiscal adjustment in an overly narrow fashion. They note that taxation of immobile land has as yet not been used on any scale to avoid accumulating heavy tax burdens on labor.

Selected Bibliography

Banco de México. Various issues. *Indicadores económicos.* Mexico City.

Blejer, Mario, and K. Y. Chu, eds. 1988. *Measurement of Fiscal Impact: Methodological Issues.* Occasional Paper 59. Washington, D.C.: International Monetary Fund.

Cardoso, Eliana A., and Santiago Levy. 1988. "Mexico." In Rudiger Dornbusch and F. Leslie C. H. Helmers, eds., *The Open Economy: Tools for Policymakers in Developing Countries.* New York: Oxford University Press.

Cole, David C., and Yung-Chul Park. 1983. *Financial Development in Korea.* Cambridge, Mass.: Harvard University Press.

Denison, Edward F. 1985. *Trends in American Economic Growth, 1929–82.* Washington, D.C.: Brookings Institution.

Deppler, Michael, and John Williamson. 1987. "Capital Flight: Concepts, Measurement, and Issues." In *Staff Studies for the World Economic Outlook.* Washington, D.C.: International Monetary Fund.

Dornbusch, Rudiger. 1988. "Mexico: Stabilization, Debt, and Growth." *Economic Policy* 3(2):231–73.

Dornbusch, Rudiger, and Alejandro Reynoso. 1988. "The Dynamics of Dollarization in Mexico and Peru." Massachusetts Institute of Technology, Department of Economics, Cambridge, Mass.

Fischer, Stanley. 1982. "Seigniorage and the Case for a National Money." *Journal of Political Economy* 90(2):295–313. Reprinted in Stanley Fischer, *Indexing, Inflation, and Economic Policy.* Cambridge, Mass.: MIT Press, 1986.

Fry, Maxwell. 1988. *Money, Interest, and Banking in Economic Development.* Baltimore, Md.: Johns Hopkins University Press.

Giovannini, Alberto. 1985. "Saving and the Real Interest Rate in LDCs." *Journal of Development Economics* 18(2–3):197–217.

Hierro, Jorge. 1988. "Financial Liberalization and Inflation." Massachusetts Institute of Technology, Department of Economics, Cambridge, Mass.

IMF (International Monetary Fund). Various issues. *International Financial Statistics.* Washington, D.C.

Krueger, Anne O. 1974. "The Political Economy of the Rent-Seeking Society." *American Economic Review* 64(3):291–303.

Lanyi, Anthony M., and R. Saracoglu. 1983. *Interest Rate Policies in Developing Countries.* Occasional Paper 22. Washington, D.C.: International Monetary Fund.

McKinnon, Ronald. 1973. *Money and Capital in Economic Development.* Washington, D.C.: Brookings Institution.

Mundell, R. A. 1971. *Monetary Theory.* Pacific Palisades, Calif.: Goodyear.

Reynoso, Alejandro. 1988. "Saving and Real Interest Rates: The Laffer Curve." Massachusetts Institute of Technology, Department of Economics, Cambridge, Mass.

5

Exchange Rate Policy: Options and Issues

Rudiger Dornbusch and Luis Tellez Kuenzler

THIS CHAPTER discusses alternative exchange rate arrangements. We present the options, some country illustrations, and a firm set of recommendations. Our chief conclusion is that economies with a proliferation of multiple rates or black markets waste resources. Whatever policymakers believe about their ingenuity and creativity in managing multiple rates, the attempt almost always falters on political grounds. The end result is a drain on the budget and a massive misallocation of resources.

A streamlined exchange rate system must strike a balance between two considerations: microeconomic efficiency and macroeconomic stability. We argue that a dual-rate system (with a market-determined rate for capital account transactions at a moderate premium over the official rate) best serves that objective.

We start with a general discussion of the role of the exchange rate in the economy. The next section discusses multiple rates. From there, we move to black markets and the associated problem of misinvoicing of trade flows. A comparison of unified flexible rates and dual exchange rates follows.

The Role and Influence of Exchange Rates in the Economy

Exchange rates (the price of foreign currency in terms of home currency, say, pesos per dollar) are one of the key linkages between a small, open economy and the rest of the world. In a world of barter, because there are no monies, there are also no exchange rates. In reality, every country in the world uses money, and most countries use their own monies.[1] Hence there are also exchange rates. The exchange rate links a country's macroeconomy to the rest of the world through the asset market and the goods market. It also connects individual countries through the microeconomic channels of the goods market and the asset market. Throughout the discussion below we refer to the home currency as the peso (pesos/dollar).

Macroeconomic Linkages

Linkages between the rest of the world and the macroeconomy arise in two ways. In the goods market, the exchange rate establishes linkages between prices in the home economy and the given prices in the world market. The higher the exchange rate, other things being equal, the higher the price of foreign goods in home currency. For a given level of domestic costs and prices, a higher exchange rate makes foreign goods less competitive in the home economy and makes the home economy's goods more competitive in the rest of the world. The linkage to the goods market can be formalized in terms of the real exchange rate, R. The real exchange rate is the ratio of domestic prices in pesos to foreign prices in pesos, or, in symbols,

$$(5\text{-}1) \qquad\qquad R = P/eP^*$$

where P is the domestic price level in pesos, e is the exchange rate (pesos/dollar), and P^* is the foreign price level in dollars.

The real exchange rate measures competitiveness by showing the number of units of foreign goods required to buy one unit of domestic goods. An increase in the real exchange rate, or a real appreciation, means that it takes more units of foreign goods to buy one unit of domestic goods. Thus real appreciation is tantamount to a loss of competitiveness. Conversely, if the real exchange rate declines, we speak of a real depreciation. The home economy becomes more competitive because it now takes fewer units of foreign goods to buy one unit of domestic goods.

Much of the discussion in this chapter deals with how the choice of an exchange rate regime can influence a country's competitiveness. For example, if domestic prices are rising because the government is pursuing an inflation policy, but the exchange rate is fixed, then equation 5-1 will show real appreciation. Inflation under fixed exchange rates is tantamount to declining competitiveness; sooner or later (mostly sooner) that leads to problems of financing a growing trade deficit. This raises the question of how a country should conduct its exchange rate policy. The first answer is to avoid overvaluation or a loss of competitiveness. But imagine that noneconomic considerations make a move in the exchange rate undesirable despite domestic inflation. Often a system of multiple exchange rates for various separate classes of goods seems to be an answer; however, we will see that multiple rates have many shortcomings and are rarely desirable.

There is a separate macroeconomic concern with exchange rates. A depreciation of the exchange rate tends to raise the domestic level of prices—that is, it is inflationary. This happens directly because the prices of imported goods in home currency rise when the currency is depreciated. But indirect channels also exist: domestic firms can afford to raise their prices when competitors' prices rise, and, in the labor market, workers may ask for wage increases when higher import prices (especially for food) raise their cost of living. Thus exchange rate movements tie in very strongly with inflation policy.

Governments, which are naturally aware of this connection, would prefer to stop exchange depreciation so as to avoid the inflationary impact, but if they do so in the face of domestic inflation, they risk a loss in competitiveness. Once again, multiple rates often appear to be an answer. They appear to be an answer because they allow a competitive real exchange rate for some goods (say, the export sector) without risking the inflationary impact of import price increases associated with depreciation. As we will see, however, a policy that allows real exchange rates for different groups of goods to diverge widely inevitably leads to large costs, because it involves a misallocation of scarce resources.

Often there is also an important impact on the budget. Specifically, if the government buys foreign exchange at a high price from exporters and sells it at a low price to importers, a budget deficit is inevitable. The budget deficit, in turn, needs to be financed by higher taxes or by inflationary money creation. Thus, exchange rate regimes are also linked to inflation.

The asset market also has an exchange rate linkage. Domestic wealth holders must choose how to hold their wealth. They can hold real assets (houses and land) or claims on real assets (stocks of corporations). They can hold domestic financial assets, such as deposits at banks or government bonds; or they can hold a range of foreign assets, from deposits in banks in Miami or Geneva to U.S. Treasury bills.

The choice among assets will depend on the tradeoff between risk and return. One simple rule is clear: when foreign assets yield a higher return (in home currency) than domestic assets and are no more risky, then many domestic residents will shift sooner or later (probably sooner) into foreign assets. That much is clear, but how do we compare the return on a dollar deposit in Miami with the return on a peso deposit in Mexico? To make a comparison we have to translate the returns on the two assets into the same currency, which introduces the effect of the expected changes in the exchange rate over the investment horizon. For example, if the interest rate in Miami is 25 percent a year in dollars and the peso/dollar rate is expected to depreciate at the rate of 150 percent a year, the peso return on a Miami dollar deposit is 175 percent. If the return on peso deposits is only 160 percent, wealth holders would prefer dollar deposits. Domestic residents would shift their wealth, at least partially, abroad. Conversely, if Mexican interest rates exceed the peso return on an investment in Miami, there would be no tendency for capital to flow out.

In general, we can express the asset market linkage in terms of a critical condition for domestic interest rates. For investment in peso-denominated assets to be competitive, the peso interest rate, i, must exceed the dollar interest rate, i^*, *plus* the expected percentage rate of peso depreciation, σ. In symbols,

$$(5\text{-}2) \qquad\qquad i > i^* + \sigma$$

If this condition is not met, but capital can move across borders in an unrestricted fashion, then a country would soon find that it loses reserves selling dollars to domestic residents who prefer them as an investment over the low-yield, domestic currency assets. The issue for exchange rate policy becomes whether and how domestic and foreign asset markets might be segmented, or how the exchange rate policy that is chosen for trade can be separated from the exchange rate relevant for calculations of asset market profitability. Capital controls or dual-exchange-rate systems, as we will see, are a potential means of achieving this end.

Microeconomic Linkages

The microeconomic linkages of exchange rates involve resource allocation. The issues here closely mirror the macroeconomic issues already discussed. When the real exchange rate makes the economy highly competitive, resources are drawn into the tradable goods sector (the notion of what a tradable good is expands). Many goods become exportable, and fewer goods are imported. Goods that used to be imported are domestically produced or even become exportable. In the factor markets this is mirrored by a new allocation of resources. When the real exchange rate is highly competitive, the economy is highly trade-oriented; employment of capital and labor in the export sector and in import-competing industries is high. Conversely, when the real exchange rate is highly uncompetitive, resources are primarily employed in the home market, imports are high, and export production is unprofitable.

The distribution of income between different groups or sectors often depends on the level of competitiveness. For example, if the country has a traditional export sector (say, agriculture or mining), then a very competitive exchange rate (meaning that the exchange rate is high in relation to wages) will make traditional exports extremely profitable. Owners of the traditional industries earn rents, and workers perceive that their purchasing power is very low. Conversely, when the exchange rate is highly uncompetitive or overvalued, workers' wages have a very high purchasing power (if workers can find a job!), whereas firms in the traded goods sector are unprofitable and hence cut back on investment.

Because of these sectoral and income distribution issues, governments often look for ways to avoid what they perceive to be adverse effects of a competitive exchange rate. They may introduce multiple exchange rates to tax traditional export industries or to raise artificially the purchasing power of wages in terms of imported food. Policies of multiple rates, if pursued for a long time, can ultimately distort the use of resources and lead to low investment and investment in the wrong sectors.

There is also a microeconomic counterpart to the asset market linkage. In economies in which domestic returns invariably fall short of returns abroad, capital flight will take place. This may take time, but in the end people do get their money out—if necessary, by faking trade invoices. That means fewer resources are available for investment in the home economy. Moreover, those who get their money out often do so at the expense of those who cannot (we will see examples of this below). Hence distribution issues are important here, as well.

Alternative Exchange Rate Regimes

We can classify alternative exchange rate regimes in terms of two dimensions. The first dimension has to do with whether the exchange market is unified or segmented. In a unified market all transactions occur at the same rate; in a segmented market different transactions take place at different exchange rates. The second dimension concerns the supply of foreign exchange. In one classification, it is rationed to those who have specified eligible transactions, and recipients of foreign exchange are required to surrender it at a specified price. The alternative is a system in which foreign exchange is freely available at a specified price from the central bank, and owners or recipients are not subject to a surrender requirement (see table 5-1).

Table 5-1. Alternative Exchange Rate Regimes

	Foreign exchange market	
Foreign exchange supply	*Unified*	*Segmented*
Rationed/requisitioned	I	II
Unrestricted	III	IVa

a. In practice, IV does not exist as a system.

Among developed countries, case III is the most common: exporters have no need to surrender foreign exchange, and importers can buy it freely in the market. There will typically be no difference (except in Italy or France, on occasion) in the treatment of trade transactions and financial transactions. We refer to such a system as unrestricted convertibility. In this case, the central bank may be actively involved in the market by fixing the exchange rate, may be totally absent with a flexible exchange rate clearing demand and supply, or may intervene, buying and selling to influence the level of the equilibrium exchange rate.

Most developing countries do not have unrestricted convertibility. Even highly efficient surplus countries such as the Republic of Korea maintain restrictions on payments as, indeed, did Japan in the 1970s. For most developing countries, exchange rate regimes tend to fall into the other boxes. The most straightforward is case I. Here the government draws up a list of specified transactions (an import list, an authorized transfer list, and an authorized capital outflow list) for which foreign exchange is supplied at a specified rate. Exporters have to surrender all foreign exchange they receive at the same specified rate. For unauthorized transactions, no foreign exchange is available (and hence a black market springs up). This exchange rate regime is a reflection of an overvalued currency: at the specified price, foreign exchange is in short supply; therefore, rationing and requisitioning are required. Although using a disequilibrium exchange rate may help a government equalize income distribution, the system misallocates resources: goods that do not make the import list cannot be obtained, and, if the list is poorly done, it may exclude, for example, essential intermediate inputs, not just "dispensable luxury goods."

When the black market for foreign exchange (and the associated smuggling and faking of trade invoices) becomes a major issue, as happens in a system like case I, governments often move to a case III regime. Or, they might adopt multiple exchange rates for commercial transactions and maintain the rationing and requisitioning of foreign exchange, or they might have a uniform rate for specified commercial transactions and another for capital account transactions and all those commercial transactions not taking place at the commercial rate. This is the system that prevailed in Mexico, for example, after 1982. The difference between these modalities primarily concerns the question of whether the authorities administer each of the rates or whether they administer some and allow the exchange rate to find the equilibrium level in the remaining markets, perhaps with some intervention. Thus the segmentation case will tend to be a mixed system, with an administered commercial rate, for example, and a free rate for all other transactions. The case of unrestricted, segmented markets (case IV), with a flexible rate for each separate market, is in principle possible but is not a reality. That case does not exist, because governments get into the practice of segmenting markets for the purpose of actively maintaining a disequilibrium rate for some particular class of transactions.

There is another way of classifying exchange rate systems, based on whether the rates are fixed or flexible in nominal or real terms (table 5-2). Fixed nominal exchange rates (case I) arise when a country has a strong economic relationship with a particular industrial country. For example, in most African countries that were former colonies of France, exchange rates are fixed in relation to the French franc. Similarly, Panama and several Caribbean islands have fixed dollar parities. Other countries maintain an exchange rate fixed in terms of some basket of foreign currencies rather than a single currency. The distinction is important, because in a world where the dollar-franc rate moves wildly, there are clearly important exchange rate issues for a country that trades with both France and the United States. If that country fixes the rate to one currency, it has wild swings in competitiveness in relation to the other. Fixing an exchange rate in terms of a trade-weighted basket of currencies helps avoid some of these vagaries for countries that do not have an overriding relationship with one single industrial country. It does not, however, totally eliminate the exchange rate difficulties of developing countries that arise from the instability of exchange rates among major industrial countries.

A fixed real exchange rate (case II) is an exchange rate regime in which the nominal exchange rate is automatically depreciated at a rate that offsets inflation differences between the country and its trading partners.[2]

Fixed exchange rates are administered rates, whether fixed in nominal or real terms. Flexible rates, shown as case III, are determined by the market. A government may or may not influence the rate through intervention or through its domestic monetary policy, but the basic point is that the rate is market-determined. Few developing countries have a fully flexible exchange rate.

We now turn to specific policy situations and cases to examine, in greater detail, the costs and benefits of alternative exchange rate systems.

Multiple Exchange Rates for Commercial Transactions

In this section, we look at an exchange rate system in which the government administers specific exchange rates for different commercial transactions. We leave issues of capital flows to a separate section.

Table 5-3 shows the Peruvian system of the mid-1980s in all its complexity. The system had two basic rates and many variations. One

Table 5-2. Fixed and Flexible Exchange Rates

Exchange rate	Fixed	Flexible
Nominal	I	III
Real	II	

was the "official rate" that applied to all "essential" imports and at least partially to other transactions. The other was the "financial rate." Most transactions were undertaken at a mix of these two rates. Thus in 1987, for example, petroleum exporters had to surrender 55 percent of their foreign exchange at the official rate and 45 percent at the financial rate. In addition to the two basic rates, there was a super rate for financial transactions. The difference between the lowest and highest exchange rate was 60 percent in May 1987.

Table 5-3. Exchange Rate Regime, Peru, 1984–87

	Applicable exchange rate			
Transaction	1984	1985	1986	May 1987
Imports				
Essential	O	O	O	O
Other	O	O	F	F
Exports				
Traditional				
From mines				
Small	O	95/5	45/55	35/65
Large	O	95/5	65/35	55/45
Petroleum	O	O	O	55/45
Nontraditional	O	80/20	P	P
Invisibles	O	O	O	O
Authorized transfers	O	O	O	O, F
Capital				
New loans	O	O	O	F
Bank accounts	O	O+3%	O,F	O,F,SS
Repatriation	n.a.	n.a.	n.a.	S
Rates in effect (intis/dollar)				
Official	5.20	13.95	13.95	15.42
Free	5.38	17.38	17.45	19.28
Premium	5.92	19.12	19.20	21.21
Special	n.a.	n.a.	n.a.	24.70
Super special	n.a.	n.a.	n.a.	28.40

n.a. Not applicable.

Note: O = Official; F = Free; P = Premium; S = Special; SS = Super special. Where transactions are undertaken at a mix of official and free rates, the ratio of the two weightings—O (Official) to F (Free)—is given.

Source: IMF files.

Two points should be immediately obvious from the table. The first is that the average rate at which the central bank bought intis from importers is far below the average rate at which it sold intis to exporters. Thus, the exchange rate system had adverse fiscal consequences for the central bank. The second is the large variability in the applicable rates over time.

Figure 5-1 shows the result of these exchange rate policies (and the accompanying tariff and licensing policies): the real price of imports and exports in terms of domestic goods. These prices are calculated (by the World Bank) as the averages, using all applicable exchange rates and tariffs for each of the separate commodity groups. Note that from 1985 to mid-1987, the real prices of both exports and imports declined by more than 35 percent. In response to these price changes, the demand for imports increased sharply and export profitability fell off. As a result, a growing foreign exchange problem developed. In late 1987 the government started responding to the problem by increasing the real prices of both exports and imports, but the correction did not last long. Soon the policy of cheap imports resumed. The real prices for exports moved sharply up as export exchange rates increased ahead of domestic prices. Import exchange rates, on the other hand, lagged far behind the domestic rate of inflation.

Why Countries Use Multiple Rates

The complexity of the exchange rate arrangements shown in table 5-3 immediately raises the question of why governments opt for multiple rates. Do multiple exchange rates achieve economic efficiency, or are there other reasons why governments use multiple rates? The answer is that far from bringing the economy closer to efficiency, multiple rates are likely to create waste, yet they are a way of affecting resource allocation and income distribution.

By interfering with free market prices a government can reallocate resources, direct resources into alternative uses, and affect the real incomes of different sectors and the factors of production. The basic instruments for redirecting resources are taxes, subsidies, tariffs, and quotas, on the one hand, and special exchange rates, on the other. Anything that can be done with tariffs can be replicated with a special exchange rate. Thus, if an industry is to be protected against foreign competition (thereby giving the owners of resources in the industry higher real incomes), a tariff can do the job, but so can a high exchange rate for this particular type of good. Likewise, if the objective is to raise workers' real incomes in terms of a particular traded good (say, food), this can be done by a consumption subsidy. But it can

Figure 5-1. Real Prices of Exports and Imports, Peru, 1985–88
(1986 = 100)

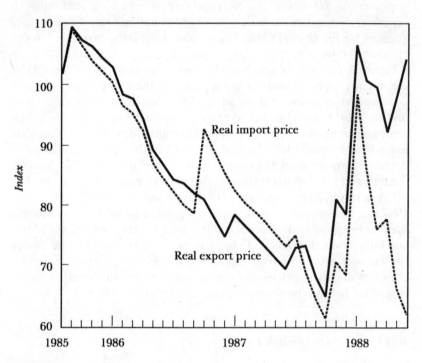

Source: World Bank data.

also be done by an especially low exchange rate for imports of this particular good.

In the absence of other instruments, governments find multiple rates to be a ready way of achieving noneconomic objectives. Governments often fool themselves, however, because they underestimate the cumulative economic costs of a distortionary exchange rate system. We will discuss the costs in a later section.

Mechanisms for Special Exchange Rates

There are a number of mechanisms for special exchange rates.

EXCHANGE RATES FOR IMPORTS. Special exchange rates for particular groups of imports involve two separate issues: the purchasing power of wages and industrialization.

The typical situation is one in which a country has a trade imbalance. That means that the level of spending is too high in relation to income (perhaps because of a budget deficit) and that traded goods are underpriced (imports are too cheap, and exports are priced so low that exporting is unprofitable). An adjustment is needed, and the clean way is to have a real depreciation that reduces the purchasing power of income and increases the competitiveness of the tradable goods sector.

Governments are rightly concerned, however, that an across-the-board increase in import prices will have adverse political consequences: increased prices of imports will reduce the purchasing power of wages and create political problems. Governments therefore look for a more selective way to ration foreign exchange—one that attempts to skirt the political problem. The immediate step is to distinguish between "essential" and "nonessential" imports. For essential imports, the exchange rate is held unchanged, whereas for nonessential imports, it is increased sharply so as to reduce foreign exchange outlays and thus solve the trade deficit problem.

Does such a policy work? Often one finds that the purchasing power of wages in terms of essential goods stays unchanged and that it declines sharply in terms of all other goods. The poorest groups in society might be protected, but the vocal middle class is being squeezed, and that poses new problems. Of course, we would want to check whether multiple rates at least succeed in attaining the government's objectives. In many instances they have not and may, in fact, have hurt the very group they were designed to benefit, as well as making everybody else worse off.

The other important motivation for special exchange rates on the import side is industrialization. A government may feel that domestic industry should be protected. Rather than pursue a policy of trade-oriented growth (often declared to be a low-wage strategy), the government may want to promote more rapid economic growth. Industries are designated as plausible development targets and are favored with a special exchange rate. Here the special exchange rate plays exactly the same role as a tariff, except that (in a context of import licensing) using special exchange rates may be easier administratively.

As a result of the special exchange rate, domestic firms in the protected industry can charge higher prices and can thus afford to produce at a cost that is higher than the world market's. In time they may go through a learning process, reduce costs, and ultimately become world class. More likely, they will keep producing at high cost, enjoying protection at the expense of consumers and at the cost of a waste of resources.

EXCHANGE RATES FOR EXPORTS. Special exchange rates are used for exports primarily for several reasons.

One reason is to encourage industrialization. Particular export industries are given an implicit subsidy that allows them to sell at world prices. This typically applies to manufacturing or nontraditional export industries.

Another reason concerns traditional export industries (oil in Venezuela and Peru and agriculture in Argentina). A government may believe that these industries should not enjoy a windfall gain from a general exchange depreciation because their output is not very price-responsive. Thus, the government may use a special exchange rate to tax any windfall profits away from these industries. For example, if the currency is depreciated to eliminate a trade deficit, agricultural exporters will face higher prices in pesos. If their harvests have already been planted (or even harvested), the entire price increase might represent windfall profits, with no favorable effect on dollar earnings. Moreover, the increase in pesos of agricultural export prices would raise the prices at which the agricultural sector would sell in the home economy, because farmers clearly would not sell below what they could earn abroad. But that would imply a reduction in the standard of living for consumers of agricultural goods—hence the politically attractive argument for a "compensated devaluation," namely, a devaluation for all sectors except agricultural exports.

The argument becomes even more attractive when it applies to foreign oil companies. Why create windfall profits for them (which they might take out of the country) rather than administer a low, special exchange rate at which they are required to surrender foreign exchange revenues?

The Costs of Multiple Rates

We have seen the political reasons for multiple rates. We next look at the costs—the misallocation of resources, rent seeking, and the budget problem.

THE MISALLOCATION OF RESOURCES. Multiple exchange rates have important implications for resource allocation. The (competitive) market solution is to allocate resources so that, on the export side, the marginal cost (in relation to the domestic resources required) to produce an extra dollar of foreign exchange is equalized across all export activities. In this way, expanding one industry just a little and contracting another slightly leave the total resource costs of obtaining a given dollar of revenue unchanged. The resource cost of earning foreign exchange is effectively minimized.

In an economy that allocates resources efficiently, the marginal cost of an extra unit of output equals the price a firm receives, and that price equals the value a buyer places on an extra unit of output. This is the crux of microeconomics. When this equality of price and marginal cost prevails, there is no way of reshuffling productive resources— producing more of one good and less of another—in a way that makes one person better off without making someone worse off. This, in a nutshell, is the economic case against multiple rates.

Multiple exchange rates interfere with the optimal allocation of resources because for the same good—a dollar—different sectors or groups in society pay or receive different amounts of pesos. As a result, people or activities that get cheap dollars will spend too much on dollar goods. People or industries that receive high peso prices for the dollars they surrender will produce too much of the goods that are earmarked for especially high exchange rates. Resources could be reshuffled, and they would be if the economy went to unified rates, so as to reduce the resource cost of earning dollars and to spend the dollars earned in a better way. The government resists this "better way" because, although it makes society better off, it may make particular groups (low-wage labor) worse off.

Export activities with relatively favorable exchange rates overexpand in relation to those with less favorable exchange rates. Thus it takes a larger amount of domestic resources to earn a given amount of foreign exchange. This is because in the industries with a favorable exchange rate the marginal cost of earning a dollar can be much higher than in the industries with the unfavorable rate. Equalizing rates would contract high-cost production and expand low-cost production, thus lowering the total cost of earning foreign exchange.

The same reasoning applies to imports. Imports of goods favored by relatively cheap foreign exchange expand, and those with a high price of foreign exchange contract. Domestic resources are drawn into the areas in which the exchange rate is unfavorable; they cannot compete where the exchange rate is particularly favorable. Once again, equalizing the rates would tend to expand the relatively low-cost import substitution industries and contract the industries in which import substitution is subsidized (implicitly) by the highly protective exchange rate.

Resource misallocation between exportable and import-competing industries also occurs. With a large spread between (average) import and export rates, the export sector will overexpand and import competition will be underdeveloped. Exchange rate unification would move resources from earning foreign exchange through exports to saving foreign exchange through the production of import-competing goods. The marginal cost of producing import-competing goods (and thus the marginal cost of saving a dollar by import substitution) is thus much lower than the marginal cost of earning an extra dollar by expanding exports. Exchange rate unification would lead to the equalization of the marginal cost of dollars on the saving and earning sides.

Equalization of marginal costs and benefits would not be an issue if exports and imports did not respond to prices. If they were fully unresponsive, the exchange rate system would simply be a way of distributing from one group of households or firms to another. No waste would be involved, just politics. But when activities do respond to prices, the economy is worse off with a system of multiple exchange rates. A given amount of resources produces fewer goods and services than could be obtained if marginal costs and benefits were equalized across all activities.

Why then do governments use multiple rates? The reason is a combination of two factors. First, governments are interested in redistributing income across groups, and the exchange rate system offers that possibility. Second, governments often believe (erroneously) that the resource allocation effects of a distortionary exchange rate regime are small. The reason they cite is that resources do not easily move across industries (technically, elasticities are low) and consumers are relatively unresponsive to price changes. In fact, very little evidence for low responsiveness of households or firms exists, certainly when we allow for some time to adjust to a new set of prices.

The temptation to use multiple rates is particularly strong when a country's economy has a division between traditional and nontraditional exports, and even more so when traditional is tantamount to large, rich, foreign firms or domestic landowners. In the Peruvian example cited earlier, nontraditional exports (compared with, say, exports from small mines) are heavily subsidized by the exchange rate system. Moreover, the exchange rate for nontraditional exports far exceeds the rate for imports. Thus import competition in nontraditional industries is discouraged by a cheap import policy, but at the same time, the implicit export subsidy encourages these industries to work for the world market on the export side. The system thus draws resources out of import competition (thereby increasing import spending) while expanding exports. There is a net domestic resource cost, and there may even be a loss of net dollar revenues.

Finding examples is easy. Suppose intermediate inputs, for example, are allowed a favorable exchange rate, but final luxury goods are implicitly taxed by a high exchange rate. In that case, we should not be surprised to find that the resource cost of producing luxuries may actually involve a larger foreign exchange cost than if they were allowed outright. Resources might even be spent to break up finished goods abroad, import them as intermediate goods at a favorable exchange rate, and reassemble them into finished goods at a considerable domestic resource cost. Privately, this may be entirely profitable, but from a social perspective, it wastes resources.

A particularly extreme example of the misallocation that can result from multiple rates involves negative value added. This is a situation in which an industry is privately profitable but, from the social point of view, should be closed.

Consider a specific example. A firm produces chemicals for export. A gallon of chemicals can be sold in the world market for $20. The export exchange rate at which the revenue is converted is 20 pesos per dollar, so that for each gallon exported, the revenue is 400 pesos. Next consider the cost side. A gallon of chemicals requires one person's day of labor at 60 pesos a day and two barrels of oil at $15 a barrel. For imports of intermediate goods the government allows a favorable exchange rate of only 10 pesos per dollar. Hence a barrel of oil costs the chemical company 150 pesos. The two barrels of oil required to produce one gallon of chemicals will cost the company 300 pesos, which, together with the labor cost of 60 pesos, brings the total cost to 360 pesos. Subtracting the cost from the revenue of 400 pesos leaves a profit of 40 pesos. Thus, with the particular set of exchange rates, producing chemicals for export is profitable (privately!).

But now consider the social costs and benefits. To earn the $20 of export revenue per gallon of chemicals there is an expenditure of $30 to buy the oil, which is an indispensable input. Therefore, of every dollar of chemicals exported, the country loses $10, not even counting the labor effort. Privately, exporting chemicals is profitable because the multiple exchange rate makes oil (in pesos) cheap in relation to the export price (in pesos). Socially, the undertaking is a big waste. If the operation were closed, the economy would be ahead.

This example seems farfetched. It is not. In many countries, the exchange rate structure produces this extreme kind of distortion of negative value added. With a unified exchange rate (and in the absence of subsidies), such a possibility cannot arise.

RENT SEEKING, RED TAPE, AND CORRUPTION. The costs of multiple exchange rates go beyond those caused by the direct waste of distorted production and consumption patterns. Additional costs result from what Krueger (1974) has called rent-seeking activities. Because multiple exchange rates create economic rents for those factors of production that are specific to activities receiving special protection, economic agents will devote real resources to obtaining exchange rate protection. In plain language, they will spend resources on lobbying.

Lobbying may appear to be a relatively innocuous activity, but it does absorb scarce resources. Not only do lobbyists spend time and effort, they also divert policymakers' attention from their primary tasks to a negative-sum redistribution. In countries with highly distorted and discretionary exchange rate systems, the management of the redistribution implied by the exchange rate pattern almost becomes a full-time activity.

The red tape that comes with implementing a complicated exchange rate system adds to these costs. All firms have paperwork to show their compliance. Verifying the paperwork incurs costs, as does falsifying the paperwork. Bureaucracies spring up around this paperwork, and ultimately they become a raison d'être for the exchange rate system, because the bureaucrats would lose their jobs if the economy were run more efficiently. In countries where administrative capital is scarce, these considerations are decisively important.[3]

The costs increase even more in that discretionary distortions open the door to corruption. Economic agents will lobby and pay (in one form or another) for exchange rate protection or to avoid the implicit taxes that come from some other sector's protection. Corruption, in turn, affects the public sector's morale and efficiency and may disrupt economywide tax compliance. Corruption need not take the form of explicit cash payments; other ways are available: gifts, power, or simply the good feelings of administrators. If corruption becomes the routine way of paying civil servants, then the exchange rate structure (and all other taxes and subsidies) is motivated not by economic merits, but by the potential for extracting payoffs.

These aspects of discretionary exchange rate regimes create instability in economic rules and sharply raise the costs and uncertainty of doing business. They therefore have adverse effects on investment, profitability, and real wages.

THE BUDGET PROBLEM. When the central bank sells foreign exchange to importers there is a receipt, and when it buys foreign exchange from exporters there is an outlay. We are interested in how multiple exchange rates affect the net outlay.

Let X denote the total dollar value of exports, and e_x denote the weighted average exchange rate paid to exporters. On the import side, M is the dollar value of total imports, and e_m is the weighted average exchange rate for imports. The net outlay of the central bank as a result of foreign exchange transactions thus becomes:

(5-3) $$\text{Net outlay} = e_x X - e_m M$$

or, adding and subtracting $e_m X$ and collecting terms,

(5-4) $$\text{Net outlay} = X(e_x - e_m) + e_m(X - M).[4]$$

Suppose now that trade in dollars is balanced so that $X = M$. In this case, equation 5-4 for net outlay simplifies to $X(e_x - e_m)$. Thus, if the average export exchange rate exceeds the average import exchange rate, the central bank will be making losses on its foreign exchange transactions.

The larger the discrepancy between the rates, the greater the losses. To finance these losses, the central bank will print money. This money creation, brought about by the foreign exchange regime, in turn proves a source of inflation. This is almost certainly the case when the central bank's losses are very large. The World Bank estimates that central bank losses from exchange transactions in Peru were, as a percentage of GDP, 1.5 in 1985, 0.4 in 1986, and 2.0 in 1987. A loss of 2 percent of GDP, financed by money creation, is barely compatible with moderate inflation. But when the deficit that requires financing exceeds 10 percent, as it did in Peru in 1987, high and rising inflation is inevitable. Just how costly the budget financing turned out to be is apparent from Peru's experience in 1988. Inflation in August 1988 reached 2,500 percent! In September, the government unified the exchange rate in a last attempt to stem hyperinflation.

Black Markets and Trade Misinvoicing

Black markets exist because of a combination of factors. First, the rationing of foreign exchange by quotas, licenses, absolute restrictions, or special exchange rates gives rise to a demand for foreign exchange to finance illegal imports and outlays abroad. Second, there is a portfolio demand for foreign exchange that needs to be satisfied in a black market if the government does not sell foreign exchange for that purpose, but economic agents want to hold foreign assets. Third, if the black market rate exceeds the official exchange rate (or rates), exporters have an incentive to underreport their true exports and surrender their foreign exchange to the black market rather than the central bank; likewise, firms find a way to overstate the costs of authorized imports, diverting part of the foreign exchange obtained at the official rate toward the black market.[5]

The Black Market for Dollars

To understand the operation of a black market, it helps to separate the portfolio aspects and the current flows in and out of the black market. On the right-hand side of figure 5-2 we show as a hyperbola the stock demand for foreign exchange, that is, the amount of pesos people want to hold in the form of dollar-denominated assets. The vertical axis shows the black market exchange rate (pesos/dollar), and the horizontal axis shows the number of dollars. The product eB, where e is the exchange rate and B the stock of dollars, thus represents the value in pesos of a given dollar portfolio. The schedule VV shows a given level of the stock demand. This stock demand is determined by the expected profitability of holding dollars rather than pesos and thus depends on interest rates at home and on the expected rate of exchange depreciation. The higher the foreign interest rates and expected depreciation are in relation to the home interest rate, the farther out and to the right is the value of black dollars (in terms of pesos) that residents want to hold. The vertical schedule BB denotes the existing stock at a point in time. Short-run equilibrium in the black market occurs at an exchange rate e_0.

The left-hand side of the diagram shows current flows in and out of the black market. The schedule SS shows the current inflows of dollars from export underinvoicing and import overinvoicing. The higher the black market rate is in relation to the official rate, the larger is the flow supply. The flow demand for dollars for tourism and for import smuggling, DD, is a declining function of the black market rate. The lower the black market price of dollars, the cheaper it is to buy in restricted goods or buy foreign exchange for tourism.

The stock and flow markets are connected by the fact that the price at which the existing stock of dollars is held, e_0, determines the current amount of inflows and outflows, S_0 and D_0. The way we have drawn the schedule, the difference between the quantity supplied and demanded ($S_0 - D_0$ or $C - A$) is positive. This means that inflows exceed outflows,

Figure 5-2. A Model of the Black Market

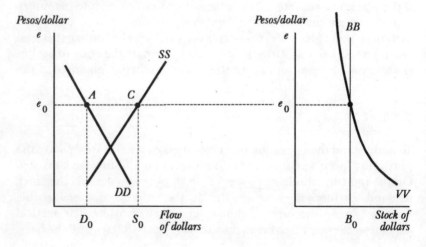

and hence the stock held in portfolios increases. This will show over time as a rightward shift of the stock supply, *BB;* a declining exchange rate; and declining net inflows until the market achieves the steady state.

These bare bones of a black market model help to identify the main determinants of the black market exchange rate (or the premium over the official rate):

- The higher the interest rates abroad and the expectations of depreciation are, the higher is the stock demand and hence the price of black market dollars. Figure 5-3 shows the black market premium in Brazil. Note the premium of nearly 100 percent at the end of 1986. This premium stemmed from a widespread expectation of a large depreciation against which asset holders sought to protect themselves by a flight into dollars. As the supply of dollars was fixed, the flight into dollars pushed up the premium. Thus monetary instability is the prime reason for a large black market premium. Political instability works in the same direction.
- An increase in trade restrictions increases the flow demand for dollars for purposes of financing smuggling. Over time, the higher flow demand leads to a rising premium, because the net inflow into the market falls off. The black market for foreign exchange typically finances all imports that are subject to high duties.
- Greater ease in supplying the black market by misinvoicing shifts the flow supply curve out and to the right and thus reduces the long-run premium.

Misinvoicing

There are basically two reasons for misrepresenting trade data. One is capital flight; the other is the desire to evade import or export duties or to capture export subsidies. These reasons, summarized in table 5-4, are discussed in more detail below.

CAPITAL FLIGHT. Residents of a country where exchange control prohibits the free export of capital for portfolio purposes might attempt to acquire foreign assets for several reasons. The three most important are fear of political instability, anticipated financial instability, and the laundering of assets. Shifting into foreign assets, in terms of currency denomination and location or jurisdiction, shelters the portfolio holder against the vagaries of domestic political and economic disturbances or against inspection by the tax authorities.

Figure 5-3. Black Market Premium, Brazil, 1962–89

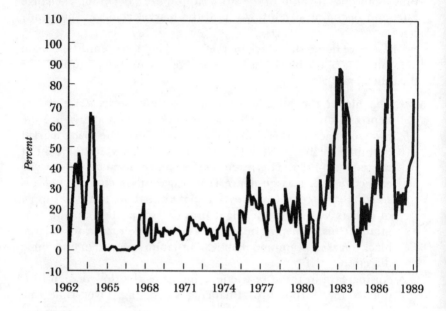

Source: Bank of Brazil data.

Interest in sending assets abroad in anticipation of political changes is apparent when one thinks of the extreme cases of Marcos or Duvalier, but such interest is also manifested, in a less extreme fashion, among asset holders who fear that their wealth or their previous dealings might become exposed in a regime change. For example, a significant political capital fight from Brazil in 1986 was motivated by the business community's fear that the left-wing parties might gain a large share of the seats in the Constitutional Assembly.

Financial instability is perhaps the most important reason for capital flight. When asset returns in a country are negative because interest rates are outpaced by inflation, asset holders are keen to protect their

Table 5-4. Principal Motives for Overinvoicing and Underinvoicing

Category	Overinvoicing	Underinvoicing
Exports	Capturing export subsidies	Capital flight
		Avoiding export taxes
Imports	Capital flight	Evading import duties

wealth by moving into dollar-denominated assets. This is the capital flight typical of Mexico in 1980–82 or of Argentina in 1979–83. Figure 5-4 shows the high Argentine black market premium during the latter part of this period of instability. This kind of capital flight is particularly vigorous when a large overvaluation of the currency makes it almost certain that holdings of dollars will carry a large return because of the anticipated depreciation of the home currency.

Capital flight to launder assets is common whenever a country starts enforcing its tax laws and institutes an improved system for monitoring tax compliance. When that happens, offenders have to take their undeclared assets out of the local jurisdiction to avoid detection and prosecution. Imagine what would happen in Argentina, for example, if bank secrecy were abolished and tax laws were, for the first time, seriously enforced. An immediate wave of capital flight would result as the business community sought to shelter its previous fraud. (Laundering of assets also applies, of course, to public officials who take abroad the revenue from corruption.)

Capital flight for these various motives needs a vehicle. When exchange control means that foreign exchange cannot be bought freely and anonymously, then the misinvoicing of trade transactions becomes the means for generating the foreign exchange that is sold in the black market to those individuals seeking to move money abroad. Whenever it is possible to buy foreign exchange freely at the official rate, and with not too many traces left behind, there is no advantage to using trade flows as a means of acquiring foreign exchange.

Exporters can generate foreign exchange to finance capital flight by underinvoicing their exports. Rather than surrender the full value of export revenues to the official foreign exchange authorities, as they are required to do, they understate the export revenue on their invoices and instruct their trading partners to deposit the balance in a foreign account for their benefit. This balance, in turn, might be held by the actual exporter or sold in the black market to someone else who wishes to acquire foreign exchange.

The incentive for an exporter to engage in underinvoicing is quite obvious. Take the case of Brazil in the last quarter of 1986. The premium in the black market was 100 percent. Underinvoicing an export by 25 percent would mean making an extra 25 percent profit over and above the normal commercial profit. With so large a profit margin for an activity that is widely considered to be a sport rather than a criminal activity, underinvoicing of exports becomes pervasive. This is made easier when exports are diversified manufactures rather than homogeneous primary commodities with commonly known world prices. Although it is apparent that export underinvoicing will take place when its rewards are as extreme as in Brazil, one wonders what

Figure 5-4. Black Market Premium, Argentina, 1960-88

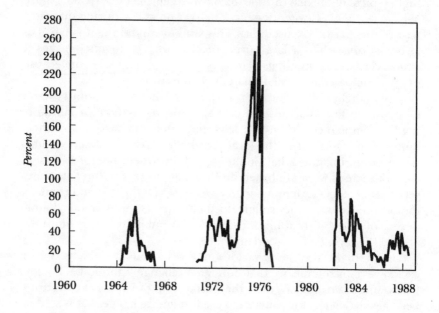

Source: Central Bank of Argentina data.

the threshold is in Argentina. Experts maintain that export underinvoicing starts when the black market premium goes beyond 25 percent.

Overinvoicing of imports, just like underinvoicing of exports, can serve as a vehicle for capital flight. An importer, when applying for foreign exchange to the authorities, will overstate the value of the import shipment. Depending on the country's procedure, the authorities will directly instruct payment to be made or they will put at the importer's disposal foreign exchange in an account abroad. In one case, the importer directly acquires the foreign exchange in excess of actual import costs. In the other case, cooperation with the foreign shipper is required. Whichever is the case, defrauding the foreign exchange authorities is a routine activity. Once again, the proceeds might be held by the actual importer or sold through the black market to other residents who wish to acquire foreign exchange but cannot obtain it freely or discreetly from official sources.

International transactions are natural vehicles for tax fraud, because domestic tax authorities do not have access to trading partners' business records as they do for domestic ones. In the domestic market, one person's receipts are another person's outlays, a fact that sharply reduces the opportunity for fraud.

IMPORT DUTIES. High import duties are a common feature in many developing countries. One reason is that trade taxes remain an important part of public revenues. The other reason is a long-standing policy of import protection. For all of Latin America, taxes on international trade are 12 percent of total government revenue. In some countries, the share is more than 25 percent, as in Bolivia or Costa Rica.

When import duties are high, importers have an incentive to cheat on import duties by underinvoicing. By simply understating the value of imports, the importer reduces the amount that must be paid in duties. As a result, the average burden of the duty, expressed as a fraction of the true value of imports, is reduced. For example, if the duty is 70 percent, and underinvoicing amounts to 25 percent, an importer pays only 52.5 percent effective duty rather than the 70 that is owed.

So far we have assumed that the importer can freely obtain foreign exchange to finance the part of the import bill that is underinvoiced, but, of course, that may not be the case. When there is exchange control, the importer has to buy the extra foreign exchange in the black market at the cost of a premium over the official rate. To know whether underinvoicing remains profitable, we must compare the black market premium with the tariff rate. If the tariff rate exceeds the black market premium, then underinvoicing saves more in import duties than it costs in the black market to make up the difference in the foreign exchange required. This points to goods with very high tariffs—of 100 percent or more—as the items most likely to attract fraud on import duties. By contrast, goods with no import duties serve as vehicles for underinvoicing to generate foreign exchange for sale in the black market.

We have discussed how import duties are avoided by understating the value of shipments, but an important, parallel alternative occasionally applies. Often tariff rates differ significantly among different goods that might pass for being the same. Whenever that is the case, the incentive goes strongly in the direction of misstating the exact nature of the imported goods. By representing the commodity as belonging to a low tariff category rather than to the appropriate high tariff category that actually applies, the importer saves tariff costs.

EXPORT DUTIES. In some countries, the government levies export duties. For example, in Argentina agricultural exports are typically taxed and so are, on occasion, some manufactures. In such a situation, when export duties are ad valorem, the exporter has an incentive to understate the true value of an export shipment to reduce the amount of duties paid. Thus, underinvoicing of exports reduces the effective tax rate that the government collects.

EXPORT SUBSIDIES. When a government grants export subsidies, for example, to nontraditional exports, the incentive runs the other way. To increase the effective subsidy rate, the exporter will overstate the value of a shipment.

OTHER TAX FRAUD. Overinvoicing or underinvoicing occurs for other, more specific reasons. Some are worth mentioning if only to show that in a society in which tax fraud is common, overinvoicing or underinvoicing will tend to appear in a very significant association with trade transactions. One example is abuse of investment tax credits. Suppose a country pursues an investment strategy and for that purpose allows a tax credit against equipment purchases that also applies to imported equipment. By overstating the value of imports, the firm obtains a larger amount of tax credit or a higher effective investment tax credit. As another example, consider corporate income tax fraud. A company that routinely imports materials has an interest in overstating the cost of materials to reduce its before-tax profits and hence the effective tax on profits. This is difficult to do within a country, but overinvoicing is an obvious means.

One can imagine that in the case of multinational corporations, misinvoicing of imports and exports is simply a means of shifting their tax liabilities from one jurisdiction to another. By overstating import costs from their foreign headquarters or by understating export value, they shift corporate profits abroad to take advantage of lower tax rates that may apply there.

EMPIRICAL EVIDENCE. The significant misrepresentation of trade data in developing countries is well known. Bhagwati and Krueger (1974) documented extensive underinvoicing, and more recent work by Gulati (1987) shows that the practice flourished in the late 1970s and 1980s.

There are no direct measures of underinvoicing or overinvoicing in international trade. The only method is to compare one country's trade data with the data of its trading partners. Any discrepancy is a guide to the extent of overinvoicing or underinvoicing, although it may represent, to a small extent, other factors. (See Gulati 1987 and Bhagwati and Krueger 1974 for a more detailed discussion of the statistical issues.) The International Monetary Fund (IMF) reports trade data by country and region. Using these data, it is possible to calculate the amount of overinvoicing or underinvoicing for a particular country, say, Argentina. One simply compares the value of exports to industrial countries and imports from industrial countries reported by Argentina (on the basis of invoices presented to the Argentine authorities) with corresponding data reported by industrial countries. Table 5-5 shows the average level of underinvoicing of exports for a number of countries.

At a more aggregate level we can look at Latin America's trade with the industrial countries. We take 1982 to 1985 as years in which currency disturbances were particularly important. Interestingly, both export and import underinvoicing occurred throughout the period (table 5-6). Export underinvoicing points to continuing, steady capital outflows. Import underinvoicing means that tariff evasion dominates capital flight motives. Thus, looking at the trade account, export underinvoicing finances the tariff evasion by supplying the black market dollars required when the import value is understated. It is striking and depressing that a whole continent's tax fraud should be so simple to document.

The Mexican data show substantial export underinvoicing and hence evidence of steady capital flight. Persistent underinvoicing of imports points to tariff evasion. The huge underinvoicing of 1983 presumably indicates that the system of rationing foreign exchange was particularly vulnerable to fraud.

The Macroeconomic Effects of Black Markets

The preceding section showed pervasive evidence of capital flight via underinvoicing of exports. In countries where exporters are required

Table 5-5. Underinvoicing of Exports, Selected Countries, 1977–83

(percentage underinvoicing)

Country	1977	1978	1979	1980	1981	1982	1983	Average
Argentina	20.6	21.2	18.9	17.4	19.2	21.0	19.5	19.6
Brazil	11.2	9.0	17.1	14.5	11.4	15.9	9.8	12.7
Chile	14.0	23.5	14.8	13.8	9.6	12.0	6.5	12.8
Korea, Rep. of	2.0	−0.9	−0.7	0.5	−3.5	−6.1	−5.1	−2.5
Mexico	77.9	26.8	42.4	27.6	26.9	26.5	33.8	33.6
Peru	20.8	15.6	8.9	14.4	18.1	10.0	9.6	12.9
Uruguay	15.0	13.5	13.7	14.3	19.5	64.1	52.6	27.8
Venezuela	7.6	6.1	0.7	4.2	9.5	8.9	9.4	6.9

Note: Because exports are recorded f.o.b. and imports c.i.f., a difference of approximately 10 percent is to be expected. Thus only magnitudes above 10 percent should be regarded as capital flight.

Source: Cuddington (1986).

Table 5-6. Average Underinvoicing, Mexico and Latin America, 1982–85

(percentage of exports and imports, respectively)

Category	1982	1983	1984	1985
Export underinvoicing				
Mexico	25.0	32.0	17.0	17.5
Latin America	9.3	8.5	7.3	8.3
Import underinvoicing				
Mexico	34.0	84.0	39.0	19.7
Latin America	18.9	23.8	27.9	15.8

Source: IMF data.

to surrender their full export proceeds at the official exchange rate, underinvoicing implies that the government receives less than the full export revenue. What are the macroeconomic implications? One immediate implication is that the government does not collect all the revenue that is due. The other is that the reduced foreign exchange receipts imply the need for extra exchange depreciation, which brings with it a reduced standard of living and inflationary pressure. Each of these has adverse effects on the budget and, from there, on macroeconomic stability.

LOSS OF REVENUE. Table 5-7 shows data on the share of trade taxes in total revenue and the ratio of trade taxes to GNP. These data show that import duties are an important element of the government revenue base. Accordingly, widespread underinvoicing is a major issue in public finance and macroeconomics.

The averages in table 5-7 conceal the fact that some countries are much more dependent than others on trade taxes for government finance. In Africa, for example, trade taxes provide almost 50 percent of Mauritania's revenue and 30 percent of Senegal's. In Asia, the revenue share of trade taxes in Pakistan and Sri Lanka exceeds 30 percent. In Latin America, and especially Central America, the smaller countries derive a large share of their revenue from duties.

Table 5-7. Trade Taxes as a Share of Government Revenue and as a Share of GNP, 1982

Region	Trade taxes as a percentage of revenue	Revenue from trade taxes as a percentage of GNP
Africa	15.5	2.9
Asia	19.1	3.2
Latin America	14.4	2.9

Source: IMF (1986).

We saw earlier that underinvoicing of imports for Latin America averages 30 to 40 percent. What is the budgetary implication of these losses in duty revenue? A crude estimate, using table 5-7, is revenue losses on the order of 1 percent of GNP! In countries where budget balancing and revenue collection are major problems, a revenue loss of 1 percent of GNP is an extraordinary shock to public finance.

LOSS OF FOREIGN EXCHANGE. When a firm underinvoices exports, it withholds foreign exchange receipts from the exchange authorities. This foreign exchange might be used to build up external assets or perhaps sold to importers who are underinvoicing. For the government, the reduction in foreign exchange receipts implies that, at the going exchange rate, there is now a shortfall of export revenue in relation to the foreign exchange required to finance the existing level of imports. The foreign exchange deficit forces one of two policy measures: the imposition of extra protection to cut selectively the level of imports or a depreciation of the currency so as to increase export competitiveness and reduce import dependence. The economy must make up the foreign exchange deficiency caused by underinvoicing of exports either by saving on foreign exchange through restrictions or by finding extra ways of earning and saving foreign exchange through currency depreciation.

It is immediately apparent that overinvoicing imposes an important social cost. Protection is costly not only for consumers at home but also for foreign exporters who are barred from a market in which capital flight absorbs the foreign exchange that otherwise would have been available to finance extra imports. Depreciation achieves much the same end, because the only way to close the foreign exchange gap is to sell more and buy less.

There is an obvious cost to foreign exporters who are forced out of the home market by the gain in competitiveness of extra depreciation. There are also losses to foreign firms whose products now have to compete with the more competitively priced imports from the developing country. The simple way to think of this process is that the developing country must earn the extra foreign exchange that is now diverted to capital flight: extra exports or cuts in import spending must supply the dollars that are absorbed by capital flight through export underinvoicing.

In the country suffering the capital flight, the costs go much further. Real depreciation reduces the purchasing power of wages; that is, after all, how depreciation makes a country more competitive in world trade. Thus there is a redistribution of income from wage earners and the public at large to the firms that practice capital flight. There is an economywide cut in real income, the proceeds of which are indirectly and illegally appropriated by the firms that practice capital flight.

The cut in the standard of living has inevitable budgetary effects. Spending decreases, and much of the reduction in spending falls on nontraded goods. Domestic activity therefore tends to decline. The reduced level of activity reduces budget revenues and hence contributes to a deficit. In addition, the reduced standard of living often forces the government to adopt selective subsidies for food or public transport. Thus an increased budget deficit almost certainly emerges as one effect of capital flight.

INFLATION. The inflationary effect of the depreciation required by increased capital flight is also important. The inflationary pressure stems from two sources. First, depreciation raises the price of traded goods and the cost of living. Then, assuming the increased cost of living results in wage demands, a wage-price spiral is triggered. That wage-price spiral is fed by the money creation that stems from enlarged budget deficits, as noted earlier.

Thus an increase in inflation—possibly a major increase—inevitably appears. This inflation, in turn, promotes further capital flight. There is, accordingly, a vicious spiral of capital flight and instability that can be stopped only by both working directly on the budget and curbing capital flight. To place the burden exclusively on the budget raises the social costs of making illegal trade transactions unprofitable. The better way is to make at least some effort at directly stopping the faking of export invoices.

AGGREGATE COSTS. To obtain an impression of the aggregate effect of capital flight on an economy, it is helpful to compare capital flight to a loss of export revenue caused by a decline in export prices. Imagine a country that suffers a 20 percent decline in the price of an export product that accounts for 70 percent of total exports. The total reduction in dollars in export revenue accruing to the central bank is 14 percent. This loss can easily result in a foreign exchange crisis with devaluation, budget deterioration, and inflation.

Underinvoicing of exports at the rate that is evident for Latin America in table 5-6 is strictly equivalent to a fall in export prices, and the social consequences are quite the same. But there is a difference: when export prices decline, the country at large, including exporters, loses. With export underinvoicing and capital flight, by contrast, the exporters gain and force not only the direct costs of what they misappropriate but also the excess burden of the macroeconomic adjustment required by the foreign exchange shortage onto the country.

We have emphasized here the macroeconomic costs of export underinvoicing. In addition, there are microeconomic or welfare costs. Underinvoicing of exports can be thought of as a privately collected export tax. Interpreted in this way, there is an identifiable deadweight loss for consumers as well as a transfer of resources from the community at large to exporters.

One might be tempted to conclude that because black markets have adverse macroeconomic effects and lead to a misallocation of resources, they should be vigorously repressed. Economists will give a different answer. Repressing black markets is rarely successful; therefore, it is better to repress the causes rather than the symptoms. More financial stability and less restrictive trade regimes will vastly reduce the demand for foreign exchange that gives rise to a black market.

Dual Exchange Rates and Unified, Flexible Rates

In this section we discuss what exchange rate system is suitable when the capital account plays an important role in the economy and when capital controls are ineffective either because of a lack of administrative infrastructure or because geography (as with Mexico) makes controls implausible. The discussion compares two alternatives: a system of dual exchange rates or one of unified, flexible rates.

Dual Exchange Rates

A system of dual exchange rates has only two rates: an "official" rate that applies to most, if not all, trade transactions and a "financial" or "free" rate at which all other transactions take place. Mexico produces a good example of such a system.[6] From 1955 to 1976 and again from 1976 to 1982, Mexico maintained a fixed exchange rate in relation to the United States. But as figure 5-5 shows, in the early 1980s, the real exchange rate appreciated massively, and this led to a payments crisis. The government responded in August 1982 with a devaluation and the adoption of a split exchange market. Approved trade transactions were to be financed at the official rate and all other transactions at a "market" rate.

Figure 5-6 shows the premium of the market rate (in New York) over the official rate. It is interesting to note that with the exception of isolated crises in 1982, 1985 (when oil prices declined), and late 1987 (when private external debt payments fell due) the premium was quite moderate. This is the main point: a combination of a realistic commercial rate and a realistic interest rate ensures that the gap between the commercial and financial rate will be moderate and that distortions are unlikely to become major.

Before we return to the Mexican case, we briefly look at Venezuela (figure 5-7) to see an alternative. Here the gap is persistently large, and, as a result, inefficiency in resource allocation and underinvoicing have to be major issues.

Figure 5-8 gives further insight into how the Mexican system operates. This figure shows two "market" rates, one in Mexico and the other in New York, in addition to the commercial ("controlled") rate. The movements of these rates show clearly that the Mexican market rate is also a controlled rate. Rationing of foreign exchange at the posted price allows a smooth pattern compared with the New York rate. The divergence is particularly striking in late 1982, when the New York rate is far higher than the rate in Mexico.

We saw in the previous two sections that multiple exchange rates or black markets involve a misallocation of resources. That would seem to make the case for a uniform exchange rate, whatever the political costs. Here we go the other way to argue that a well-managed system of dual rates may function as a sensible shock absorber in economies in which capital is highly mobile and capital controls are ineffective. The key qualification, of course, is the term "well-managed." We mean by that a premium that never exceeds a 15 to 20 percent range except temporarily. A small premium implies little incentive for overinvoicing or underinvoicing and hence involves small resource costs. In such a situation, it is worth asking what the benefits are, if any.

The chief benefit of a dual-rate system is avoiding situations in which transitory shocks in the capital account significantly affect the exchange rate and hence prices and wages. Such a situation might be one in which a temporary event (say, political uncertainty or uncertainty about future oil prices) leads to capital flight and then the need to devalue the exchange rate. If the exchange rate and prices and wages come to be driven by portfolio holders' expectations and the price and wage adjustments lead to expectations of further depreciation, the economy easily loses the anchor of nominal stability. If capital flows are potentially unstable and wages and prices are extremely responsive to movements in the nominal exchange rate, and if controlling capital flows is nearly impossible, then dual rates are probably the only modus vivendi.

In a dual-rate system the commercial rate remains stable, whereas the free rate reflects the instability of portfolio holders' expectations, and hence of capital flows. Because the commercial rate is detached from the influence of capital flows, shifts in portfolio preferences cease to affect wages and the prices of traded goods. The commercial rate thus provides a nominal anchor.

Clearly, such a system works well if capital account disturbances are short-lived; if, however, they primarily reflect expectations about the

Figure 5-5. Real Exchange Rate, Mexico, 1970–88

(1980–82 = 100)

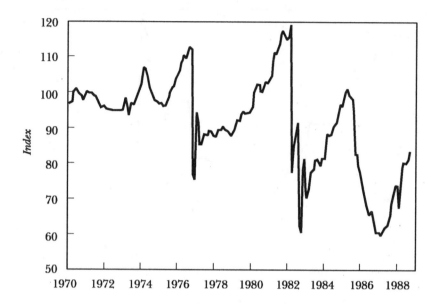

Source: Morgan Guaranty data.

Figure 5-6. Free Market Premium, Mexico, 1982–88

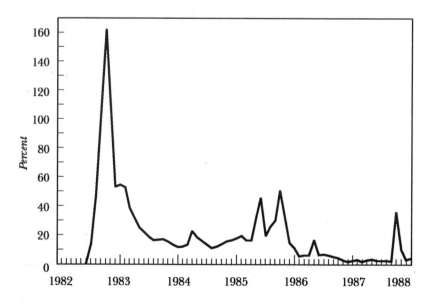

Source: Central Bank of Mexico (various issues).

Figure 5-7. Exchange Premium, Venezuela, 1983–88

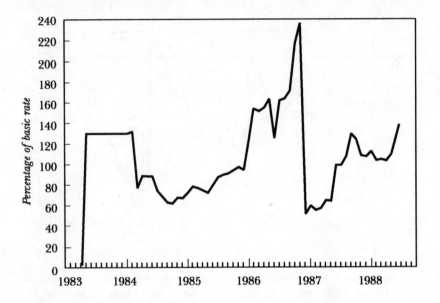

Source: Central Bank of Venezuela data.

Figure 5-8. Exchange Rates, Mexico, 1982–85

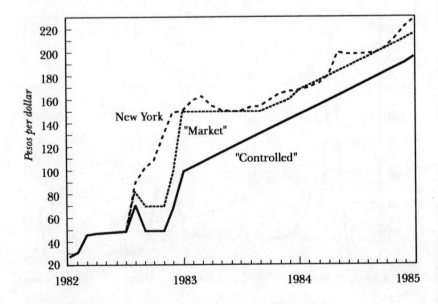

Source: Central Bank of Mexico data.

viability of the commercial rate, a large, persistent premium develops, and this leads to distortions. For example, if oil prices decline permanently, the commercial rate for an oil-exporting country ultimately has to depreciate. Asset holders anticipate this event, and therefore the free rate (pesos/dollar) immediately rises, opening up a persistent premium. Unless the authorities adjust the commercial rate, inefficiency and misinvoicing soon become a major headache. This highlights the critical role of a moderate premium.

Considering the need to keep a moderate premium, is a dual-rate system really useful? The answer is yes. Under a dual-rate system transitory disturbances in the capital account do not affect the macroeconomy. At the same time, the free rate suggests what the commercial rate should be whenever the premium becomes sizable.

The Mexican system involves central bank intervention in the free market along with an exchange rate rule for the controlled rate. Normally the spread between the New York rate and Mexico City rate is very small or even negligible, but when major disturbances do open a gap, the rationing of foreign exchange at the free rate in Mexico leads to a double premium and thus to an extra shock absorber. As long as such a situation does not persist for long, the system is quite desirable in that it minimizes the exceptionally disruptive effects that would come from either a major collapse of the exchange rate or the news of massive exchange reserve losses. The key point is the need for an anchor, and a dual-rate system provides precisely that service.

Unified, Flexible Rates

Faced with complicated distortions in many exchange rate regimes, numerous observers conclude that simplification of the exchange rate system down to a single rate is desirable. They argue further that governments are excessively tempted to maintain overvalued rates whenever exchange rates are fixed. Hence they advocate a move to a unified, flexible exchange rate.

Advocacy of flexible exchange rates for developing countries is a new development. The traditional view has been that exchange markets in developing countries are too "thin" and that, accordingly, exchange rates might fluctuate excessively. The new view challenges that belief, and its proponents might add that in a comparison of the volatility of one system and the wasteful resource allocation of another, why conclude that volatility is the worse evil? (For a review of the arguments and some case studies see Quirk and others 1987, 1988.)

The emphasis on thin exchange markets takes the discussion about fixed, versus flexible, rates in the wrong direction. The United States, under flexible rates, experienced extraordinarily large fluctuations in the real exchange rate during 1980–87, and these rate movements are hard to rationalize in terms of fundamentals. Yet nobody doubts that the world market for dollars is large and deep. The main issue is really the underlying volatility of fundamentals and the extent to which government policy measures are endogenous or exogenous.

If government policy—the budget and the money supply—is totally independent of what happens in the economy, and if fundamentals such as the terms of trade vary little, then speculation is easy and stabilizing. Speculators have little room to guess what the equilibrium price will be. But if policy responds to what happens in the economy and speculators start anticipating policymakers' responses, there is no assurance that the economy will have a stable equilibrium. In this case, the economy has no stable anchor, and any level of wages, prices, and exchange rate is equally plausible. In such a system, flexible exchange rates can be immensely volatile, as can prices and wages. The exchange rate system actually interferes with economic performance.

The case for unified, flexible exchange rates in developing countries is therefore implausible. Thus the choice is between a unified, fixed rate, and a dual-rate system. The need for some flexibility in the capital account, without macroeconomic feedback, makes the case for dual rates. But efficiency needs to be addressed by arguing for a limit on the size of the premium. The best way to handle this issue is by an informal rule that has two features. First, major events that are relevant to the commercial rate should trigger an immediate devaluation or revaluation. Guessing whether the disturbance is transitory or permanent and the appropriate size of the exchange market is difficult. Mistakes will occur, but this is unavoidable. Second, when major shocks in the absence of the premium diverge from a moderate bound, depreciation of the commercial rate should gradually speed up to reverse the buildup of the premium.

Conclusion

The exchange rate is a central price linking an economy to the rest of the world. Although exchange rates are always important, they become especially important when misaligned. In that case, they create a wasteful allocation of resources and lead to capital flight. The economy's productive potential deteriorates, and ultimately the realignments force major devaluation, which brings about massive inflation and disarray. Managing exchange rates along simple, stable rules is thus critical. These stable rules must assure that cumulative overvaluation is ruled out by a policy of devaluation that keeps in line with domestic inflation.

The rate system should also be uniform as it applies to commercial transactions. There may be (in isolated circumstances) a case for taxes or subsidies to promote specific economic or noneconomic objectives, but using explicit taxes and subsidies rather than the disguised form of multiple exchange rates is almost always preferable.

Finally, realism requires governments to recognize that portfolio holders have the option of holding external assets and that they will acquire them if domestic assets are unattractive because of low returns or exchange rate overvaluation. To avoid the distortionary effects of black markets, a realistic exchange rate system should build on a dual rate. A dual rate strikes a compromise between the microeconomic case for unified rates and the macroeconomic need for an anchor.

Notes

1. For a discussion of a cost-benefit analysis of having a national money, see Fischer (1982).

2. There are various ways of calculating trading partners' inflation using export weights, import weights, or both, including or not including services. For a discussion see Williamson (1982) and Wickham (1985).

3. The issue of red tape goes further when we note that there will be important incentives to misinvoice products or even to devote real resources to modifying products so as to take advantage of special exchange rate regimes.

4. We need not be concerned with the second term, $e_m(X - M)$. If this term is positive, the outlays arise from a trade surplus in dollars and the central bank should contemplate exchange appreciation or unification. If the term is negative, then the central bank faces a trade deficit in dollars and must finance this by running down reserves. The reserve losses reduce the inflationary effect of the multiple rates, but they have their own problem. Specifically, what happens when the central bank runs out of reserves?

5. On the economics of black markets for foreign exchange, see Pechman (1984), Dornbusch and others (1983), and Dornbusch and Pechman (1985) and the references given there.

6. There are many practical issues in the administration of such a system. They include whether investment income and services such as tourism should be financed at the controlled or the free rate. They also include the important question of which rate applies to the amortization of private debts. For a discussion of some of these questions and for references and a formal model, see Dornbusch (1986).

Selected Bibliography

Banco de México. Various issues. *Indicadores económicos*. Mexico City.

Bhagwati, Jadish, and Anne O. Krueger. 1974. "Capital Flight from LDCs. A Statistical Analysis." In Jadish Bhagwati, ed., *Illegal Transactions in International Trade*. Amsterdam: North-Holland.

Cuddington, John. 1986. *Capital Flight: Estimates, Issues, and Explanations.* Princeton Studies in International Finance 58. Princeton, N.J.: Princeton University Press.

Dornbusch, Rudiger. 1986. "Special Exchange Rates for Capital Account Transactions." *World Bank Economic Review* 1(1):3–33.

Dornbusch, Rudiger, and Clarice Pechman. 1985. "The Bid-Ask Spread in the Black Market for Dollars in Brazil." *Journal of Money, Credit, and Banking* 17(4, Part 1, November):517–20.

Dornbusch, Rudiger, Daniel V. Dantas, Clarice Pechman, Roberto de Renzende Rocha, and Demetrio Simões. 1983. "The Black Market for Dollars in Brazil." *Quarterly Journal of Economics* 98(February):25–40.

Fischer, Stanley. 1982. "Seigniorage and the Case for a National Money." *Journal of Political Economy* 90(2):295–313. Reprinted in Stanley Fischer, *Indexing, Inflation, and Economic Policy*. Cambridge, Mass.: MIT Press, 1986.

Gulati, Sunil K. 1987. "A Note on Trade Misinvoicing." In Donald R. Lessard and John Williamson, eds., *Capital Flight and Third World Debt*. Washington, D.C.: Institute of International Economics.

IMF (International Monetary Fund). 1986. *Government Finance Statistics Yearbook 1986*. Washington, D.C.

Krueger, Anne O. 1974. "The Political Economy of the Rent-Seeking Society." *American Economic Review* 64(3):291–303.

Pechman, Clarice. 1984. *O dolar paralelo no Brasil*. Rio de Janeiro: Paz e Tera.

Quirk, Peter J., Benedicte V. Christensen, Kyung-Mo Huh, and Toshihiko Sasaki. 1987. *Floating Exchange Rates in Developing Countries*. IMF Occasional Paper 53. Washington, D.C.: International Monetary Fund.

Quirk, Peter J., Graham Hacche, Victor Schoofs, and Lothar Weniger. 1988. *Policies for Developing Forward Foreign Exchange Markets*. IMF Occasional Paper 60. Washington, D.C.: International Monetary Fund.

Wickham, Peter. 1985. "The Choice of Exchange Rate Regime in Developing Countries: A Survey of the Literature." *IMF Staff Papers* 33(2 June):248–88.

Williamson, John. 1982. "A Survey of the Literature on the Optimal Crawling Peg." *Journal of Development Economics* 11(1 August):39–61.

6

Protection in Developing Countries
Paul Krugman

ALTHOUGH ECONOMISTS have long advocated free trade as an ideal, nearly all market economies protect at least some industries from foreign competition. Developing countries generally provide higher levels of protection, to a wider range of industries, than do advanced economies. When governments instituted protectionist policies, particularly in the two decades following World War II, economists hoped that they could serve as instruments of development, helping to close the gap between developing nations and the industrial world. Today these same policies are widely viewed more as obstacles to advancement than as desirable parts of development strategy. Appropriate trade policy remains a subject of considerable dispute, however, and in any case trade liberalization presents difficult problems both of economic management and of political economy.

The Costs of Protection

In protecting a domestic industry from import competition, a country risks imposing a series of costs on its economy. These costs may usefully be divided into four categories. First, by raising the price of imports and import-substituting goods relative to their world prices, protection distorts incentives, leading the economy both to produce and to consume the wrong mix of goods from the point of view of economic efficiency. Second, protection fragments markets, so that the economy typically ends up producing too many products at too small a scale, with a resulting loss of production efficiency. Third, because protection lessens the competition from abroad, it leads to an increase in the monopoly power of domestic firms. Fourth, protection typically creates "rents"—extra returns to those who receive privileges from the protecting government. Resources that could have been used productively may be dissipated in pursuit of these rents.

Against these costs, offsetting benefits may sometimes occur; however, we postpone consideration of the benefits until the next section and begin by considering the costs in more detail.

The Distortion of Incentives

The most straightforward cost of protection is that it gives false signals to the economy, which lead it both to produce and to consume the wrong mix of goods. Suppose, for example, that a given set of resources could be used to produce either soybeans for export or oil to replace imports. Suppose, also, that the soybeans that these resources could produce are worth $1 billion at world prices, whereas the oil they could produce are worth only $500 million. Then the country clearly ought to use the resources to produce soybeans and buy the oil from abroad. Yet a tariff of 100 percent on oil imports makes it more profitable to produce oil, leaving the country $500 million poorer.

The point of this example is that the tariff, by driving a wedge between the prices that a country faces on world markets and the prices facing individual firms, also drives a wedge between the actions that maximize national income and those that maximize the income of individuals. As a result of this distortion of incentives, resources may be diverted away from their most productive uses.

The example emphasizes the distortion of production incentives that results from protection. Similar distortions, however, will also occur on the demand side. Suppose that instead of being able to produce oil, the domestic resources could only produce gasohol, which is an inferior substitute for oil, but that a tariff makes oil so expensive that consumers choose to buy the gasohol to replace $500 million worth of imported oil. Again the country is worse off: consumers have shifted to an inferior substitute, even though the resources used to produce that substitute could have been used to produce exports that more than paid for the imports eliminated as a result of the tariff.

The effects of distorted incentives are most dramatic when imports of intermediate goods are restricted. In highly distorted economies, millions of dollars of exportable output may be stranded because transportation networks or processing industries are unable to obtain fuel or spare parts costing only a fraction of the value of the exports.

The distortion of production and consumption incentives that results from protection is often quite substantial. As we will see later, effective rates of protection in developing countries can lead to an allocation of resources to sectors in which they are less than half as productive as they would be if used elsewhere. Yet most students of protection believe that the costs are considerably larger than the distortion of incentives alone.

The Fragmentation of Markets

Protection is often described as an "inward-looking" policy: it induces a country's producers to look toward the domestic market and tends to make a country more self-sufficient. A completely protected economy would produce everything it consumed. One problem with such an inward orientation has already been noted: an economy may be able to "produce" many goods more efficiently by producing other goods for export and using the earnings to buy imports. Protection distorts incentives, inducing countries to forgo some of the benefits of specialization in accord with their comparative advantage. Another important cost is that developing economies are simply too small to combine self-sufficiency with an efficient scale of production.

A sense of the numbers may be useful. The world's two largest free trade areas are the United States and the European Economic Community (EEC), each of which provides a market in excess of $4 trillion. Trade in manufactured goods between these areas and other industrial countries is fairly free (with a few exceptions), so that the advanced-country market in which manufactured goods can be sold may be said to exceed $10 trillion annually. Meanwhile, only four developing countries—Brazil, China, India, and Mexico—offer home markets with even 1 percent of this purchasing power. Thus, an industry that develops behind a protectionist barrier in a developing country must operate on a scale that is tiny by world standards.

The result is that many protected industries are unproductive because of their very small scale. In many manufacturing industries the minimum efficient scale of plant is believed to be 5 percent or more of the U.S. or EEC market, which means that most developing countries cannot support even one plant of efficient scale if the plant is oriented wholly toward the domestic market. Much less can they achieve economies of multiplant operation or support competition among a number of efficient producers. Instead, production takes place at a small fraction of the scale that manufacturers in advanced countries regard as desirable. In the automobile industry, for example, manufacturers in advanced countries typically regard output of several hundred thousand vehicles a year as necessary to achieve full production efficiency; yet in the protected automobile industries of Latin America, manufacturers have often produced less than 20,000 units annually.

In addition to the direct costs in terms of efficiency, the fragmentation of markets that comes with protection in developing countries typically leads to problems in maintaining effective competition. Although this is closely related to the problem of inefficient scale, it deserves treatment as a separate cost of protection.

Monopoly Power

In a small economy, which even the largest developing nations are when compared with the major advanced countries, industry will inevitably be relatively highly concentrated. Because of the economies of firm size, a country with a GNP of $20 billion cannot support as many firms as one with a GNP 200 times as large. The same is true of small advanced countries: Sweden's industrial structure, for example, has a far more concentrated ownership than that of the United States.

When an economy has relatively free trade and is highly open to the world economy, however, a concentrated industrial structure does not create much monopoly power. Swedish manufacturers cannot sharply raise prices to domestic consumers because if they did the consumers would turn to imports instead. In any case, the typical Swedish manufacturer sells as much or more in foreign as in domestic markets, and in foreign markets the firm is usually a small player rather than a monopolist. So despite a relatively concentrated industrial structure, Swedish industry is not characterized by any unusual degree of monopoly power.

When a small economy follows a protectionist policy, however, it simultaneously ensures that domestic firms are strongly oriented toward the domestic market and that they are insulated to at least some degree from foreign competition. The result is that monopoly power is a much greater concern in protectionist developing countries than in advanced countries.

At first glance, monopoly might appear to be purely a distributional issue: the monopolist is better off at the expense of the consumer, but is the country as a whole any poorer? Monopoly, however, imposes net costs for two reasons. First, the exercise of monopoly power distorts prices and hence incentives: by making their goods expensive, monopolists induce consumers to shift to other goods that yield less satisfaction yet are more costly to produce. Second, the possibility of monopoly profits leads to wasteful efforts to obtain or secure these profits. Too many firms may enter an industry in an effort to share in the monopoly profits that a cartel could provide, dissipating these profits in wasteful duplication and an even more inefficient scale of production than necessary. Or established firms may invest in excess capacity to discourage additional entrants.

An important aspect of monopoly power in both advanced and developing countries is that it often seems to be shared by firms with some of their workers. In highly concentrated industries that are insulated from foreign competition—whether in the U.S. automobile and steel industry or in the manufacturing sectors of most developing countries—organized labor often seems able to achieve the position of a partner in the exercise of monopoly power, receiving wages that are considerably higher than what the same workers could receive elsewhere in the economy. As we will argue below, the wage differentials thus created may exacerbate the labor market distortions that are sometimes used to justify protection in the first place.

Rent Seeking

Protection generally generates some benefits to particular groups. These benefits are a function of the policy rather than of the groups' actual contribution to the economy. The most notable example is the value of licenses to import when imports are restricted: anyone who receives a license can purchase imports at world prices and sell them at a higher price internally. More generally, industries that receive protection will at least temporarily earn higher rates of profits, be able to pay higher wages, or both. These benefits conferred through government policy may be referred to in general as "rents."

Economists have argued that a major cost of protection lies in the resources used up by groups attempting to ensure that they receive such rents. The classic example is India's allocation of foreign exchange to firms. In the 1960s, the government allocated foreign exchange for imported inputs, spare parts, and so on to firms in proportion to their installed capacity. This provided firms with an incentive to build excess capacity in an effort to increase their share of the valuable foreign exchange. This excess capacity represented a waste of resources over and above the usual costs of distorted production and consumption, market fragmentation, and so on. The rent seeking induced by protection may thus be considered an extra cost.

Although most examples of rent seeking are less clear-cut, they are nonetheless important. Examples include the tendency of firms to locate in or near the capital city in order to have greater access to political influence, even when doing so is uneconomic; the tendency of workers to leave rural areas for cities, even when they have a high probability of being unemployed, to have a chance at high-paying jobs in protected industries; and the expense of retaining lobbyists to affect decisions.

There is an obvious similarity between the costs of protection that are a result of rent seeking and the costs of monopoly that arise from efforts to acquire or secure monopoly power. Indeed, the term "rent seeking" itself is now widely used in the literature about industrial organization to refer to the costs associated with monopoly, even though these costs may arise without any government action. In developing countries, however, because protection is a major source (probably the major source) of monopoly power, one may regard all these costs as being of like kind.

As we have seen, protection is likely to be harmful. Yet protectionist policies remain widespread in the developing world. No doubt much of this represents a failure to understand not only the costs but also the realities of political economy, in which economic efficiency is far from the only criterion of economic policy. Nonetheless, examining the purely economic arguments for protection is also important, because these arguments have played a large role in influencing or at least rationalizing protectionist policies.

Arguments for Protection

Nearly all intellectually respectable arguments for protection, whether for advanced or developing countries, have a common conceptual basis. This basis is the view that the domestic economy is subject to some kind of failure of markets, so that the market left to itself does not allocate resources efficiently. If a government can correctly diagnose the market's failure, it can use protectionist policies as a partial correction: the distortion of incentives that is a result of protection can "lean against" the inherent distortion in the market, moving the economy closer to, rather than farther from, the resource allocation it should have had in the first place.

This broad view is often referred to as the domestic distortions argument for protection. Two points should be immediately apparent. First, it is by no means a blanket argument for protection: a randomly chosen protectionist policy is surely as likely to aggravate a domestic market failure as to cure one. Thus, this is at best an argument for a selective, targeted trade policy. Second, if the justification for an active government policy is a failure of domestic markets, trade policies are unlikely to be the best possible answer. Instead, the best answer will be to fix the market failure directly, if that is possible, and if it is not, to target policies specifically toward the source of the problem. In general, trade policies will turn out to be a blunt instrument for dealing with market failure.

The general description of the domestic distortions argument is important, because it helps us to see the common themes among various specific arguments. Most discussion of justifications for protection, however, hinges on more specific kinds of market failure:

distortions of factor markets and possible spillovers resulting from learning and technological change.

Factor Market Distortions

In many developing countries the labor market exhibits two characteristics that suggest a significantly distorted market. First is the presence of large differentials between wage rates in the relatively advanced manufacturing and urban sector and those in the traditional and agricultural sector. Second is the presence of substantial persistent unemployment, especially in urban areas. Each of these has been seen as a possible justification for some kind of protection of the manufacturing sector.

The reasons for a large urban-rural wage differential are still disputed. It seems unlikely that all of the differential is attributable to the skill levels of workers. The prevailing explanations rest in part on firms' need to pay high wages to discourage turnover and to encourage high-quality work (the so-called "efficiency wages" argument) and in part on the market power of unions, reinforced by government actions such as the enactment of minimum wage rates well above the normal wage in the traditional sector. Whatever the reason for the wage differential, it is an important source of divergence between private and social costs, leading to a suboptimal level of urban employment. A firm considering hiring an additional worker in the urban sector will do so only if that additional employee yields additional revenues that exceed the urban wage rate; but because shifting a worker from rural to urban employment greatly increases the worker's wage rate, it would be worth doing from a social point of view even if the value of the urban worker's addition to output were somewhat less than the wage.

Ideally, a developing country could eliminate the wage differential through institutional reform. Failing that, a subsidy on urban employment would be the next best policy. A subsidy to manufacturing production would not be as good, because it would have the unintended by-product of shifting other factors of production to manufacturing as well. Finally, a tariff protecting manufacturing from foreign competition could have the desirable effect of increasing manufacturing employment; unfortunately, it would have the undesirable side effects of also shifting other factors and of distorting consumption.

Thus we see that the existence of wage differentials provides a possible justification for protection, but only as a crude (strictly speaking, a fourth best) instrument to be used if no others are available.

The existence of substantial unemployment in urban areas seems at first sight to reinforce the case for government intervention, including protection if nothing better, such as wage or production subsidies, is available: any such policy may now draw workers out of unemployment, a situation in which they produce nothing, instead of from traditional occupations that still have some positive product. Some economists, however, have challenged this, arguing that urban unemployment in developing countries is itself a consequence of the wage differential: workers move to urban areas to have access to higher paying jobs than are available elsewhere. In this case an increase in urban employment, by inducing more rural-urban migration, may actually increase the number of urban unemployed.

An important critique of arguments for protectionist policies based on labor market distortions is that these distortions are themselves exacerbated by protection. In particular, the urban-rural wage differential, which is a problem in itself and may underlie some of the persistent urban unemployment, probably arises in part because of the monopoly power of industrial unions. As we have argued in the previous section, however, protection increases monopoly power and is therefore likely to make the wage differential larger than it would otherwise be. Quite conceivably, a government that protects its manufacturing sector helps engender a wage differential that in turn leads to rural-urban migration, creating as a result precisely the labor market distortions that are often used to justify protection.

The Infant Industry Argument

Among the oldest arguments for protection is the idea that new industries need a period of being sheltered from their established competitors in other countries in order to become established. The infant industry argument, which was used to justify the tariffs that protected manufacturing in the Federal Republic of Germany, Japan, and the United States in the past, continues to have popular appeal.

That the infant industry argument is a domestic distortions argument for protection may not be readily apparent. In the absence of any domestic market failure, however, there would be no reason to give special protection to infant industries. If an industry were worth developing, in an undistorted economy it would be privately profitable to do so. For the infant industry argument to be valid, there must be some divergence between the private and social benefits of investing in a new sector.

One kind of divergence might be a failure of the capital market. Suppose that a firm entering a new industry must go through an extended period of losses before eventually becoming profitable and that for some reason capital markets in a developing country will not finance it through this entry period. Then entry of new firms may be facilitated by temporary protection that makes firms profitable even during the breaking-in period. The question is whether the capital markets are in fact inadequate in this way and, if so, why. In practice, there are reasons to doubt the inadequacy: many "infant" industries in developing countries are made up of subsidiaries of multinational firms, which presumably have little problem of access to capital, and even domestic firms often have close links to banking groups that could presumably finance them if the prospect of future profitability were fairly likely. In any case, the substantial imperfections of capital markets in developing countries are in large part the result of government regulation, so that the appropriate policy would be one of institutional reform rather than protection.

Another reason why infant industries may need help lies in external economies of learning and technological change. Creating a new industry in a developing country generally requires some investment in adapting the technology to local conditions. Yet a firm that makes this investment may find that it is unable to appropriate the benefits fully because other firms can follow its lead and benefit from its efforts. Thus private agents may fail to develop an industry even when this is socially desirable. In this case, a temporary period of protection can help correct the market failure.

Two points need to be emphasized, however. First, the need for such temporary protection is almost inevitably difficult to ascertain. Nobody knows how to put a value on spillovers of knowledge between firms with any accuracy, especially in a prospective rather than an established industry. Thus the infant industry argument is a highly speculative one, easily abused to justify protection for other reasons.

Second, the justification offered by the infant industry argument is not really for protectionist trade policy, but for a policy specifically aimed at encouraging investment in knowledge. Even a less targeted policy of encouraging production would be preferable to limitations on imports. This is particularly true if one remembers that infant industries could be aimed at exports rather than import substitution.

"Strategic Arguments"

Recent work in the theory of international trade has emphasized the importance of imperfect competition and increasing returns to scale in the world economy. Out of this new theory emerges a new class of arguments for government intervention in international trade. These arguments arise from the potential "strategic" role of government action in shifting the terms of competition to the benefit of domestic firms. We shall refer to them in short as "strategic arguments." The most widely known example is the one for export subsidies as a way of deterring foreign competition. The proponents, Brander and Spencer (1985), show that under the right circumstances, a preannounced export subsidy, by inducing foreign firms to produce less, can raise the profits of domestic firms by much more than the amount of the subsidy. The result is to raise the national income of the subsidizing country at foreign expense. Similar arguments can be used to show that a protected domestic market can give domestic firms a strategic advantage that similarly raises national income.

For the most part, trade policy arguments based on strategic needs rely on two assumptions that rarely apply to developing countries: first, the country is assumed to be a major supplier in the market for a good being produced in an imperfectly competitive market, and, second, the country's own domestic market is assumed to be a significant part of the world market. As already emphasized, developing countries are uniformly small in economic terms, so that they are never major markets for traded goods. They are also rarely major producers, except where the good is a raw material of which they happen to have a large share. Thus the particular strategic trade arguments that have attracted the most attention in discussions of the competition among the United States, Japan, and Europe are largely irrelevant to developing countries.

Some related arguments may have more relevance. One possibility pointed out in the new literature is that because of the prevalence of oligopoly in world markets even a small country may be able to affect the prices of its imports. In principle, trade restrictions or a government marketing board could induce foreign suppliers to provide goods more cheaply than they would otherwise. Also, entry into some industries may yield rents to specific factors of production even though monopoly profits are competed away, so that a policy of export promotion based on strategic needs can still raise national income. These possibilities are discussed in Krugman (1989).

Overall, however, the new strategic arguments seem unlikely to add much force to the argument for protection in developing countries. This argument still rests primarily on considerations of factor market distortions and infant industries. If these considerations seem dubious when compared with the costs described earlier, this simply says that in the current state of knowledge, the case for protection as a tool of development strategy is not a very strong one.

Forms of Protection

The effects of protection often depend crucially on the specific character of the protectionist policy. We therefore turn next to a review of some of the main forms of protection and their effects.

Tariffs

A tariff—a tax levied on imported goods at the border—is the oldest form of protection. The effect of a tariff is usually straightforward: it raises the price of the imported good by an amount equal to the tariff. There are only two exceptions. First is where the importing country is a large share of the world market for the imported good, in which case the tariff will lower world prices somewhat and be less than fully passed on in domestic prices. This case is of little importance for developing countries. The other is where the good is supplied by monopolistic or oligopolistic firms that may choose to absorb part of the tariff rather than raise prices by the full amount. The importance of this effect in practice is not clear.

Tariffs were the main instruments of protection before the 1930s and in particular were the basis of the import-substituting industrialization the United States and Germany pursued in the nineteenth century. In most of the world, however, tariffs have become less important than administrative protection that sets quantities rather than simply taxing goods at the border.

Import Quotas and Exchange Controls

An import quota sets a limit on the quantity of a good that may be imported during a given period. Control of foreign exchange, under which the quantity of foreign exchange available for imports within a particular category is restricted, has a similar effect.

The most common misunderstanding about import quotas is the view that, unlike tariffs, they do not raise prices. In practice, by restricting the supply of imported goods to the domestic market, an import quota raises the price that domestic residents are willing to pay for the good by at least as much as a tariff that restricts imports by the same amount.

Because a quota raises domestic prices, the right to import a restricted good is valuable: the good may be sold on the domestic market at a price higher than its purchase price. Thus, to administer a quota, the authorities must allocate the rights to import, usually through a system of import licenses. These licenses are sometimes auctioned off; more often they are allocated through some administrative procedure.

The first difference between a tariff and an import quota is immediately apparent. A tariff yields revenue to the government, whereas a quota, unless it is auctioned off, yields rents to the recipients of import licenses. In highly protected economies these quota rents are often a substantial share of national income, and their allocation is therefore a key government policy. As already mentioned, rent seeking is a possible source of additional costs to protection. Most economists believe that quotas are much more likely to generate rent-seeking activities than are tariffs.

An additional difference between tariffs and quotas lies in their effects on domestic monopoly power. Consider a firm that has a domestic monopoly position protected by a tariff. Although this firm can raise its price to a certain point, if it raises its price too high customers will shift to imports despite the tariff. If the same firm is protected by an import quota, customers will be prevented from shifting to imports; when the firm's price is increased, the premium charged by holders of import licenses will rise again. As a result, a firm protected by a quota will, other things being equal, find it more profitable to exercise its monopoly power and raise domestic prices. It is in this sense that a quota, which does not directly tax imports, will often raise prices more than a tariff will.

Finding reasons for preferring an import quota to a tariff is difficult. The loss of revenue, the costs of rent seeking, and the increase of monopoly power all point toward the conclusion that tariffs are at any rate less costly than quotas for any given degree of protection. The popularity of quotas and exchange controls thus lends credence to the most cynical interpretations of protectionism in developing countries: Either the countries do not know what they are doing, or their governments are actually eager to create the private rents associated with import licensing.

Content Requirements and Trade Offsets

In some cases, the authorities allocate import licenses according to a formula that makes their receipt conditional on other actions by firms. In this case the quota rents are in effect used to subsidize some other desired activity. The most familiar schemes of this type are content restrictions on sales and the more general category of trade offsets.

A content restriction requires that some minimum fraction of a product category sold in the country represent domestic value added. For example, a country might require that 80 percent of the value of an automobile sold in the country represent domestic content, with only 20 percent being imported. If the required local share is larger than what unrestricted firms would have chosen to do, the effect of the scheme is like a tariff on imports whose proceeds are used to subsidize domestic production. Producers would like the right to import, because imports are cheaper than their domestic substitutes; they are therefore willing to sell domestic production at a loss, because this gives them the right to bring in imports.

A trade offset is a generalization of a content restriction that allows exports to be traded off for imports. For example, one might have a scheme that required only that a firm produce 80 percent of domestic value added per unit of domestic sales, without requiring 80 percent content on those sales themselves. Then the firm might choose to have some exports, say, equal to 10 percent of domestic sales, allowing it to have imports equal to 30 percent. The advantage of trade offsets over content requirements is that they allow more flexibility. Firms can specialize in the products for which the country's cost disadvantage is smallest, and they can also produce a narrower product range to achieve greater economies of scale.

Both content restrictions and trade offsets differ from straight import quotas in not generating quota rents. In effect, firms compete for import licenses by engaging in domestic production, so that the quota rents are redistributed in an implicit subsidy.

The Extent of Protection

Considerable effort has gone into measuring the actual extent of protection in developing countries. One might think that this would be a straightforward matter of simply cataloging the trade policy measures in place. In fact, the issue is fairly difficult. First, the use of a variety of forms of protection (tariffs, quotas, content requirements, and so on) poses the problem of establishing a common measure of protective impact. Second, the degree of protection provided to any given activity depends not only on the direct protection given to that activity but also on the indirect effects of tariffs and import restrictions on other sectors.

Measuring Protection: Tariff Equivalents

As we have noted, actual systems of protection mix a variety of tools. To come up with meaningful estimates of the extent of protection, the usual method is to calculate what system of tariffs would have provided industries with the same incentives and then to measure the extent of protection by the percentage of tariff equivalents thus calculated.

The basic idea is straightforward. Suppose that an import quota raises the internal price of the restricted import 60 percent above the world level. Then the import quota is considered equivalent to a 60 percent tariff. Three issues complicate this measurement in practice, two of them issues of principle, one an issue of practicality.

First, the effects of other protective measures may not be fully equivalent to those of tariffs. As noted earlier, most economists believe that an import quota creates more monopoly power and raises internal prices by more than a tariff that limits imports to the same amount. As a result, there may be no meaningful equivalent tariff into which to convert a quota. Using the implicit rent on quota licenses, which is how it will be done in practice, will not tell the full story.

Second, complex schemes such as content requirements will be different from tariffs in their relative effects on consumer and producer prices. A simple tariff on automobiles will yield revenue to the government. A local content requirement will in effect distribute that income as a subsidy to domestic producers, so that domestic producer prices rise by more than the rise in consumer prices. The normal convention in measuring protection is to focus on the effects on producer incentives rather than on consumers. This represents a judgment about relative importance that is defensible, but not entirely satisfactory.

Finally, measurement of tariff equivalents is difficult. A regulation that limits imports does not specify the equivalent tariff that results, so the economist must study not only the government's actions but also the effect of these actions in the marketplace. Economists frequently discover that the rates of tariff-equivalent protection resulting from the administrative restriction of imports are substantially larger than the government had realized, so that when countries replace quotas with tariffs they often lower the rate of protection without meaning to.

Despite these problems, the measurement of protection is a useful exercise, giving at least a rough idea of the quantitative importance of the kinds of trade policy discussed earlier.

Effective Protection

If all goods were produced entirely from capital and labor inputs, without the use of intermediate inputs that might be imported or exported, computation of tariff equivalents would complete the job of calculating rates of protection. Because this is not the case—especially in manufacturing in developing countries, where industries may add only a thin slice of value added to a product—the notion of protection must be elaborated on. The basic tool used to do this is the concept of effective protection, which measures the degree of protection offered to particular activities rather than simply the tariff rate.

Probably the best way to understand effective protection is to look at a simple example. Suppose that a country can buy complete automobiles on the world market for $10,000. Suppose, alternatively, that it can purchase the parts needed to construct an automobile for $8,000. Finally, suppose that the domestic automobile assembly industry, which is inefficient by world standards, cannot assemble a vehicle for less than $4,000. To encourage the domestic assembly of automobiles, the government would have to make the price of an assembled import equal to $12,000, the price at which a domestic firm could sell a vehicle assembled from foreign parts. This can be done by imposing a 20 percent tariff or equivalent on imported automobiles.

What rate of protection is the domestic automobile assembly industry receiving in this case? The tariff rate on automobiles is 20 percent, but this tariff allows the domestic industry to assemble a car despite the fact that its costs are twice the value added it provides at world prices. Therefore, the 20 percent tariff provides the domestic industry with an effective rate of protection of 100 percent.

This example shows that the effective rate of protection provided by a tariff may differ substantially from the nominal tariff rate. It should also be apparent from the example that tariffs on the inputs used to produce a good, as well as the tariff on the good itself, enter into the determination of the effective rate. For example, a 5 percent tariff on imported automobile parts, other things being equal, would reduce the margin on which domestic assemblers can work from $2,000 to $1,600, that is, it would amount to a negative 20 percent rate of effective protection for domestic automobile assemblers. Overall, assessing effective protection thus requires measuring tariff equivalents not only on an industry's output but also on all its inputs.

Evidence on the Extent of Protection

Table 6-1 presents some estimates of effective rates of protection in several developing countries. Although calculating effective rates does not tell us whether the costs of protection exceed its benefits, evidence

Table 6-1. Effective Rates of Protection in Selected Developing Countries, Selected Years, 1967–81

(percent)

Country and year of estimate	Average rate for manufacturing	Spread across industries
Brazil, 1980–81	23	−85 to 219
Chile, 1967	217	−23 to 1,140
Colombia, 1979	55	25 to 127
Korea, Rep. of, 1978	5	−38 to 135
Nigeria, 1980	82	−62 to 1,119
Philippines, 1980	44	—
Singapore, 1967	0	−7 to 21

— Not available.
Source: World Bank (1987).

such as that summarized in table 6-1 has been widely used to make the case that protection in developing countries is harmful. Three points stand out. First, effective rates of protection for some industries are very high. Recall that an industry receiving an effective rate of protection of 100 percent is in effect producing goods that are worth only half as much at world prices as they cost to produce. One must place very great weight on the arguments for protection described earlier to second-guess market prices this much. Yet effective rates of protection exceeding 100 percent are quite common. This observation suggests that justifying the protective structures of these countries on a cost-benefit basis must be hard.

Second, the rates of protection are highly variable across industries within each country. Are governments really well enough informed to know that one industry needs no protection whereas another is worth an effective rate of several hundred percent? Again, one cannot avoid a heavy dose of skepticism.

Third, the most successful manufacturing nations in the table, Singapore and the Republic of Korea, have, on average, virtually no protection rates for manufacturing. This apparent correlation of relatively free trade and economic success lends some weight to the view that protectionism is associated with large costs, although economists have offered other explanations for the relative success of outward-looking economies.

A Broader Analysis of Protection

Although the concept of effective protection is a useful tool for measuring the protection of particular activities, economists have long recognized that it gives only an incomplete picture of the way in which protection affects a country's industrial structure. There are other channels—more indirect, but ultimately equally powerful—through which protection of one sector affects the output of others.

One such channel is the exchange rate. Protection, other things being equal, reduces imports and tends to create a trade surplus. Such an effect is always transitory, however. Either the currency appreciates as a result of the trade surplus, or its rate of depreciation fails to keep up with inflation, which has the same effect. The end result is a stronger real exchange rate. This in turn makes unprotected sectors less competitive: Both import sectors that receive low rates of effective protection and export sectors find that their costs rise in terms of foreign currency, and thus they are actually taxed when some sectors receive high rates of effective protection. World Bank estimates find that every percentage point of taxation of imports translates into a tax of 0.4 to 0.8 percentage points on exports.

Protected sectors also compete with other sectors for scarce inputs. A policy that creates capital-intensive industries behind tariffs or quotas will make capital scarcer, and this scarcity will affect the incentives for production throughout the economy. Sometimes such effects may be indirect and surprising. Consider the following hypothetical example. Argentina protects its manufacturing sector, which draws labor away from agriculture. The shortage of labor that results forces a shift away from labor-intensive cultivation, such as wheat farming, toward livestock raising; thus, in an indirect way, protecting manufactures actually encourages beef exports.

In principle, fully specified "general equilibrium" models can keep track of all these indirect effects. Such models have been developed for several countries and ultimately represent a better approach. Because the models are difficult to construct and rely on assumptions that are often disputed, however, they have not yet displaced calculations of simple effective protection as a tool of practical analysis.

Cost-Benefit Analysis of Protection

A tariff or import quota normally produces a mixture of costs and benefits to different groups in the economy. Higher prices hurt consumers while benefiting import-competing producers. In addition, either the government gains revenue from a tariff or the holders of import licenses gain rents.

The net costs of a tariff or import quota are measured by the difference between the consumer costs and the benefits. In the simplest analysis, net costs arise from the distortion of incentives described above. There is a producer distortion loss because producers manufacture goods that could be imported at a lower cost. And there is a consumer distortion loss because consumers shift away from imports on the basis of an internal price that exceeds the true cost of the goods to the economy. Standard techniques exist for calculating these costs, and, although the amount is sometimes a matter of dispute, the costs themselves are not controversial in principle.

Many of the effects of protection, however, go beyond these distortion losses. On the cost side, the gain to producers may be dissipated by firms' efforts to compute monopoly profits. As discussed earlier, the proliferation of firms of inefficient size and the maintenance of excess capacity in order to deter competition may absorb much of the initial gain. Increased wage differentials and the increased unemployment that results may also effectively wipe out some of the gain.

When protection takes the form of an import quota rather than a tariff, the rents may also be dissipated by firms' efforts to secure import licenses, whether through the emergence of excess capacity or through resources expended on lobbying.

On the other side, there may be benefits from protection. Empirical estimates of the costs and benefits of protection start with the consumption and distortion losses caused by distorted incentives. They then proceed to make the best imputations they can of the other effects. In general, researchers have to rely heavily on plausible assumptions in doing this; thus, wide uncertainty surrounds any estimates of the cost of protection. Most empirical studies give short shrift to the potential benefits. This reflects the judgment of the researchers that protection has had little success in countering domestic distortions and may have actually aggravated them in many cases. Although this is a plausible view, the estimates of the costs of protection are not only based on many assumptions but also somewhat incomplete. Nonetheless, it is worth considering some sample calculations of the costs of protection (none of the empirical estimates for developing countries find net benefits).

Table 6-2 shows estimates of the costs of protection in several developing countries at various times, measured as a share of the gross national product. The estimated costs are in general several percent of GDP, but less than 10. That is, these costs are significant but not overwhelming.

What conclusion should one draw from the range of costs? Keeping in mind the caveats about the estimates, the general conclusion is clearly negative for advocates of protection as part of a development strategy. In practice, countries have done themselves significant harm rather than good with protection. Anyone advocating protectionist development policies must explain why future results should be any different.

The costs of protection are not so large, however, that one could describe protectionism as the principal obstacle to development. The largest estimates of costs are no more than two year's growth differential between the successful outward-oriented economies and some of

Table 6-2. Estimated Costs of Protection in Selected Developing Countries, Selected Years, 1960–78

Country and year of estimate	Percentage of GDP
Brazil, 1966	9.5
Mexico, 1960	2.5
Pakistan, 1963	6.2
Philippines, 1978	5.2

Source: For Brazil, Mexico, and the Philippines, Belassa (1971); for Pakistan, Clarete and Whalley (1985).

the countries where import substitution has had the worst failures. This poses a puzzle: if protection has only the moderate importance we see here, why is the apparent difference in performance between outward-oriented and inward-looking countries as large as it is? From 1973 to 1985, countries that the World Bank classified as strongly outward-oriented experienced real per capita growth at more than 5 percent annually, whereas those classified as strongly inward-oriented experienced a slight decline in per capita output. Why this is so is still a matter of dispute. Some economists argue that there are additional dynamic costs of protection. Others argue that the correlation between protection and growth is accidental and that other policies— or cultural factors—play the key role in rapid growth.

The Political Economy of Protection

Theory and evidence both suggest that protectionist policies in developing countries, at least on the scale practiced by many nations, have costs that substantially exceed their benefits. Yet such policies remain in place, and major trade liberalizations are infrequent. No discussion of protection in development can be complete without some explanation of why protection persists despite its costs.

Broadly speaking, the political economy of persistent protection has three levels. At the highest level, liberalization imposes transition costs that may deter a government: The short-run costs may look larger and more certain than the eventual gains. Less charitably, we may note that even if the nation as a whole benefits from liberalized trade, important groups may suffer losses, at least at first, and a government may not be willing or able to face the political costs of income redistribution. Finally, protectionist trade policies, especially those involving substantial administrative discretion, provide opportunities for influence and profit to government officials. These officials will often oppose reforms that deprive them of that role.

Transitional Costs

The transitional costs associated with trade liberalization arise from two main sources—the balance of payments and transitional unemployment.

Other things being equal, trade liberalization will lead to a worsening of the liberalizing country's trade balance. The public will demand more imports, which will place a strain on the country if it is facing constraints on its international financing.

The import boom that follows a trade liberalization may, perversely, be exaggerated if the liberalization lacks full credibility. When tariffs are reduced and quotas lifted, imports become cheaper. If the public does not regard this state as permanent and expects controls to be reimposed, it will rush to buy imports, especially of durable goods, while it can. In some cases this lack of confidence in liberalization has been a self-fulfilling prophecy, in which an inrush of imports leads the government to reimpose controls.

The authorities can avoid the balance of payments effects of trade liberalization if the trade reform is accompanied by currency devaluation. Indeed, a devaluation-cum-liberalization strategy is precisely the orthodox one. Countries facing inflationary pressures are usually reluctant to make the steep devaluations that they may need to accompany a trade liberalization, whereas countries facing external financing problems are reluctant to count on a devaluation to offset the increase in imports. Thus, as a practical matter, the balance of payments problem cannot be easily dismissed.

Aside from the balance of payments issue, there is the problem of transitional unemployment. This may best be understood by considering our earlier discussion of wage differentials. Suppose that a country has built up a protected manufacturing sector that pays wages well above what the same workers could receive elsewhere. With trade liberalization the wages of those workers will no longer be sustainable at the same level, yet their wage rates may be slow to come down. In the meantime, employment in the manufacturing sector—particularly in the protected sectors—may fall sharply, leading to a rise in unemployment. Unlike the balance of payments problem, this transitional unemployment may be unavoidable even with appropriate currency and monetary policies, because it ultimately stems from the need to get some workers to accept a decline in real wages (which one hopes is offset by real wage increases for others).

The transitional problems associated with trade liberalization are certainly real. Yet they do not fully account for the unwillingness of countries to dismantle costly protectionist regimes. We need to turn next to less creditable explanations.

Income Distribution

Any change in trade policy creates winners and losers, with the redistribution normally large relative to the net gain. So considerations of income distribution clearly matter. When a country liberalizes trade, firms—and to some extent workers—in protected sectors lose, whereas the rest of the economy gains.

The key question is why the losses often seem to outweigh the gains in political calculations, even though in terms of national income the rewards from freer trade should be larger than the costs. One answer might be social concern: If protection generally helped the relatively badly off at the expense of the more affluent, one could understand a reluctance to liberalize. This does not, however, seem to be true in general; if anything, the evidence suggests that protectionist economies have a less equal income distribution than those with freer trade.

A better explanation may be a general dislike on the part of political actors for large changes, regardless of who is affected. To remove protection, once it has become established, would shake up existing political and economic compromises, and leaders are reluctant to take the risk of doing so.

Finally, the beneficiaries of protection usually have an organizational advantage over their opponents. The benefits of, say, an import quota are concentrated on a few firms and labor unions, whereas the costs are broadly diffused over the population. The beneficiaries are usually therefore better informed and better organized than those who are hurt. Indeed, consumers may not even realize the effect of trade policy on their standard of living.

Influence and Corruption

In discussing protection in practice, it is impossible to avoid the blunt fact that some government officials value protection because of the privileges and power it gives them. The preference of countries for administrative measures rather than tariffs to protect industries, despite an overwhelming economic case against this practice, makes sense only if one thinks of the greater role for officials in an administration system. Most charitably, one may assert that officials find ways to convince themselves that a system that makes their decisions important is desirable. Least charitably, one may assert that quota rents have a way of being appropriated by those who allocate the rights to import. To suggest that bad policy results from the desire of public servants to enrich themselves at public expense is embarrassingly crude, but it is not irrelevant.

The unfortunate fact is that long-standing protectionist regimes end up being defended by "iron triangles" of interested groups— firms that depend on the barriers, organized labor that extracts wages above the level in unprotected sectors, and government officials who gain influence and perhaps profit from their role in controlling trade. The strength of these triangles is such that major trade reforms usually occur only following severe political or economic crises.

Conclusion

Despite movements toward liberalization in some developing countries, high rates of effective protection remain in much of the developing world. Although some intellectually respectable arguments favor limited, selective protection, the protectionist policies actually pursued in developing countries are almost surely the cause of significant economic costs.

Unfortunately, protection is not continued simply because countries are misguided in their economic analyses. The main problem in the political economy of protection is that any long-established protectionist regime tends to generate a set of economic and political interests that make it self-perpetuating except under crisis conditions.

Selected Bibliography

Banuri, Tariq, ed. 1991. *Economic Liberalization: No Panacea.* New York: Oxford University Press.

Belassa, Bela. 1971. *The Structure of Protection in Developing Countries.* Baltimore, Md.: Johns Hopkins University Press.

Brander, James L., and Barbara J. Spencer. 1985. "Export Subsidies and International Market Share Rivalry." *Journal of International Economics* 16(1-2):83–100.

Clarete, Ramon, and John Whalley. 1985. *Interactions between Trade Policies and Domestic Distortions.* Centre for the Study of International Economic Relations Working Paper 82550. London, Ontario: University of Western Ontario.

Dornbusch, Rudiger. 1992. "The Case for Trade Liberalization in Developing Countries." *Journal of Economic Perspectives* 6(1):69–85.

Krueger, Anne O., ed. 1988. *Development with Trade.* San Francisco: Institute for Contemporary Studies.

Krugman, Paul. 1989. "New Trade Theory and the Less Developed Countries." In Guillermo A. Calvo, Ron Findlay, Pentti Kouri, and Jorge de Macedo, eds., *Debt Stabilization and Development.* Oxford, U.K.: Basil Blackwell.

Thomas, Vinod, and James M. Nash, eds. 1991. *Best Practice in Trade Policy Reform.* New York: Oxford University Press.

World Bank. 1987. *World Development Report 1987.* New York: Oxford University Press.

7

The Other Side of Tax Reform

Arnold C. Harberger

ECONOMISTS DEALING with public policy, public finance, economic development, and related topics confront the subject of tax reform time and again. Mostly, the confrontation has taken place in an arena defined by economic treatises, textbooks, and journals. Within that arena, economic efficiency has been the guiding star, the dominant criterion governing the discussion.

This essay deviates from the standard practice just described and views tax reform from different vantage points. Simply put, it examines tax reform from the standpoints of people who are involved in different layers of the process—from the finance ministers who sponsor the reforms, to the taxpayers who have to live with them. In between are at least two other important groups: the administrators who must implement the reforms and the interest groups that are principally affected.

My comments about tax reform will not be highly structured and formal. Rather, consider them as the musings and reflections of someone who has witnessed many efforts at tax reform and participated in more then a few.

The Moral Flavor of Tax Reform

To me, the key to the success of many tax reform efforts lies in the moral dimension. We start from a point at which an old system of gathering revenue has broken down. The taxes that are on the books are subject to widespread and quite open evasion. Administration has become lax. Rumors, and often far more than just rumors, abound of corruption on the part of those who administer the taxes.

Usually part of the fault lies in the bad design of existing taxes—bad design by technical standards and bad design in terms of how various groups of taxpayers perceive these taxes. The seeds of evasion are often sown when different groups of taxpayers come to feel that they have been singled out for unfair treatment. They then try to "correct" the unfairness by simply not paying the full tax that is legally due.

On the whole, when the need for reform is greatest, the most important sources of the problem go far beyond simple issues of bad design. In the process of the breakdown of a system, quite ordinary people—who generally think of themselves as honorable and honest—end up participating in gross evasion of taxes. Why? How? Their standard answer is, "I would be a fool to pay the full tax when nobody else does." Once this idea gets around, it is like a virus; anybody can become infected. The judges in the tax courts may themselves be evading, but even if they are not, they know their brothers and sisters and friends are doing it. So the honest judge becomes the one who looks on evasion as something that almost everybody does and who lets evaders off with a small fine or a warning. The dishonest judge becomes the one who extracts a bribe for doing so. No judge actually makes a serious attempt to enforce the law as it stands.

The problem can get considerably more complicated if a "tax-and-evasion race" between the fiscal authorities and the taxpayer ensues. The authorities, finding that the taxpayers are paying only half of what they should according to law, respond by doubling tax rates. But now taxpayers react by evading more, triggering yet another increment in rates by the authorities. The end result of such a vicious cycle is a set of tax rates so high that even the most conscientious taxpayers are driven to evasion. As is so often the case with major policy mistakes, no straightforward solution to the problem exists.[1]

I do not like to use the word "corrupt" to characterize societies that end up in the situation just described. Too many fundamentally decent, ordinary people are involved to warrant so harsh a term. I prefer to say that such a society has lost its moral tone—has become demoralized—in tax matters.

Perhaps the biggest task that faces the tax reformer in such a case is to rekindle the society's moral tone: to turn it from a society composed mainly of tax evaders to one in which most people comply with the tax law. It would be naive to think that a spiritual conversion is all that is required here. Most successfully administered tax systems anywhere in the world incorporate penalties for noncompliance. On examining these tax systems a bit more closely, however, we find that the affected populace typically considers them to be reasonably fair in their design and administration.

By fairness I mean "absence of capriciousness" or, in a very basic sense, "justice." I do not mean fairness in the sense of exactly the right sharing of the tax burden among different groups and categories of taxpayers (what we used to call vertical equity). Nor do I mean fairness in the sense of people in similar situations being treated equally by the tax law (what we used to call horizontal equity). As an example of vertical equity, a well-administered, flat-rate income tax could easily fit into my definition of fairness, even though the society might in some sense prefer (and maybe even in the next election vote to institute) some degree of progression. As an example of horizontal equity, I can imagine a tax law being fair, according to my definition, and yet giving substantial tax breaks, say, to farmers or to people living in remote regions of the country, even when the society at its next election opportunity would eliminate these preferences.

"Capriciousness" is present when large numbers of individual taxpayers experience a sense of injustice concerning the way the system treats them. Mainly this occurs through differential evasion by different groups, some groups being able to get away with paying little or no tax, and others (usually wage and salary earners), having no easy escape route, being forced to comply. But it can also occur in an exacerbated fashion if tax collectors go around soliciting bribes for special favors.

To turn around a demoralized tax system is a major task. It requires working at all levels, from the tax collector down to the most inconspicuous individual taxpayer. The surest (and most humane) method is to go after the most flagrant violators first. A good starting place is with the most corrupt officials on the one hand, and their biggest and most notorious clients on the other. Severe penalties should be imposed on such people, not just for their own sake but as a warning to other administrators and taxpayers who are not quite such blatant violators. Step-by-step, the cutting edge of enforcement is moved closer and closer to the average administrator and the average taxpayer. As this happens, more and more of these people modify their behavior so as to conform to the law. In the process, the demoralized society becomes remoralized.

Designing a Tax System for Efficiency and Fairness

The more I have looked at situations in which reform has been the aim and the watchword, and the more I have reflected on the solutions adopted or recommended by wise and observant people, the more I have come to feel that these solutions embodied important criteria above and beyond pure economic efficiency. Let me begin this topic by setting out what I believe to be the "expert consensus package" for the 1990s. I am thinking here particularly of small, open, developing economies. The experts are those from the countries themselves; from the World Bank, the IMF, and other international as well as bilateral economic assistance agencies; and from the segment of the academic world that deals with the economic policy problems of actual countries.

Where has the thinking of these experts been heading over the last decade or so? As I perceive it, the emerging consensus includes a broadly based value added tax, a tariff structure that moves over time toward uniformity, and a set of sumptuary and "luxury" taxes to deal with consumption of special items. At the level of enterprises, there is an increasing recognition of the folly of levying progressive taxes on the income of business firms. The consensus is definitely for a uniform rate (perhaps with a minimum exempt amount), with the rate itself established with an eye to the tax situations of foreign and multinational firms that have invested or may invest in the currency in question. The experts are virtually unanimous in deploring the widespread use of tax incentives aimed at all kinds of (real or alleged) special objectives.

The Value Added Tax

The value added tax is an interesting case study in itself. In textbooks and classrooms this tax is almost invariably expounded as if it were a fully general tax on all production of goods and services in the economy. Given that at each level of production, inputs (including capital goods) purchased from other levels are deductible in the computation of value added, the fully general tax on all productive activities becomes a fully general tax on consumption. Typically, textbook and classroom presentations will at this point note that even this tax of maximal generality does not reach the leisure (nonmarket) time of workers and their families, so that one cannot assert that it is completely neutral. But their argument for a value added tax nonetheless rests on its coming just about as close as is possible in the real world to an idealized vision of a neutral tax.

There is a sharp contrast between the foregoing picture of a value added tax and what one sees when one looks at value added taxes in practice. The striking feature of real-world value added taxes is how much their actual revenue yield differs from what would be generated by a fully general tax. Take, for simplicity, a case in which a uniform rate of value added tax is in effect. If it were a fully general tax of the consumption type, its theoretical yield would be equal to the tax rate multiplied by total consumption in the economy. When we perform this exercise, however, we find that actual tax yields rarely reach half of the theoretical yield.

Why do actual yields fall so far short of the hypothetical yield of a fully general tax at a similar rate? Part of the answer lies in evasion, which is important in some countries. But the bulk of the answer, universally among countries (even those with superb tax administration and hence minimal evasion), is that the tax, far from being fully general, covers an amazingly moderate part of the total consumption.

Looking simply at the part of consumption that is counted as such in the calculation of national income, we find that such activities as medical services, educational services, charitable institutions, and so on are universally exempt. So, often, are other professional services and those of craftsmen and tradesmen. Domestic service, which is quite important in many developing countries, is almost never reached by the net of a value added tax. Finally, there is the imputed income from owner-occupied housing, that proverbial wraith of the tax world that seems to elude the tax collector's grasp, no matter what, no matter where.

Coverage of the Value Added Tax

Apart from the sectors and activities that are more or less routinely left aside in the laws defining the base of a value added tax, other activities exist whose treatment is the result of more conscious decisions by policymakers. In this vein, sometimes all agriculture is left out of the network and sometimes farms below a certain economic size. The areas producing financial services—banks, *financieras,* insurance companies, and so on—are almost invariably left out of the jurisdiction of the value added tax. These sectors, particularly agriculture and finance, have the curious attribute that one actually does not know whether one gains or loses tax revenue by leaving them out of the value added tax net.

The apparent paradox of actually gaining revenue by leaving a productive sector uncovered by a tax is easily explained. The key lies in the credit method, by which most real-world value added taxes are administered. Under the credit method, each enterprise that is covered must pay tax on the value of all its production (sales). It can then claim credit for the value added tax paid by supplier enterprises on the various inputs (including investment goods) that it bought from them during the tax period.

Suppose that we have a flour mill that buys wheat from farmers. The mill always pays tax on the flour it produces. If the wheat farmers who supply it are part of the tax network, they pay tax on the value of their wheat, and the mill gets to deduct this tax from the amount it owes to the government. If, on the contrary, the farmers are not included in the tax network, the mill is not able to deduct any tax previously paid. The mill in effect ends up paying the farmers' tax for them. So far, we have no paradox. The farmers pay tax on the output if they are in the system, and the mill pays tax on the same output if the farmers are out of the system. But now consider the tax treatment of the farmers' inputs. If the farmers are included in the value added tax network, they get to deduct the tax paid on their inputs; if they are excluded from the network, they receive no deduction, and neither do the mills that process their wheat into flour. When the farmers are out of the system, they constitute a break in the value added tax chain. Because of this break, neither they (the farmers) nor the food processors who buy their output receive a credit for the tax embodied in purchased farm inputs.

Leaving farmers out of the system does not always yield greater tax revenue. Offsetting the greater tax that the government gets on purchased farm inputs is the fact that direct sales by farmers to consumers (or to other entities out of the tax network) do (or at least should) result in tax liabilities if the farmers are in the network but quite obviously do not generate any tax liability if they are out of the network.

Thus the key to whether the government gets more or less tax revenue by leaving farmers out of the tax network lies in whether the tax embodied in purchased farm inputs exceeds or falls short of the potential tax that would be paid on direct sales by farmers to consumers or other purchases outside the network. This principle applies to any activity or sector.

The Financial Sector under a Value Added Tax

The financial sector is perhaps the most interesting case, mainly because of the complication of defining inputs. Clearly, the Canon or Xerox copiers, the IBM computers, and the tons of paper used by financial institutions are inputs that are as easy to identify as the wheat used by a mill or the flour used by a baker. But what about demand deposits, time deposits, and savings deposits? What about CDs? Are they inputs into banking operations in the same sense as computers and paper? If so, are interest payments by banks to business firms supposed to embody a value added tax that should then be creditable against the value added tax that they owe? And should banks in turn pay value added tax on the interest they charge on their loans, with this tax then being creditable by firms that are part of the value added network but not so by firms and families that are outside it? These questions are really conundrums, ideal for occupying insomniac economists during their sleepless nights.

Insurance companies are not easier to fit into a scheme of administering the value added tax through the credit method than are banks. The problem here is that the premiums charged do not simply cover purchased inputs plus the firm's value added. They also cover reserves of all sorts against future claims, reserves that in turn function also as investments on which interest, capital gains, and possibly other financial income accrue.

Compounding the problems connected with incorporating financial institutions into a value added tax network is the fact that corresponding to any treatment accorded to items such as interest received and paid by banks, or premiums received, claims paid, or reserves formed by insurance companies, is a counterpart treatment to be applied at the level of the financial entity's client firms.

Public finance experts have studied and restudied these problems, and the invariable answer is that just leaving the financial sector out of the network is much simpler. Then we do not have to define its value added for tax purposes. For analytical purposes, we can simply call it x. The analyst can then use the results of, say, our farm example and state that whatever x may be, the business firms that are members of the value added network do not get to claim a credit for tax paid on whatever part of x they buy. On this part of the financial sector, the government gets the same revenue regardless of whether the financial sector is in or out of the network. At the same time, for the services rendered directly by the financial sector, consumers go without paying any tax if the financial sector is out of the network. Finally, if the financial sector is out of the network, it does not get credit for its inputs purchased from firms that are members of the network. Some of these inputs, such as paper, copiers, and computers, are easy to define and identify; others are subject to the same questions as enter into the definition of value added for the financial sector. To any definition of value added, x, is added a corresponding definition of purchased inputs, y. What we know is that while part of x (that part sold to entities outside the network) goes untaxed when financial services are left out, part of y (that part provided by firms that are in the network) pays tax that would not be paid if the financial sector were itself covered.

Retailing under the Value Added Tax

The case of retailing is not nearly as complicated as that of the financial sector. Analytically, it is a straightforward application of the results presented earlier. The problem is that retailers sell an overwhelmingly large fraction of their output to final consumers. Because retailers have no corresponding sales (or at least hardly any) to firms that are in the value added network, nobody else within the network pays tax, as it were, on their behalf. Therefore, leaving retailing out of a value added network means, in general, the outright loss of the tax that would accrue on the basis of the retail sector's value added. Fortunately, leaving retailing out does nothing to impinge upon the tax already collected at earlier stages.[2]

Sometimes retail enterprises below a certain size (usually measured in terms of annual sales) are excluded from the tax net. Excluding these enterprises saves administrative costs but also encourages economic inefficiency. In effect, this differential treatment amounts to taxing one mechanism of providing retailing services (the value added by a firm of medium or large size), while leaving untaxed an alternative close substitute (the value added by a smaller firm that provides the same or similar services). Moreover—and once again human ingenuity comes into play—it stimulates the destruction of medium-size and large firms as their owners create new entities, involving many small firms, to do the same work previously done by a single firm. One partial solution to the efficiency problem, and its corollary the artificial fractionalizing of larger enterprises, is to place on smaller firms of a given type a simple tax (such as 1 percent of sales, as estimated by the tax assessor), with the firms being allowed to comply in full with the record-keeping and other requirements of the value added tax should they find that alternative preferable.

Different Levels for the Value Added Tax

Another way of dealing with the difficulty of collecting from vast numbers of tiny retailers is to leave all retailing out of the value added network. In effect, this creates a value added tax at the manufacturer and wholesale level. The problem here is one of enterprises trying to define themselves out of the tax category. In particular, integrated firms will try to use artificially low transfer prices between their wholesale and their retailing divisions so as to minimize value added up through the wholesale level. This minimizes their tax payment, because they report that value added is located at the retail level.

It is, of course, the task of the tax authorities to track down the sort of abuse just mentioned and to stamp it out. On the whole, conscientious enforcement is considerably easier at the wholesale than at the retail level, simply because of the vast differences in the number of taxpaying firms.

When problems of administration loom large, as in populous countries with low levels of per capita income and with gross shortages of competent administrators, the alternative of a value added tax at the manufacturer level is sometimes adopted. This tax usually covers the manufacturing sector, broadly defined to include modern food processing and mining, perhaps even modern forestry and fishing operations. As in all other cases, imports of the affected items are subject to the tax, and the tax is rebated on exports of such items.[3]

The Strategy of Value Added Tax

I hope that you can extract from the preceding commentary some sense of the different considerations that enter into the design of a modern value added tax. From the outset, I have emphasized that the tax is far from being fully general. Whole sectors, such as domestic service and the imputed income from owner-occupied housing, are left out of the tax net without a moment's hesitation and virtually without discussion. Underlying such wholesale sectoral preference seems to be some combination of a "sacred cow" image (spelling severe political difficulties for the government that is rash enough to meddle) plus an inchoate, unarticulated sense of vast enforcement difficulties.

Once past the sacred cows, one confronts a series of questions about how the base of the value added tax should be defined. Here administrative issues interplay with those of equity and efficiency. All these questions have come up many times in the context of a value added tax with a single uniform rate. They are not issues of pure equity, nor of pure efficiency, nor of pure administrative convenience. In the end, I would risk the judgment that tax experts facing these problems try to establish a workable, robust set of rules that specify in a simple way what should and should not be directly taxed, where this distinction is workable from an administrative point of view, and where it does not lead to any gross, easily avoidable production inefficiencies. This view carries the presumption (sacred cows aside) that a productive activity or sector should fall within the net. But experts recognize that sometimes it is not very costly in terms of either revenue or efficiency to leave an activity out. Sometimes the inclusion of an activity can itself have large efficiency costs (particularly if close substitute activities must for one reason or another be left outside the net), and sometimes it is simply a matter of fairness to put a given activity on one or the other side of the line that divides the covered from the uncovered sector.

This view also presumes that as an economy develops, the answers to the many questions concerning the inclusion and exclusion of sectors will themselves change. Taxes at the manufacturer level will probably evolve to the wholesale level, then to a partial retail coverage, and finally (perhaps) to full retail coverage. Agriculture and fishing sectors that were initially left out may also over time find themselves included in the tax net. All this is compatible with a general sense of robustness and fairness of the system prevailing at each stage. This, in my opinion, is the way contemporary tax reformers look at the problems surrounding the value added tax.

The Uniform Tariff

The political economy of tariffs is one of the more fascinating puzzles facing economists. In the first place, I believe one can say without fear of contradiction that tariffs are never, at least for a developing country, the ideal or best solution to any economic problem. Usually tariffs are motivated by a desire to protect (that is, subsidize) some domestic activity. But it is easy to show that a tariff is in fact equivalent to a subsidy to the domestic production of a good, together with a tax (at an equal rate) on its domestic consumption. Hence, if the authorities want to stimulate domestic production of a particular good, the idea of a subsidy makes sense, but why the domestic users of that type of good should be singled out as the group that has to pay for the subsidy is a question that has never had a satisfactory answer.

On the whole, one can say that tariffs exist, when and where they do, because the political influence of producers is stronger than that of consumers. High tariffs appear where producer interests are at their most powerful and where the countervailing consumer interests are at their most dispersed and least well articulated.

Facing the interests that argue and press for protection, economists have accumulated two centuries of experience pleading the case for free trade. Some may say all this effort has come to little, as in the end we still see all the signs of protectionism around us. But that sells short the efforts not only of economists but also of hundreds of wise and dedicated public servants and more than a few true political leaders. For most of the industrial countries, protectionism is today far less than it used to be, and for the developing countries, perhaps the biggest, most dramatic change in commercial policy in more than a decade has been movement in the direction of freer, not more restricted, trade.

I believe the modern view of tariff policy, and of trade restrictions in general, is more subtle and complicated than the simplistic free-tradism of earlier generations. It is not that the old arguments are wrong or that modern policy economists would negate free trade as a worthy goal. Rather, what I would call the modern view accepts the existence of protectionist pressure and finds it strategically interesting to cede a little territory to the protectionists in order to preclude their command over a much greater area.

Central to this vision is the idea of interest groups using all their powers of threat and persuasion to achieve their protectionist objectives. This is in line with modern political economy studies, which help to explain why some pressure groups succeed grandly, others manage to win some protection, and still others succeed not at all. But such studies certainly do not justify the end result as being in the social interest. To my mind and that of many others, it is the role and responsibility of the economics profession to articulate society's broader interests and to lead the resistance to pressures by special interest groups.

Wherein does the strategy call for ceding a little? In granting some protection to essentially every import-substituting activity in the economy. How does it thereby gain a lot of territory? By limiting that protection to whatever is provided by a moderate, uniform tariff. What is the logic behind this? It provides a natural guarantee against the huge efficiency costs (as well as the gross inequities) involved in the exaggerated rates of effective protection that flow from grossly differentiated tariff structures. What is the key political economy tactic that the strategy invokes? Putting each individual protectionist interest group on the defensive. How is this accomplished? By asking them to justify why their group should be singled out for special protectionist treatment while all other import substitutes are given the effective protection implied by a standard uniform tariff rate.

Of course, a strategy to limit protection to whatever is provided by a moderate, uniform tariff cannot be implemented unless the government adopts and supports it. If the government has already sold out to the protectionist interests, the strategy has not a chance. This strategy is not for such governments, but rather for those that actually have had the general interest at heart yet have been unable to overcome the many political obstacles in the path of liberalization. For them, adopting a uniform tariff has the effect of splintering the opposition into separate groups, each favoring special treatment for itself. This, of course, is the way interest groups typically behave, but fighting for differentiated treatment when such treatment is the norm is one thing; fighting for it against the backdrop of uniform tariff protection for everybody else, with special treatment just for one's own group, is quite another.

In a sense, a uniform tariff policy gives the government the high ground in its struggle against special interest groups. The government adopts a policy of uniform effective protection of import substitutes, then challenges the opposing interest groups to come up with a clear alternative criterion. In general, they will not easily discover such a criterion, and if one is found that favors one group, it is likely to disfavor another (relative to the uniform tariff).

Uniform Effective Protection

The idea of a uniform tariff as a practical, real-world policy measure received great impetus from the development and elaboration of the concept of effective protection. I think of this as the really great advance of international trade theory of the 1960s, at least in its real, as distinct from monetary, dimensions. To me, the big lesson of effective protection analysis is that without something like a uniform tariff, one is not even able to interpret the protective "content" of a given and known tariff structure. Consider a 30 percent tariff on men's shirts (a favorite example). If the country in question produces its own cotton, a 30 percent tariff on shirts represents 30 percent effective protection. But suppose the country does not produce its own wool, silk, or cashmere and that yarns of these various kinds enter duty free. If the wool to make a woolen shirt accounts (at international prices) for half the cost of the shirt, the 30 percent tariff on men's shirts will amount to 60 percent effective protection of local value added in making woolen shirts out of imported yarn. The same 30 percent tariff will give 120 percent effective protection to the making of silk shirts, if the silk yarn accounts for 75 percent of the international cost of the shirt. And it will provide an astounding 300 percent effective protection to the making of cashmere shirts, if that particular yarn accounts for 90 percent of the international cost of the cashmere shirt.

Not only does effective protection thus vary greatly, even within a quite narrow tariff category such as men's shirts, but also the degree of effective protection moves up and down capriciously with movements in world prices. If silk yarn accounts for 75 out of 100 percent of costs for a silk shirt at some initial point in time (yielding 120 percent effective protection), a fall of a third in silk prices will shift that to 50 out of 75 percent (yielding 90 percent effective protection), whereas a rise of silk prices by a third will make it 100 out of 125 percent, bringing to 150 percent the degree of effective protection provided by a 30 percent tariff on the final product. This means that even if one wants to aim for a particular rate of effective protection of an operation using imported inputs, achieving that rate in practice is impossible as long as the international prices of the relevant inputs and outputs are subject to even reasonably modest fluctuations.[4]

Not all the lessons of effective protection analysis are so disheartening, however. We can use the same analysis to show that a uniform tariff will rescue policymakers from the mare's nest of effective protection rates that seems to be the inevitable outcome of traditional tariff setting. It is easy enough to visualize: if all final products receive 30 percent protection and all imported inputs are likewise subject to a 30 percent tariff, the domestic value added process that converts the imported inputs into a final product will also be given protection of 30 percent.[5]

A few technical caveats should accompany any statement concerning the virtues of a uniform tariff. The first and most important of these is that although the uniform tariff in principle treats all import-substituting activities alike, it obviously discriminates against export activities. If the exchange rate in a developing country is 10 pesos to the dollar, setting a uniform tariff of 30 percent stimulates import-substituting activities, paying them, in effect, up to 13 pesos for saving a dollar's worth of foreign exchange. At the same time, export activities receive only 10 pesos for each dollar's worth of foreign exchange they generate. Such discrimination in favor of import substitution and against exports is the inevitable result of protectionist policies. Uniform tariffs make protection more rational and less costly, but they do not eliminate distortions altogether.[6]

At another level, when imposing a uniform tariff, the authorities must ensure that the tariff costs embodied in the prices of export products are reimbursed when the goods are in fact exported. This treatment has been incorporated in the "rules" of the General Agreement on Tariffs and Trade (GATT) from its very inception. If such treatment is not given, then export goods that use imported raw materials or components will receive negative effective protection.[7]

A final caveat is in a sense the obverse of the previous one. If export goods are sold inside the country at world market prices while import goods (and their substitutes) sell for world market prices plus 30 percent, then an import-substituting activity can end up being favored if it uses one or more export goods as an input. In principle, for a uniform 30 percent tariff always to yield 30 percent effective protection, the tariff should be accompanied by an internal tax (a quasi tariff) on the use of exportable goods as inputs into import-substituting activities. No one has ever seriously suggested that this be done. I note it here as a source of deviations from full uniformity of effective protection in the real world, even in countries that have adopted uniform tariff policies.[8]

Tariffs on Imported Inputs: Today's Big Debate

As countries drift toward more uniform tariff structures, there is relatively little resistance to the reduction of the highest rates of tariffs. These usually fall on finished products of a luxury nature. Sometimes the prevalence of contraband in such highly protected products causes even firms that are beneficiaries of protection to question the merits of extremely high tariffs. In any case, the nature of a differentiated tariff structure means that only a relatively few activities receive the highest rates of protection. Hence reducing the highest tariffs has been a relatively easy task for governments that are determined to liberalize their trade restrictions.

By contrast, raising the tariffs on imported inputs to levels that are close to the target level for final product tariffs has been far from easy.

The difficulty stems from a number of quite distinct factors. First, the interest groups that benefited from the tariff structure in the first place have, in general, also benefited from being able to buy imported inputs that enter with low or zero tariffs. (This is the historic pattern of protection: highest on luxury goods, next highest on other final products, lowest on certain key "necessities" and on all or most imported inputs.) These interest groups can coalesce on the general principle of keeping tariffs on inputs low, even while they may be forced to accept lower tariffs on final products.

Second, many imported inputs do not have domestically produced substitutes. It is hard for people to understand the "need" for having tariffs on products that are required for some local productive activity and that are not actually produced, or even foreseeably producible, at home. Typically, only those who are familiar with the mechanisms of effective protection can see the logic behind that "need," and they, sad to say, are invariably a small minority, composed mainly of economists and other technocrats.

Finally, even economists typically fail to reach consensus on the desirability of raising tariffs on imports, because some economists remain swayed by the arguments for fully free trade and see any raising of any tariff as unwanted deviation from that goal. Some of these economists remain unconvinced, even after all technical demonstrations, but others change their view once they see the positive merits of raising tariffs on inputs in the presence of higher tariffs on outputs.

A tariff on an imported input of a domestically produced good is a simple, straightforward distortion. It does nobody any good except the local producing interests (if any) that it protects. When the tariff is on an input of a good produced for export, GATT-rule treatment (called border tax adjustments) should guarantee that it will not interfere with the international competitiveness of such exports (see above). With respect to the exports that are given GATT-rule treatment, tariffs on imported inputs are, in effect, nullified.

We come finally to tariffs on inputs used to produce import substitutes. The proposition here is that raising such tariffs is always welfare-enhancing, at least up to the level of tariffs affecting the final product in question. This much should be clear from our earlier example of the tariff on men's shirts: raising the input tariff to 30 percent lowers the effective rate of protection to 30 percent. This represents a benefit (that is, a welfare enhancement), regardless of whether the initial rate of effective protection was 60 percent (woolen shirts), 120 percent (silk shirts), or 300 percent (cashmere shirts).

What many people do not understand is that raising the tariff rate on the input in question continues being beneficial considerably beyond the point at which the input tariff equals the output tariff.

However, this result should be intuitively obvious. If by raising the tariff on wool from zero to 30 percent, we can reduce the effective protection of woolen shirts from 60 to 30 percent, should we not be able to reduce that effective protection all the way to zero by pushing the tariff on wool still higher? Indeed, this is the case. Effective protection for the woolen shirt industry reaches zero when the tariff on wool is 60 percent; for the silk shirt industry it reaches zero when the tariff on silk yarn is 40 percent; and for the cashmere shirt industry it becomes zero when the tariff on cashmere yarn is about 33 percent.

Now it would be absurd to argue for a set of differentiated tariffs on all sorts of imported inputs as a device for reaching lower rates of effective protection on final products. But the fact remains that the optimal levels for tariffs on inputs, given the tariff rates on their outputs, are higher, not lower, than the output tariff rates. Realizing this, many who espouse free trade on general philosophical grounds are swayed to support raising input tariffs up to the standard uniform tariff level and thus give up their initial resistance to the idea.[9]

The Taxation of Income from Capital

Nowhere in the field of taxation can we find, in my opinion, a sharper contrast between appearance and reality than in capital income taxation. Taxing capital income appears to be an excellent way to introduce progression into the tax structure—to make the rich bear a heavier relative tax burden than the middle classes and the latter a heavier relative burden than the poor. The reality is quite the opposite. In every small country, at least in the Western world, anyone with funds to invest can easily place those funds in New York or London or Zurich. There is really nothing that policymakers can do to prevent such a "portfolio diversification" on the part of the nationals and other residents of developing countries.[10]

Because the relevant rate that can be earned abroad is something that is totally beyond the control of any developing country's government, it must be taken as given in any analysis of developing-country policy.[11] From this it follows that the heavier the taxation of income from capital in the developing country, the greater the incentive to hold assets abroad. In the simplest analytical case, one can take the required expected net of the tax rate of return in the developing country to be equal to that available abroad plus a fixed risk premium or differential. In this case, each increment of the tax placed on the income from capital in the developing country leads to a capital outflow from that country. The outflow continues until the gross of tax return has risen so as to fully reflect the increment of tax. In this way the net of tax return in the developing country is restored to its equilibrium level (equal to the "given" foreign rate plus the required differential).

Thus the higher the tax on the income from capital in a developing country, the smaller will be the stock of capital that is occupied there. Because labor is, in general, much less mobile internationally than is capital, the consequence of having less capital occupied in the country is a lower scale of real wages and salaries. Thus it is really labor that bears the burden of taxation on capital income in developing countries.[12]

This is the irony of policies such as heavy taxation of capital income. They have the appearance of being "populist" policies yet end up hurting mainly the wage and salary earners of the country. It follows that if one wants truly to help these groups, one should tread very lightly when it comes to capital income taxation.

It would appear to follow from the above that one should, in principle, reduce corporate income taxes to zero. This would generate an "optimal" capital stock and would produce a distinctly positive effect on real wages and salaries, in contrast to the present situation in most countries. Two considerations, however, weigh against this option: first, the presence in most developing countries of a significant sector composed of multinational corporations and, second, the existence of a greater problem of monopoly power (and hence monopoly profits) than is common in more advanced countries because of the small economic size of most developing countries.

Income of Multinational Companies

The first problem—that of multinational companies—derives from the fact that they are, in principle, subject to tax in their home (base) countries on the profits they earn via their subsidiaries located in developing countries. Typically, the multinationals are also eligible in their home countries for tax credits that reflect the taxes they pay to developing-country treasuries. These credits generally apply only up to the amount of tax that would be due to the home country government on the profits in question. The end result of this tax treatment is that a developing country, by lowering its tax rate below that applying in a company's home base, simply gives up the tax money. The company still pays the tax, but now it goes to the treasury of its home base country instead of to the developing country where the operations in question are located.

The obvious way for a developing country to avoid simply giving up money to the treasuries of the advanced countries where the multinationals are based is (a) to have a corporate income tax of its own and

(b) to set the rate of tax at a level approximating those prevailing in the most important base countries.

At first sight, the above solution appears to handle well the problem of loss of revenue to industrial-country treasuries but to leave unsolved the problem (referred to earlier) of reduced holdings of capital assets by nationals and other residents of the developing country. Happily, there is an easy way to handle both of these problems. It consists of maintaining the corporate income tax as part of the legal tax structure but of providing also for the integration of the corporate and personal income taxes as far as local resident taxpayers are concerned. Under full integration of the two taxes, the corporate income tax would turn into a simple withholding device. Local shareholders in a local corporation would be asked to declare as their own income their proportionate share of that corporation's profits. Then, once their tax liability was determined, the corporate tax paid on the basis of their shares would be creditable toward what they owe in personal income tax, in just the same way as the amounts withheld by employers are creditable against employees' tax liabilities.

A similar effect would be obtained by simply exempting from personal income tax the dividends received from domestic corporations plus the capital gains on their shares. This treatment works best when the top bracket rate of the personal income tax is equal to the rate of the corporate income tax.[13]

Monopoly Profits

The second issue with respect to the taxation of capital income has to do with monopoly profits. Many people now recognize that the economies of scale that exist in many activities are operative for smaller firms but do not continue to be significant once the firm (or the productive operation, as the case may be) reaches a certain critical size. The critical size in most industries is such that monopoly problems are not severe in advanced economies. There, demand is sufficient to allow several firms above the critical size to coexist in the market and compete with one another. In smaller countries, particularly developing countries, the demand from within the country may not be large enough to warrant several firms of efficient size. Thus one quite commonly finds in such countries a number of activities in which only one or two firms play a significant role.

In these circumstances monopoly power becomes a matter of significant policy concern. The standard economist's answer to this problem is for small countries to use the world market as their principal instrument for control of monopolies. To the extent that the potential monopoly power occurs in the tradable goods area, a policy of free trade (or of a relatively low uniform tariff) will do a great deal to limit the monopoly potential that would otherwise exist. The obverse of this proposition is that the freehanded application of protectionist measures is typically an open invitation to the exercise of monopoly power by protected local firms.

The monopoly problem is thus greatest under protectionist regimes and least under free trade or low uniform tariff policies. Nonetheless, even under the latter type of policy, the governments of smaller countries probably have more reason to worry about monopoly power than do those of larger countries. Now one thing that a well-administered corporate income tax will do, automatically, is to take its bite out of monopoly profits, just as it will out of any other category of profits. This is the most natural way for a small developing country to approach the monopoly problem. Price fixing and rate fixing are approaches that may work (if well administered) in basic public utilities such as telephone and electricity companies. It is very difficult to administer beyond this range, particularly with respect to activities whose output consists of a number of different products, with numerous variants of each with respect to quality, design, and so on. In such cases, price regulation has proved to be unworkable and often directly counterproductive (when the monopoly succeeds in flouting the controls, but only by incurring significant real costs).

Under the circumstances, the course of greatest wisdom for a developing country with a perceived problem of monopoly control is to use the corporate income tax as a device by which the public at large gains command over at least a certain share of such profits, wherever and for whatever reason they may occur.

This is the only argument I know of for limiting the degree of integration between the corporate income tax and the personal income tax in a developing country. Full integration by the withholding method would only ensure that shareholders in such enterprises pay their full personal tax on their full profits, including monopoly profits. As one pulls back from full integration, the total tax paid by enterprises gets correspondingly higher. Policymakers concerned with monopoly in developing countries thus face an interesting policy question. How much of the benefits of full integration are they willing to give up in order to obtain a greater bite into the monopoly profits of corporations? I will not attempt to answer this question here. Let me simply point out that a number of policy devices and packages are available, all of which succeed in taking a greater share of monopoly profits, but at the cost of making the country a less hospitable place for local residents to invest their capital. A brief listing of a few such schemes follows:

- Make the corporate tax rate higher (say, 40 percent) than the highest personal tax rate (say, 30 percent) with the corporate tax being creditable only up to the percentage rate (here, 30 percent) of the personal income tax.
- Make only a specified fraction of corporate taxes creditable against the personal income tax liability of domestic nationals and residents. Introduce integration of corporate and personal income taxes only with respect to dividends, with dividends being grossed up to reflect the profits on which they were based. This would mean that with a 40 percent tax rate, there would be a tax credit of 40 for each 60 percent of dividends received. No tax credit would be received by local residents with respect to profits retained within the corporation.
- Introduce integration of corporate and personal income taxes only with respect to dividends, without the dividends being grossed up. In this case, and again with a 40 percent corporate tax rate, there would be a tax credit of 24 (60 x 0.4) for every 60 percent of dividends received.

Clearly, these devices provide a wide range of options for the policymaker. At the same time, it is equally clear that any gain made with respect to getting a greater share of monopoly profits comes at the expense of reducing the incentive for local investors to keep their money in the country.

Conclusion

The foregoing discussion of policy issues will, I hope, give readers something of the flavor of the issues facing tax reformers in developing countries. On the whole, the scope for tax reform is enormous, in the sense that actual tax structures are grossly inferior in almost any dimension to those that could be achieved simply by implementing the reforms suggested in this paper. Yet, and this too is worthy of note, the devices on which we have concentrated—a uniform value added tax; a uniform tariff at a moderate rate; and a moderate corporate income tax that is fully or partially integrated with a personal income tax, both with similar (and moderate) maximum rates—are themselves not "optimal" in a formal, technical sense.

Tax reform in today's world is, I believe, more appropriately focused on the giving of robust signals that will improve the private sector's allocation of resources than on the niceties associated with formal, technical optimization.

Notes

1. Experts are unanimous in advising against the granting of tax amnesties as a general policy. Such amnesties typically allow taxpayers to bring their taxes up to date with little or no penalty. Sometimes they even collect no interest and make no inflationary adjustment on back taxes due. Thus the evaders of the past end up paying less real tax at its total present value than did the compliers who made every payment in full and on time. But the tax-and-evasion race referred to in the text takes away all moral absolutes. If past taxes were set at high levels in anticipation of evasion, the argument for a partial forgiveness of such taxes becomes stronger, especially when such forgiveness is thought to clean the slate for a "new future" in which everybody pays taxes due in full. But granting partial forgiveness once can easily leave taxpayers with the idea that evasion yields a positive payoff. This can set in motion yet another tax-and-evasion race, with successive increments of evasion triggering successive upward shifts of the entire tax rate structure. The only happy solution to such a problem is one in which taxpayers somehow are brought to believe that the future will be very different from the past, so that they shift their behavior at some point from wholesale evasion to something close to full compliance. It takes a government with great credibility and moral authority to accomplish such a feat.

2. An individual's ingenuity blooms in full flower when it comes to tax evasion. One of the great virtues of a value added tax administered by the credit method is that if one stage of production understates its sales (and therefore underpays its tax), the error will tend to be compensated at the next stage, which will, as a consequence of the understatement, receive a correspondingly smaller tax credit. This self-correcting feature works well up to the last stage. But what about an understatement of sales by a retailer? Obviously, there is no compensating correction here, and value added tax administrators are well aware of this fact. In theory, cunning retailers could not only fail to pay tax on their own value added but even end up collecting money from the treasury by having sales consistently lower than purchases of inputs. Fortunately, this would show up as negative value added.

In general, value added tax legislation does not permit instantaneous crediting of taxes paid on inputs when these exceed the tax due on a firm's output. Rather, the excess must be carried over to future tax periods. In this way, the worst that even the shrewdest retailers can do is to reduce the tax on their own value added to zero; they cannot, under the treatment, eat into the tax already paid by another. Note also that cases of consistently negative or zero value added are highly likely to trigger an audit by the tax authorities, even when they are no more than mediocre in the conscientious execution of their duties. Persistently negative value added is a phenomenon too conspicuous simply to overlook. Hence, even at the last and most vulnerable stage, the value added tax has some sort of built-in insurance against the loss of revenues garnered at previous productive stages.

3. Imposing a value added tax on imports and rebating it on exports does not protect import substitutes or subsidize export activities. These so-called "border tax adjustments" are simply ways to permit the tax to show up as part of the domestic prices of the affected products without giving up the artificial stimulus for users to seek substitute goods through importation and without putting artificial trammels on export activities.

4. The price movements dealt with here should be thought of as movements in real or relative prices, not as a reflection of international inflation. An easy rule of thumb is to think of the price of wool, the price of silk, and so on, and the international prices of the corresponding shirts, as being expressed in relation to an index of world market prices of tradable goods.

5. If r_j is the nominal rate of protection on final product j, r_i the nominal rate of protection on input i, and a_{ij} the fraction of the cost of j accounted for (at international prices) by input i, domestic resource costs can extend up to the domestic currency equivalent of

$$(1 - r_j) - \Sigma_i\, a_{ij}(1 + r_i)$$

per dollar's worth of final product displaced. The net saving of foreign currency obtained in the process is equal to

$$1 - \Sigma_i\, a_{ij}$$

This pattern of protection therefore allows for domestic resource costs of up to

$$[(1 - \Sigma_i\, a_{ij}) + (r_j - \Sigma_i\, a_{ij} r_i)]/(1 - \Sigma_i\, a_{ij})$$

per net dollar of foreign exchange saved. This implies a rate of *effective* protection of

$$(r_j - \Sigma_i\, a_{ij} r_i)/(1 - \Sigma_i\, a_{ij})$$

Thus, this rate of effective protection will be equal to r_j, whenever all the relevant r_i are also equal to r_j. This says that the effective protection of a final product will be equal to its nominal protection whenever the relevant imported inputs into its production have tariffs equaling (or averaging) the rate that applies to the final product. Thus if all final products and all imported inputs carry the rate r^*, then all domestic value added (in processes of import substitution) receives protection at that same rate.

6. The famous "Lerner theorem" of the 1930s points out that a uniform 30 percent tariff accompanied by a uniform 30 percent subsidy to exports would in principle be nondistorting. Indeed, it would be equivalent to free trade. As far as trade items (imports and exports) are concerned, a country could equally well (a) institute a uniform 30 percent tariff plus a uniform 30 percent subsidy to exports or (b) devalue the currency by 30 percent while in all other respects maintaining free trade.

7. The effective protection level of an export good x_j is found by substituting the export subsidy rate z_j for the tariff rate r_j in the formula for effective protection. The effective protection rate on an export good x_j is then

$$(z_j - \Sigma_i\, a_{ij} r_i)/(1 - \Sigma_i a_{ij})$$

Normally, z_j will be zero for the typical export good. Effective protection can then be made equal to zero by rebating the tariff r_i that enters into its cost structure. Otherwise x_j will end up with negative effective protection.

8. I do not believe it is a serious flaw in these cases, at least for the developing countries with which I am familiar. On the whole, export production is far more specialized than import substitute protection. Many important exports by developing countries are agricultural products (wheat, beef, fruits, and so on), which do not typically enter as inputs into import substitute production. Other export products, such as copper and tin, do not play a major role in the costs of import substitute production. Still others (jute, forest products, and so

on) may be important as inputs into export products but not into import substitutes.

9. This is not the place to elaborate greatly on the above point, but it is worth mentioning that raising tariffs on inputs into the production of importables is *trade creating*. This is the only big and important class of trade-creating tariffs. The process works very simply. If imported inputs account for 40 out of 100 percent of total cost (at international prices) of an import substitute, then increasing the tariff on the inputs will, with fixed proportions, result in an increase of 100 percent of trade in the final product for every 40 percent of trade in the inputs. Abandoning the assumption of fixed proportions modifies, but does not annul, this result.

10. In my own experience, India of the early 1960s was a striking example. When I was there in 1961–62, capital outflows were essentially prohibited, and all kinds of controls existed. Nonetheless, a parallel or black market in foreign currency not only prevailed, but thrived. The black market premium was high, however: about 50 percent over the official rate of Rs4.75 to the dollar. I took every opportunity to ask people what rate of return they expected to get on the money they had invested abroad (mainly in London). The answer was always the same: they expected to get whatever rate of return prevailed in the London financial market. When asked if the high black market premium didn't get in the way of such an outcome, they replied, "No, we take it out over the black market, and we bring it back the same way." They did not face a significantly lower expected return, despite all the controls. All they faced was an added source of possible variability (up or down) in the rate of return, stemming from possible changes in the black market premium over the period for which the funds were invested.

11. For our purposes it does not matter whether this return is taxed or not taxed in, say, the United States. Interest earned by developing-country nationals on accounts in the United States is free of U.S. income tax, but U.S. corporate income tax is paid on the profits from their investments in corporate shares. Whatever the tax treatment in the financial market center, developing-country investors will react to the net of tax return they receive. This is what must be taken as "given" when analyzing developing countries' policies.

12. Most of the time, labor bears more than the full burden of, say, a corporate income tax. This is because the corporate sector produces mainly tradable goods, whose prices are to a large degree determined in world markets. The tax therefore cannot push up the international prices of corporate output significantly; the effect of the tax must rather be to push down wages by enough so that the tax can be paid while product prices remain substantially the same. But wages in the corporate sector do not move just by themselves. The effect we are talking about is on the equilibrium level of wages and salaries throughout the economy. Thus if the wages paid in the corporate sector fall by enough to "absorb" the tax, and if wages in the noncorporate sector fall by roughly the same percentage (reflecting continuing equilibrium in the labor market), then labor will end up bearing more than the full burden of the tax.

13. Over the past two decades or so there has been worldwide recognition of the merits of keeping tax rates relatively moderate, both on personal and on corporate income. Whereas at one time personal income tax rates ranging up to 50, 60, 70 percent and even higher were common, now most maximum rates are between 30 and 40 percent. Likewise, although corporate income

taxes of 50 percent and more were once common, today they, too, tend to be clustered in the 30 to 40 percent range. Thus, a developing country today can meet the two conditions specified in the text by setting its corporate tax rate at about, say, 35 percent and by making this also the maximum rate of its personal income tax schedule.

Selected Bibliography

Boskin, Michael T., and Charles E. McLure, Jr. 1991. *World Tax Reform*. San Francisco: ics Press.

Gandhi, Ved P. 1987. *Supply-Side Tax Policy: The Relevance to Developing Countries*. Washington, D.C.: International Monetary Fund.

Gilles, Malcolm, ed. 1989. *Tax Reform in Developing Countries*. Chapel Hill, N.C.: Duke University Press.

Harberger, Arnold A., ed. 1984. *World Economic Growth*. San Francisco: Institute for Contemporary Studies.

————. 1990. "Reflections on Uniform Taxation." In Ronald W. Jones and Anne O. Krueger, eds., *The Political Economy of International Trade*. Oxford, U.K.: Basil Blackwell.

Newbery, David, and Nicholas Stern, eds. 1987. *The Theory of Taxation for Developing Countries*. New York: Oxford University Press.

Tanzi, Vito, ed. 1990. *Fiscal Policy in Open Developing Economies*. Washington, D.C.: International Monetary Fund.

Urrutia, Miguel, Shinichi Ichimura, and Setsuko Yukawa, eds. 1989. *The Political Economy of Fiscal Policy*. Tokyo: United Nations University.

8

Adjusting to a Terms of Trade Shock: Nigeria, 1972–88

Michael Gavin

NIGERIA, the most populous nation in Africa, is one of the few countries blessed with substantial petroleum deposits. Production of petroleum started in 1958 and expanded briskly during the 1960s. By 1972 Nigeria was exporting nearly 2 million barrels a day of high-quality crude oil. Nigeria was therefore ideally situated to capitalize on the large oil price increase that the Organization of Petroleum Exporting Countries (OPEC) engineered in late 1973 and the subsequent, comparably large increase that followed the supply disruptions generated by the 1978 revolution in Iran. When the petroleum market entered its deep and protracted slump in 1981, however, Nigeria found that what commodity markets give they can also take away. Since then, Nigeria has been grappling with an economic crisis of enormous proportions.

As a result of increases in the price of petroleum, the dollar value of Nigeria's exports rose sixfold between 1972 and 1977 and doubled again by 1980. Adjusting for inflation, the value of Nigeria's exports more than tripled between 1972 and 1977 and rose another 50 percent by 1980.[1] Although oil prices fluctuated widely during the period, the decade after 1972 was one in which Nigeria's international purchasing power was increased beyond the wildest dreams of the most unreasonably optimistic planner.

By 1986 oil prices had fallen considerably from the dizzying heights reached in the early 1980s, and Nigeria's terms of trade in 1987 were substantially less favorable than in the boom years. Still, as table 8-1 indicates, the terms of trade remained better than they had been before the original petroleum price increase. The data presented in table 8-1 also, however, raise the suspicion that Nigeria captured astonishingly small long-term benefits from the twelve-year boom. By 1987 Nigeria's output had recovered dramatically from the crisis years 1984 and 1985. Nevertheless in 1987, and in an external environment that was not more hostile than that of 1973, Nigerian GNP per capita was 22 percent lower than it had been in 1973, fourteen years before.

Table 8-1. Nigeria before and after the Oil Boom, 1973 and 1987

Indicator	1973	1987
Terms of trade (1980 = 100)	22.3	49.1
Real GNP per capita (1980 naira)	577	450
Private consumption	356	334
Government consumption	48	47
Investment	100	49
Sources of per capita real GDP		
Agriculture (1980 nairas)	208	124
Industry (1980 nairas)	218	153
Services and other (1980 nairas)	165	167
Food production per capita (index)	109.7	103.1
External debt per capita (1987 dollars)	39	269
Debt-export ratio (percent)	32	369
Consumer price inflation (percent)[a]	9.7	18.8
Life expectancy (years)	44.9	51.1
Infant mortality (per 1,000 births)	143.2	102.8
Primary school enrollment (percentage of age group)	51	92

a. Inflation rates are averages for the five-year periods ending in 1973 and 1988.
Source: World Bank data.

Declines in output were pervasive, with agricultural output falling 40 percent, industrial output falling 30 percent, and only the service sector, which includes government employment, registering a slight increase. Food production per capita actually fell over the period, and Nigeria, which had been a net exporter of food, became a large net importer during the late 1970s. Both private and government consumption were smaller in 1987 than they were in 1973, and per capita investment fell in real terms from ₦ 1,001,980 in 1973 to less than ₦ 501,980 in 1987.

And the view from the financial markets was no more heartening than the view from product markets. In 1987 individuals in Nigeria owed an average of about $269 per person to foreign creditors. Inflation during the five years leading up to 1973 was just under 10 percent a year; during the five years leading up to 1988, inflation averaged almost twice that figure. And whereas the naira traded for $1.52 in 1973 (about $1.20 on the black market), it was worth roughly 14 cents by mid-1989.

Offsetting these setbacks, it must be said that Nigeria made substantial progress during that time in raising health and educational standards. Nigeria increased the number of physicians and nurses per capita by substantially more between 1965 and 1984 than did low-income developing economies as a whole. And as table 8-1 documents, life expectancy rose and infant mortality declined between 1972 and

1987, although it should be recognized that both indicators had been improving prior to 1972 as well. Most impressive was a tremendous surge in primary and secondary school enrollments, most of which occurred during the middle 1970s, when the Nigerian government embarked on the expensive Universal Primary Education policy.

But despite these very real gains in the areas of health and education, it cannot be said that Nigeria in 1987 was, on balance, significantly more prosperous than it was in 1973. And certainly the gains that should have been made possible by the relatively short-lived but nevertheless immense increase in oil earnings had not, apparently, been realized.

What happened? Although the oil boom that began in late 1973 may have fallen short of expectations raised during that period, it generated, on balance, an enormous increase in the resources available for the development of Nigeria. Why was the payoff from these resources, ostentatiously invested in far-reaching national plans, apparently so low? This essay explores the response of the Nigerian officialdom and economy to the petroleum price disturbances in order to draw lessons for other policymakers facing similar circumstances.

To discuss the adequacy of Nigerian policies, we need some normative benchmark against which to compare policies and outcomes. This is provided by the second and third sections of this essay. In the second section we review some important nonmonetary aspects of adjustment to a change in the terms of trade. We define "successful adjustment" with reference to the adjustment that would take place in a frictionless, neoclassical economy. Particular emphasis is placed on the role of foreign borrowing in the adjustment process.

Nonmonetary Aspects of a Terms of Trade Disturbance

The outstanding feature of a change in the terms of trade is that it alters a nation's disposable income. When the terms of trade improve, a country may consume more than it could previously without increasing its foreign debt. Alternatively, residents may choose to save some portion of the higher income and consume more in the future. When the terms of trade decline, however, a country must spend less than it could previously. The reduction in spending may be postponed by the expedient of foreign borrowing, but eventually a nation's spending must fall into line with its new, lower income.

This decline in national income is an inevitable consequence of altered terms of trade; it cannot be changed by the monetary and fiscal policies pursued by national authorities. Nevertheless, movements in the terms of trade require adjustment by the domestic economy that may be either facilitated or frustrated by the economic policies pursued by monetary, fiscal, and regulatory authorities. This section explores a number of issues surrounding such adjustment to changes in the terms of trade. Its purpose is to lay out the economic responses that constitute successful adjustment and to provide thereby some rough normative guidelines for the analysis of economic policy that follows.

What does successful adjustment involve? We alluded above to requisite changes in national expenditure. Such actions are clearly a central component of adjustment. But adjustment may also require important changes in the structure of production and the allocation of domestic investments, which will in turn require potentially large alterations in domestic relative prices. So one important goal of the following discussion is simply to articulate the impact of changes in the terms of trade on demand, production, and relative prices.

An issue of paramount importance is whether gains or losses in national income that are the result of changes in the terms of trade should be met with immediate changes in consumption expenditure or with changes in the rate of saving. If saved, current-income gains from an improvement in the terms of trade can be translated into higher future consumption, whereas reductions in the rate of national saving can postpone the decline in consumption necessitated by a deterioration in the terms of trade. The appropriate response of expenditure to altered terms of trade is therefore inherently a problem of intertemporal choice. Thus the second goal of this section is to lay out the simple principles that govern intelligent savings decisions.

Here we raise the crucial distinction between temporary and permanent movements in the terms of trade. We emphasize the usefulness of access to international capital markets for stabilizing the rate of consumption and investment when the terms of trade, and therefore national income, are highly variable. Because adjustment to a change in the terms of trade is costly and takes time to complete, we further argue that temporary recourse to international capital markets may be an appropriate response to both permanent and temporary changes in the terms of trade.

As mentioned, adjustment is a costly and time-consuming process, but the speed with which an individual economy adjusts depends on the policies the local authorities pursue. This section focuses on the impact of foreign borrowing on the speed of adjustment to the terms of trade disturbance. We argue that too much foreign borrowing or lending results in a suppression of the relative price signals required to effect adjustment. It may make sense, however, to use foreign borrowing to attenuate somewhat the relative price "overshooting" that would occur in the absence of international borrowing and thereby reduce the speed of adjustment. Excessively rapid adjustment is costly;

it may generate bottlenecks and expensive mistakes that could be avoided with a more moderate pace of adjustment (see the third section).

The last set of issues that we raise in this section concerns uncertainty. So far we have assumed that decisionmakers know how long the change in the terms of trade will persist. In reality, of course, nobody knows whether a change in the terms of trade will be reversed, will persist, or will deteriorate even more. Thus we cannot assess Nigeria's economic policy without an awareness of the uncertainty that surrounds future movements in the terms of trade. This uncertainty leads us to recommend a conservative approach to adjusting to a change in the terms of trade. Conservative in this context means two things. First, it means a higher rate of saving than would be appropriate under certainty; the rationale for this comes from the theory of precautionary saving. Second, it means avoiding irreversible commitments—or commitments that are costly to reverse—when there is substantial uncertainty about future developments. The practical implication is that domestic investment should respond more tentatively than would be appropriate under certainty and that savings should instead be channeled, at least temporarily, into relatively liquid foreign assets via current account surpluses.

The Effects on Income

We begin with the most basic considerations, which can be illustrated with an extremely simple framework. Consider an economy that is endowed with two tradable consumption goods that, anticipating the discussion of Nigeria, we label oil and manufactures. As with most developing countries, the economy is too small to alter the relative price of these goods, which is determined in the global commodity market. The economy is endowed with Q_O units of oil and Q_M units of manufactures each period.

Now we consider a deterioration in the terms of trade, which is here a decline in the relative price of oil. Income rises if measured in terms of oil and declines if measured in terms of manufactures. But *real* income, that is, the purchasing power of the economy's production, declines. This change in income is equal to the change in the terms of trade times the initial level of exports:

$$\Delta Y = \Delta P_x (Q_O - C_O)$$

where Δ stands for a change, Y stands for real income, P_x is the terms of trade, and C_O is the units of oil at a point in time.

This measure of the income effect of changes in the terms of trade is the right one to focus on in the following sense.[2] If the change in the terms of trade were accompanied by an increase in transfers from foreigners of the magnitude ΔY, then the initial consumption point, C, would still be (just barely) affordable, so consumers would be as well off as they were before the terms of trade deterioration. Phrasing the same point rather differently, we can say that ΔY is the amount by which the trade balance would deteriorate and foreign borrowing would have to increase if the initial level of consumption were maintained in the face of the terms of trade deterioration.

This first-order measure of the pain generated by a change in the terms of trade is easily quantified. Between 1972 and 1980 the real value of Nigeria's exports rose from about $6 billion to roughly $30 billion, a fivefold increase. With a population of roughly 80 million in the late 1970s, this increase in income amounts to about $300 per capita at 1988 prices. By 1986 the real value of Nigeria's exports had fallen to about $7.5 billion, almost their 1972 level. Compare these changes in income with the World Bank's estimate of per capita GNP, which was roughly $1,000 in the early 1980s and $370 in 1987. In other words, the change in income attributable to variations in the real value of Nigeria's oil exports was approximately equal to the level of real income Nigerians enjoy today.

This estimate is, of course, very rough and subject to all the qualifications surrounding international income comparisons, but it makes two important points. First, large changes in the terms of trade can wipe out years of economic growth. Second, the direct effect on income of changes in the terms of trade is not enough to explain the entire decline in Nigeria's economy after the oil market softened, beginning in 1982. We will therefore look for further explanations in policy mistakes.

Finance or Adjustment?

Having identified the loss in income generated by a change in the terms of trade, the next step is to determine the appropriate response.

BASIC CONSIDERATIONS. Our first concern is with the level of total expenditure and therefore the current account balance. The key question is whether an economy that has suffered a deterioration in its terms of trade should borrow from abroad to permit a higher level of expenditure or should, instead, reduce its consumption expenditure by the full extent of the loss in income, thereby maintaining balance in its international payments. We emphasized earlier that this question involves intertemporal tradeoffs, and these tradeoffs result because spending in excess of income leads to an accumulation of foreign debt, which must be serviced in the future. The following equations help to clarify the intertemporal financing problems that Nigeria must face.

(8-1) $$D_{t+1} - D_t = rD_t + (P_xC_x + C_M) - (P_xQ_x + Q_M)$$
$$= Rd_t + M_t - P_xX_t$$

where D_t stands for the country's net indebtedness at time t, and r is the interest rate on this debt. X denotes exports, M refers to imports, and C and Q stand for domestic consumption and production, respectively.

The right-hand side of equation 8-1 is the current account deficit, which can be written as the excess of domestic expenditure over domestic income and also as the excess of imports of goods (M_t) and capital services (Rd_t) over total exports (P_xX_t). Equation 8-1 emphasizes that current account deficits must be financed with increases in net foreign indebtedness or reductions in an economy's net foreign assets.

Equation 8-1 relates the stock of debt tomorrow to the stock of debt today and the imbalance between domestic income and domestic expenditure. We can also solve equation 8-1 forward to obtain an expression for debt two periods in the future as a function of today's and tomorrow's spending and income. If we continue to solve forward and make the assumption that international debt does not grow too fast, we obtain a revealing alternative expression for the intertemporal budget constraint:

(8-1′) $$\sum_{i=0}^{\infty}(1 + r)^{-i}E_{t+i} = \sum_{i=0}^{\infty}(1 + r)^{-i}(Y_{t+i} - D_t)$$

where E_t is total expenditure on consumption, and Y_t is the value of income from production. Equation 8-1′ states that the present value of expected future expenditure on consumption must be equal to the present value of domestic income minus previously contracted debt obligations, D_t. So if individuals decide to spend in excess of national income in one period, they are simultaneously deciding to spend less than the value of national income in some future period.

Another way of writing the same budget constraint is

$$\sum_{i=0}^{\infty}(1 + r)^{-i}[P_{x(t+i)}X_{t+i} - M_{t+i}] = D_t.$$

Here we see an important way of thinking about a nation's solvency constraint. The present value of expected future trade surpluses must be equal to the existing level of international indebtedness. Thus, if an economy is burdened with international debt and wishes not to default, it must plan to run trade surpluses in the future that equal, in present value, the value of the nation's international debt obligations.

To determine the appropriate response of consumption to changes in the terms of trade we need to discuss not only budget constraints but also consumers' tastes. For now we focus on the most basic motivation governing consumption decisions: the desire to spread consumption evenly among periods of life. That desire leads to a simple rule for consumption, which we know as the permanent-income hypothesis: plan to consume in each period of life a constant amount and set that amount equal to the most that can be consumed without violating the lifetime budget constraint summarized in equation 8-1'.

This simple rule for consumption expenditure gives an equally simple rule of optimal savings and therefore, in this simple economy without investment, for the optimal current account surplus. When income is transitorily high, save, which implies current account surpluses. When income is transitorily low, dissave, which implies current account deficits. When income is equal to "permanent income," neither borrower nor lender be.

This advice translates immediately into a simple prescription for responding to changes in the terms of trade. If the change in the terms of trade is permanent, it leads to a permanently lower level of income, as in the top panel of figure 8-1. In this case, the best response is for consumption to decline immediately to the new, lower level of national income; only such a policy maintains a smooth path for consumption while still respecting the lifetime budget constraint. If, however, the change in the terms of trade is expected to be transitory, then it does make sense to borrow from abroad to cushion the short-run effects on domestic expenditure. The second panel of figure 8-1 depicts the optimal response to a temporary decline in the terms of trade, which generates a temporary decline in national income.

PRODUCTION RESPONSES. The above discussion on financing versus adjusting to a terms of trade disturbance embodied a very limited perspective on the process of "adjustment," which was viewed simply as bringing the rate of consumption expenditure into line with income. In reality, adjustment also includes the need to adjust production in response to the altered opportunities presented by changes in relative prices.

A reduction in the price of oil will lead profit-maximizing producers to switch out of the petroleum sector and into the manufacturing sector, moving from one production equilibrium to another. This response of producers to the change in relative prices serves to offset the reduction in national income that would otherwise occur as a result of the terms of trade disturbance.

If adjustments were costless, then prompt and complete adjustment would be appropriate to any disturbance to the terms of trade. Such

Figure 8-1. Income, Expenditure, and Current Account Responses to a Change in the Terms of Trade

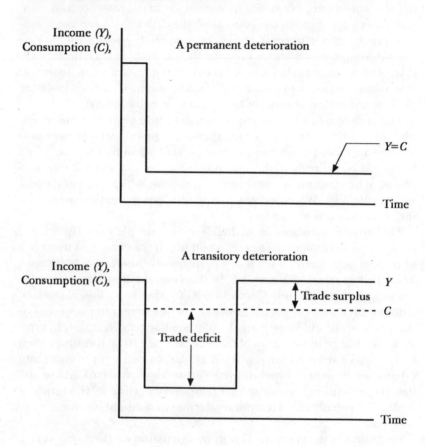

adjustment would reduce the income effects of disturbances that are adverse and allow the economy to capitalize more fully on those that are favorable. Except for altering the magnitude of the income effects of relative price changes, nothing in the foregoing analysis of financing versus adjustment would be altered. In particular, foreign borrowing would still be recommended to accompany transitory disturbances, whereas permanent disturbances would require full adjustment of production, consumption, and no foreign borrowing.

In the real world, however, moving from one production equilibrium to another takes time and is costly. This has two important implications. First, bearing these costs of adjustment will not be worthwhile if the deterioration in the terms of trade is expected to last for only a very short time. Thus rapid, complete adjustment in the production sector makes sense in response to permanent changes in the terms of trade rather than to transitory changes (see, for example, Mussa 1978). So, the adage "adjust to permanent disturbances, but not transitory disturbances" acquires a fuller meaning: not only does it apply to changes in consumption expenditure, but it applies to changes in production patterns as well.

Second, because adjustment of production to changes in relative prices takes time, so that the economy moves only gradually between the production equilibriums, a permanent deterioration in the terms of trade will have a larger adverse effect on income in the short run than in the long run, when production has had time to adjust. This has an important implication: when it takes time to adjust the production sector, even permanent changes in the terms of trade should, in part, be "financed" by foreign borrowing. Figure 8-2 illustrates the logic of this conclusion.

In figure 8-2 we consider a permanent deterioration in the terms of trade, which leads to an immediate decline in the value of national income from Y_0 to Y_1. Over time, however, the production sector adjusts, and national income rebounds partially until income eventually reaches its new, long-run level, Y_2.

The sustainable level of consumption expenditure will be somewhere between the temporarily short-run level of income, Y_1, and the long-run level of income, Y_2. As figure 8-2 makes clear, this means that

Figure 8-2. Income, Expenditure, and the Trade Balance with a Slow Adjustment of Production

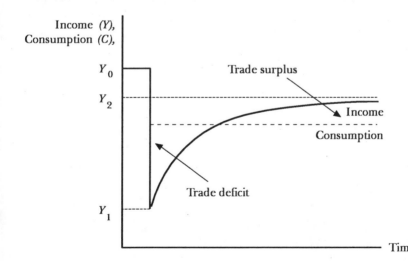

consumption will be greater than income in the immediate aftermath of the decline in the terms of trade, which implies, in turn, a period of foreign borrowing while the economy adjusts to the change in relative prices. The extent of foreign borrowing depends on the income gains $(Y_2 - Y_1)$ that come from adjusting production and on the speed with which adjustment takes place (see Gavin 1988 for a more in-depth explanation). If the gains from adjustment are small, then a small amount of borrowing is appropriate, and vice versa. If the economy adjusts to the disturbance quickly, then permanent income is close to the long-run level of income, Y_2, and substantially above the short-run level of income, Y_1. This implies that there should be more borrowing immediately following the impact of the change in the terms of trade than there would be if the speed of adjustment to the disturbance were quite slow.

This points out a key qualification of the policy advice to adjust to permanent disturbances and finance transitory disturbances. In general, even permanent disturbances will induce changes in the economy that take time to materialize and that may require resources to effect. When that is the situation, a case can be made for financing part of even permanent disturbances to the terms of trade.

Relative Prices and Adjustment

Our discussion so far has been based on a model in which traded goods are produced by a country too small to alter their relative prices. Adjustment comprised movements of factors between the export sector and an import-competing sector but involved no changes in relative prices. In reality, however, adjustment to a change in the terms of trade may require dramatic changes in relative prices; and it is by counterproductive obstruction of desirable changes in relative prices that governments make some of their most important policy mistakes. To bring out these aspects of adjustment to a terms of trade disturbance, we now introduce nontraded goods, the prices of which, unlike those of internationally traded goods, are determined by the interplay of supply and demand in the small economy that we discuss.

BASICS. For ease of analysis, let us consider an economy in which the exported good is not consumed by the domestic population and the imported good is not produced in the domestic economy.[3] We let the imported good be the numeraire, so that the price of the exported good is the terms of trade and the price of the nontraded good is likewise expressed in terms of the importable.

The supply side of the economy is easy to describe. Factors of production will move between the export sector and the nontradables sector, depending on the price of the exportable in relation to the nontraded good. When the relative price of nontraded goods increases, the nontradables sector bids factors of production away from the export sector, and vice versa. We can summarize the production side of the economy with an upward sloping curve, such as the curve labeled *SS* in figure 8-3, which gives the supply of nontraded goods as a function of the price of nontradables in relation to the price of tradables.

We will be interested once again in discussing the fact that economies adjust gradually to changes in relative prices. The practical importance of this is that the long-run supply response to a given change in relative prices will be greater than the short-run response. Thus, if we view *SS* as a short-run supply curve, the long-run supply curve will be a flatter curve such as the one labeled *LL* in figure 8-3.

The demand for nontraded goods depends on total expenditure and the price of nontraded goods in relation to the price of the

Figure 8-3. The Terms of Trade and the Real Exchange Rate

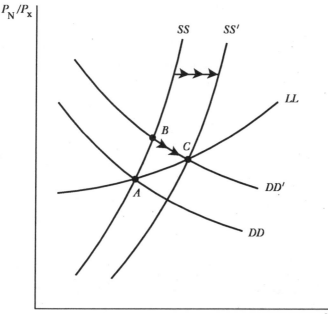

imported consumption good. Total expenditure, in turn, is equal to national income net of interest payments on foreign debt plus the rate of foreign borrowing, which is in turn equal to the current account deficit. Expressed as an equation, we have

(8-2) $$E_t = Y_t - rD_t + CA_t$$

where, as before, E is total expenditure on consumption, Y is the value of national production, D is the economy's foreign debt, and CA is the current account deficit.

Using equation 8-2, one can derive a demand equation for any given level of the terms of trade, P_x, and current account deficit, CA_t.[4] Given these two determinants, demand for nontraded goods is a downward sloping function of the price of nontraded goods, which is drawn in figure 8-3 as the curve DD. Equilibrium in the market for nontraded goods obtains, at the intersection of the short-run supply curve SS and the demand curve DD, which determines the equilibrium relative price and output of nontraded goods.

Figure 8-3 provides some important insights. First, what is the relationship between the current account deficit and the relative price of nontraded goods? An increase in the current account deficit corresponds to an increase in domestic expenditure in relation to income, which implies an increase in demand for consumption goods. Thus a current account deficit is reflected in figure 8-3 by an outward shift in the demand curve from DD to DD'. In the new equilibrium, point B, the relative price and production of nontraded goods have both risen. We therefore have the conventional relationship between real-exchange-rate appreciation and increases in the current account deficit, where the real exchange rate is defined here as the price of traded goods in relation to the price of nontraded goods. Such an appreciation leads to a movement of productive resources from the tradables sector into the nontradables sector; as the export sector shrinks, a trade deficit emerges.

An increase in foreign interest payments, holding constant the current account balance, has just the opposite effect. To generate the trade surplus that is implied by the higher foreign interest payments, domestic expenditure must decline in relation to income. Thus, the demand curve DD shifts down and to the left, leading in equilibrium to a reduction in the relative price of nontraded goods, that is, a depreciation of the real exchange rate. Foreign borrowing, therefore, has an important influence on the real exchange rate in both the short and the long run, an influence that we will want to bear in mind. In the short run, when the foreign borrowing serves to finance consumption expenditure in excess of income, the demand curve DD is shifted up and to the right; consumption is high, and the real exchange rate appreciates. Then, when expenditure is brought back into line with income to eliminate the current account deficit that corresponds to the foreign borrowing, the demand curve shifts down and to the left. It must actually shift further to the left than where it would have been in the absence of the temporary period of foreign borrowing, because the debt that was accumulated during the consumption binge must be serviced. Thus, we see that a transitory episode of foreign borrowing leads in the long run to the real-exchange-rate depreciation arising from the need to service the associated accumulation of foreign debt.

We are now ready to discuss the optimal response of foreign borrowing to a change in the terms of trade. The analysis is complicated by the fact that changes in the terms of trade have both income and relative price effects. The income effects were emphasized above; when the terms of trade improve, domestic income rises and consumers demand more of both the nontraded good and the imported consumption good. This income effect means that the demand curve *DD* shifts upward when the terms of trade improve and downward when they decline. However, an improvement in the terms of trade also makes imported consumption goods less expensive in relation to nontraded goods at any given relative price of exports and nontradables. This change in relative prices leads to substitution of the imported good for the now more expensive nontraded good. The income effect conflicts with the substitution effect; which effect will dominate depends on the degree of substitutability between the imported good and the nontraded consumption good. The most plausible supposition is that imported and nontraded goods are relatively poor substitutes in most developing economies, so this discussion will consider the case in which income effects dominate.

When income effects dominate, an improvement in the terms of trade leads to increased demand for the nontraded good. Thus, the demand curve *DD* shifts up and to the right as in figure 8-3, and a new short-run equilibrium is reached at point *B*. Thus, we see that if we maintain balance in the current account, an improvement in the terms of trade leads in equilibrium to an appreciation of the real exchange rate, whereas a deterioration of the terms of trade leads to a depreciation of the real exchange rate.

The short-run equilibrium point *B* is above the long-run supply curve, *LL*. Because the relative price of nontraded goods is higher in this short-run equilibrium than is consistent with long-run equilibrium, factors of production will gradually move from the tradables sector into the nontradables sector. This shifts the short-run supply schedule, *SS*, gradually to the right, and the economy's equilibrium moves gradually along the demand schedule *DD'* until a new long-run equilibrium is reached at point *C*, on the long-run supply schedule.

Thus, in the absence of foreign borrowing, an improvement in the terms of trade leads in equilibrium to real-exchange-rate *ap*preciation, whereas a deterioration in the terms of trade leads to real-exchange-rate *de*preciation. Because production responds only gradually, the change in relative prices may be dramatic in the short run, but over time, as production gradually responds, the exchange rate appreciation is partially reversed. Thus real-exchange-rate "overshooting" occurs in response to a change in the terms of trade, not because price rigidities occur or markets fail, but because production adjusts only gradually to changes in relative prices.

IMPLICATIONS FOR OPTIMAL FOREIGN BORROWING. The foregoing analysis assumed that foreign borrowing would not respond to the change in the terms of trade and the attendant fluctuations in relative prices. But the analysis is interesting because it reveals an additional motivation for foreign borrowing in response to changes in the terms of trade. During the transition from the short-run equilibrium, *B*, to the long-run equilibrium, *C*, the relative price of nontraded goods is gradually declining. As Dornbusch (1983) points out in a slightly different context, this gradual decline in the relative price of nontraded goods corresponds to an increase in the rate of interest, which makes it desirable for consumers to consume less in the short run in return for higher consumption in the future. This increase in savings translates in this model into a current account surplus. Thus, a permanent improvement in the terms of trade should be met with a transitory current account surplus, whereas a deterioration of the terms of trade should be met with a transitory period of foreign borrowing.

An important implication of the optimal foreign lending and borrowing just described is that they tend to dampen the real-exchange-rate overshooting that would otherwise occur. The reason for this is that borrowing, and therefore increasing spending, is desirable when the relative price of nontradables is low; foreign borrowing tends to raise the prices of nontradables. Similarly, it is optimal to save when the relative price of nontradables is transitorily high, which tends to lower the prices of nontradables compared with what they would be in the absence of the foreign lending. We see, therefore, that one result of foreign borrowing, when it is intelligently conceived and executed, is to attenuate the otherwise wild fluctuations in relative prices that might arise in the aftermath of a major change in the terms of trade.

It is also possible to show that optimal foreign borrowing tends to reduce the speed with which the economy adjusts to a change in the terms of trade. This happens exactly because the foreign lending and borrowing reduce the response of the real exchange rate to a given change in the terms of trade. This reduction in the speed with which the economy adjusts to a change in the terms of trade should not be considered a drawback of the foreign lending; instead, it is an important advantage. This is because adjusting production is costly, and the cost rises the faster the adjustment is undertaken. If an improvement in the terms of trade is met with a temporary current account surplus, the price of nontradables increases by less than it otherwise would, the speed with which resources move into the nontradables sector is reduced, and the waste and costly mistakes of excessively rapid adjustment are avoided.

Of course, an excessive amount of foreign borrowing could eliminate—for as long as the borrowing was sustainable—the real-exchange-rate depreciation that is the equilibrium response to a change in the terms of trade. In doing so it would likewise eliminate the incentives for the economy to adjust to a change in the terms of trade. We will argue that such overborrowing was one consequence of the policies the Nigerian authorities followed after petroleum prices declined in the early 1980s.

Investment

Up to now we have assumed that savings that are a result of changes in the terms of trade should be channeled into foreign investments by running current account surpluses. Changes in the terms of trade may also, however, alter incentives for domestic investment, which will have an effect on the optimal response of foreign borrowing. Although a plausible assumption is that an improvement in the terms of trade would lead to an increase in domestic investment, little theoretical justification exists for this view if one maintains the assumption of perfect international capital markets. In this case, the impact of a change in the terms of trade on the optimal rate of domestic investment depends, among other things, on the technology with which investment goods are produced and installed and on differences in factor intensities in the goods-producing sectors.

If international capital markets are imperfect, however, domestic investment in most developing countries will be constrained by low domestic saving. A presumption then arises that increases in the terms of trade that generate increases in domestic saving should lead to an increase in domestic investment as well.[5] Two questions then arise. First, of the savings generated by an improvement in the terms of trade, how much should be invested abroad and how much should be invested in the domestic capital stock? Second, in what sectors should the investment take place?

The answer to the first question depends largely on the time horizon that we consider. Just as adjusting the structure of production very rapidly is costly, so is making very rapid additions to the capital stock. The more frenetic the rate of investment, the more likely that bottlenecks will result in delay and waste and that costly mistakes will be made. These concerns are all the more important in developing countries such as Nigeria, in which the economic infrastructure is primitive and managerial and entrepreneurial resources are scarce. Thus it may pay first to divert a large share of the savings generated by an improvement in the terms of trade into the accumulation of foreign assets. These foreign assets can then be used to finance capital accumulation at a more moderate, and presumably less wasteful, pace.

The sectoral allocation of domestic investments is an equally important issue. We noted above that an improvement in the terms of trade will, assuming that income effects are dominant, lead to an increase in the relative price of nontraded goods. We argued that this would lead to a gradual movement of factors of production from the tradables sector into the nontradables sector. Similarly, the real appreciation generated by the change in the terms of trade is a signal of the desirability of allocating a substantial share of domestic investment into the nontradables sector. This makes sense: as an economy grows richer, the country's population will naturally wish to consume more of both internationally traded goods and domestically produced, nontradable goods and services. The increase in export earnings caused by an improvement in the terms of trade makes it possible to import more of the internationally traded goods, but increased production of the nontraded goods and services requires an increase in the amount of productive resources that are devoted to the production of those goods.

Investment is, of course, a forward-looking process, depending not only on the current economic environment but also on expected future conditions. One implication of this is that the extent to which investment should be biased toward the nontradables sector depends on how long the improvement in the terms of trade is expected to last. If the improvement is predicted to be permanent, one can expect that the increase in the demand for nontradables will also be permanent. Then placing a substantial portion of domestic investments into the nontradables sector may make sense. If the improvement in the terms of trade is expected to last for only a short time, it may be more logical to place a larger share of domestic investments in the tradables sector. This is because when the improvement in the terms of trade comes to an end, the demand for nontraded goods will decline toward where it was before the transitory improvement in the terms of trade. Therefore, having in place a large capital stock devoted to production of nontradables will not be desirable.

Uncertainty

In theory we can draw sharp distinctions between temporary and permanent changes in the terms of trade and derive the appropriate response for changes of either kind. In the real world, however, we do not know for certain whether a change in the terms of trade will be permanent or temporary. While we can confidently expect some disturbances, for example, weather-related ones, to be transitory, for many changes in the terms of trade it is simply impossible to know whether the terms of trade will revert fairly soon to their original level, remain at the new level indefinitely, or even move farther in the same direction as the previous change. This uncertainty is particularly salient for the changes in petroleum prices that buffeted the world economy in the 1970s and 1980s. Nobody knew in 1974 if OPEC would be able to continue extracting the monopoly rents it was then enjoying. Certainly nobody forecast the Iranian revolution or predicted its impact on oil prices. Finally, the collapse in oil prices after 1981 was a shock to almost every informed observer of the world oil market.

The theoretical literature has not emphasized the uncertainty of the terms of trade as much as it should have. Although this is not the place for a complete treatment, the implications of uncertainty are important enough to warrant at least some discussion. Here we will consider the case for a conservative policy response when there is substantial uncertainty about future movements in the terms of trade.

In this context, the first important meaning of "conservative" concerns the level of saving and consumption. The theoretical basis of recommending conservative policies is the substantial literature on "precautionary" motives for saving. When there is uncertainty about future income, the appropriate generalization of the dictum to smooth consumption is to plan on a consumption path that sets the marginal utility of consumption today equal to the expected marginal utility of consumption tomorrow. Under certainty, and assuming that tastes don't change over time, this is the same as setting consumption today equal to consumption tomorrow. But when there is uncertainty, it generally pays to forgo some consumption in the present in exchange for somewhat higher consumption in the future.[6] This is the phenomenon of "precautionary savings."

The practical importance of precautionary savings is to provide a justification for policies that aim for higher saving than would be appropriate if individuals or policymakers could be certain that the terms of trade will evolve as expected. In essence, authorities should set aside income today to ensure against a bad outcome in the future.

There is a second sense in which policies should respond conservatively to changes in the terms of trade. As stressed above, in many cases the appropriate response is sensitive to whether the change is permanent or transitory. If the improvement in the terms of trade is permanent, then it may be appropriate to expand greatly the nontradables sector. If the improvement is only temporary, investing in the tradables sector is more appropriate. If one is unsure whether the change in the terms of trade is permanent or transitory, the possibility exists that one will invest in the wrong sector. This causes no problems if investments can easily be moved between sectors, but if reversing investment decisions is very costly or impossible, then one may be stuck with the bad decision for a long time.

Recently a number of authors have pointed out that it may make sense to wait until some of the uncertainty about, for example, whether a change in the terms of trade will soon be reversed has been resolved (see, among others, Dixit 1989; McDonald and Siegel 1986). By accumulating foreign assets instead of investing domestically, it may be possible to reduce the probability of making costly mistakes in the allocation of domestic investments. Then, when the uncertainty is at least partially resolved, it will be possible to use the accumulated foreign assets to finance domestic investments.

In short, uncertainty about the terms of trade seems to support policies that encourage high savings, protect the economy against outcomes that are worse than expected, and place domestic savings in liquid form to avoid locking the economy into mistakes that are very costly or impossible to undo. In practice, this means larger current account surpluses in response to terms of trade improvements than would be desirable under certainty, and smaller deficits in response to a deterioration of the terms of trade.

Summary

Adjustment to a deterioration in the terms of trade comprises a reduction in aggregate expenditure and, under plausible assumptions, a depreciation of the real exchange rate. This depreciation will, in general, lead to shrinkage of the nontraded goods sector and a concomitant expansion of the tradables sector. An improvement in the terms of trade will generally imply an appreciation in the real exchange rate, which will lead to an expansion of the nontradables sector and a shrinkage of the tradables sector. When considering policy responses, the first and most important distinction is between disturbances expected to be permanent and those expected to be transitory. The more persistent the disturbance, the more rapid and complete the adjustment of both expenditure and production should be. This rule is summarized in the adage "finance transitory disturbances and adjust to permanent disturbances."

This advice must be qualified, however, when an economy responds slowly to changes in the economic environment. In particular, two reasons may make it sensible to engage in foreign borrowing in the immediate aftermath of a permanent deterioration in the terms of trade. First, as the economy gradually adjusts to the terms of trade disturbance, income will rise. It makes sense to borrow against that higher future income to raise consumption today. Thus, foreign borrowing may legitimately be considered to finance costly adjustment to permanent, as well as transitory, disturbances. Second, real exchange rates will fluctuate more in the short run than in the long run, because short-run supply elasticities are lower than long-run elasticities. Borrowing in response to a deterioration in the terms of trade, and running current account surpluses after an improvement, attenuates this overshooting of the real exchange rate. In doing so, it prevents what would otherwise be an excessively rapid adjustment of the real economy to the terms of trade disturbance.

While pointing out the impact of optimal foreign borrowing, this discussion incidentally brings out some implications of excessive reliance on foreign borrowing to finance a deterioration in the terms of trade. First, a high rate of foreign borrowing is associated with an overvaluation of the real exchange rate, and the overvaluation draws resources from the tradables sector, where they belong, into the nontradables. Thus, borrowing too much in the wake of a deterioration in the terms of trade will lead to a suboptimal rate of adjustment of the production sector to the terms of trade disturbance. Second, foreign borrowing cannot persist indefinitely, and when the current account is eventually corrected, the trade balance will have to improve by even more than it would have in the absence of the excessive foreign borrowing, because interest on the accumulated foreign debt will have to be serviced. This will require a greater depreciation of the real exchange rate than would have been necessary in the absence of the excessive foreign borrowing. The result will be a lower standard of living than would otherwise have been possible.

An even more fundamental qualification of the traditional policy advice derives from the simple fact that one cannot know in advance whether a change in the terms of trade (or any other change in the external environment) is transitory or permanent, or will perhaps be augmented by a subsequent move in the same direction. In the face of such uncertainty, a case can be made for policies that sacrifice consumption in the present to guard against highly adverse outcomes in the future.

Economic Policy: Money, Exchange Rates, and the Budget

In the previous section we focused on a small barter economy characterized by continuous market clearing and populated by residents with rational expectations and full access to a perfect world capital market. The purpose of that focus was to develop normative guidelines for the management of a terms of trade disturbance. We emphasized the appropriate response of foreign borrowing, although we also discussed other aspects of the adjustment process. In a sense, we may think of the previous section as defining the "external balance" toward which the authorities should steer their economies.

This earlier analysis is, however, an important step away from a serious discussion of economic policy. First, real economies are monetary, and it is through monetary and exchange rate policy that governments exert much of their influence over the macroeconomy. Second, it is misleading to think of a government determining policy for foreign borrowing and then letting expenditure and relative prices adjust to the policy. Instead, governments pursue monetary, fiscal, and regulatory policies, and the level of foreign lending or borrowing is determined as one part of the economy's equilibrium. If a government wishes to maintain the "external balance" as defined in the previous section, it must set its monetary and exchange rate policies accordingly. The purpose of this section is to clarify the link between the government's policy instruments and macroeconomic outcomes. We do so in the context of a simple monetary extension of the previous model.

Consider a small economy, very similar to the one discussed in the previous section, in which three goods are produced. Oil is produced in some exogenously given amount, Q_o, and sold on world oil markets at an exogenously given price, P_o, in terms of a second tradable good, which we label, as before, "manufactures."[7] Manufactures are, in equilibrium, imported, so the price of oil, P_o, is the terms of trade. In addition to manufactures, the economy produces nontraded goods, which in the case of Nigeria include services, many agricultural crops, and those parts of the manufacturing sector that are protected by quotas or prohibitive tariffs and face no direct foreign competition.

As discussed in the previous section, production of the tradable good and the nontradable good depends on their relative prices:

$$Q_M = Q_M(E/P_N)$$

$$Q_N = Q_N(E/P_N)$$

Production of manufactures (Q_M) is increasing in the real exchange rate, defined here as the nominal exchange rate (E) divided by the domestic currency price of the nontraded good (P_N), and production of nontradables (Q_N) is decreasing in the real exchange rate.

As in Nigeria, the government collects all the revenue from petroleum production. In addition, it collects tax revenue from the domestic private sector of amount T in terms of the nontraded good. The government spends on the nontraded good and manufactures and must pay interest on the outstanding foreign debt. We define the real government deficit as the amount by which it must increase its monetary and debt obligations to the rest of the world. This is equal to:

$$\text{RDef} = [G_N + (E/P_N)G_M + rD] - [EP_oQ_o/P_N + T + \pi m]$$

The first term in brackets is total government expenditure, which includes spending on the nontradable, the non-oil tradable, and real interest obligations on the outstanding government debt, rD. The second term in brackets is total revenue, which includes revenue from the sale of petroleum, taxes levied on the domestic population, and inflation tax revenue, πm. Here π is the rate of inflation for the prices of nontraded goods, and m is the supply of high-powered money deflated by the price of nontraded goods. This equation emphasizes the direct link between the terms of trade and the government budget; in Nigeria, for example, roughly 75 percent of government revenue comes from the oil sector. It also emphasizes the fiscal dimension of inflation. Inflation effectively cancels the government's monetary liabilities to the private sector, thereby effecting a transfer of wealth from the private to the public sector. It constitutes a tax of the private sector that is just as real as a profits tax or import tariff, and, as we will see later, recourse to the inflation tax is an important part of Nigeria's recent economic history.

The government budget deficit must be financed either by emitting interest-bearing debt or by issuing money. Although the Nigerian government does borrow, both from foreigners and domestically, it also tends to respond to budgetary imbalances by issuing money. Thus, a loose but important budgetary link exists between the terms of trade and the domestic money supply, which is exactly the reverse of the relationship under a "classical" fixed-exchange-rate regime. Under a classical fixed-exchange-rate system, defined here as a system in which domestic authorities allow the money supply to adjust automatically in response to changes in foreign reserves, a deterioration in the terms of trade would lead to reserve outflows, which would, in turn, reduce the domestic money supply. In Nigeria, however, it would be more realistic to suppose that the fiscal deficit generated by the terms of trade deterioration would lead, at least in the short run, to an increase in the money supply, because the authorities use the printing press to finance the fiscal deficits.[8]

Our second departure from the last section is to abandon the assumption that consumers operate in a world of perfect foresight and frictionless capital markets and to assume that private expenditure is determined entirely by current income and wealth. This assumption of completely myopic behavior is certainly as much a caricature of the world as was the extremely rational behavior modeled above.[9] Remembering that the government owns the oil sector, we see that income in the private sector is equal to the value of domestic production of manufactures and nontradables:

$$Y = Q_M(E/P_N) + Q_N$$

This measure of income is, in turn, a function of the real exchange rate. We can therefore write demand for tradables and nontradables as a function of the real exchange rate, domestic taxes, and real cash balances:

$$C_N = C_N [E/P_N, Y(E/P_N) - T, M/P_N]$$

$$C_M = C_M [E/P_N, Y(E/P_N) - T, M/P_N]$$

We will assume that private demand for both goods is increasing in disposable income and therefore decreasing in the level of domestic taxation, T. Demand for the nontradable is assumed to be increasing in the real exchange rate, E/P_N, because an increase in the relative price of manufactures creates an incentive for consumers to substitute in favor of nontradables. Similarly, we expect the demand for tradables to be decreasing in the real exchange rate. Finally, we assume that demand for both the tradable and the nontradable is an increasing function of the stock of real money balances held by the public. There are many explanations for why increases in money lead to increases in domestic demand, and they all boil down to reduced forms that look more or less like the equations above.

Equilibrium in the goods market requires that production of nontradables be equal to domestic demand for nontradables; this condition is expressed in equation 8-3:

(8-3) $$Q_N(E/P_N) = C_N (E/P_N, T, M/P_N) + G_N$$

Notice that the goods-market equilibrium depends on the fiscal variables (specifically, the level of taxes and the government's purchases of nontraded goods), monetary variables, the exchange rate, and the money supply. Note also that the equilibrium condition (equation 8-3) depends only on "real" quantities. In particular, a 10 percent increase in the money supply accompanied by a 10 percent increase in the price of nontraded goods will leave the equilibrium condition unaffected if there is at the same time a 10 percent devaluation of the nominal exchange rate.

Second, we note that the economy's current account can be expressed as total income (public and private) less total expenditure (public and private). Expenditure includes not only expenditure on goods but also interest payments on foreign debt, D. Imposing equilibrium in the market for nontraded goods, this can be written:

(8-4) $CA = P_oQ_o + Q_M (E/P_N) - C_M(E/P_N, T, M/P_N) - G_M - rD$

In our model, the money supply, the exchange rate, and fiscal variables are given by government policy.

Monetary Policy, Exchange Rates, and External Balance

We consider first a change in monetary policy. We begin in a position of internal and external balance, when the economy is disturbed by an expansion of the domestic money supply. As noted above, both equations 8-3 and 8-4 depend only on relative prices and real money balances. Thus, if both the exchange rate and the relative price of nontraded goods increase in proportion to the increase in the money supply, the economy remains in internal and external balance.

The exchange rate is usually not adjusted immediately, however. As long as it is held fixed, the relative price of nontraded goods increases, but not by as much as the increase in the money supply. Therefore, real money balances increase. When the nominal exchange rate is not changed, the increase in the price of nontraded goods implies an appreciation in the real exchange rate. This appreciation, with the increase in real balances, leads to an increase in demand and a reduction in the supply of traded goods. The increase of demand over supply in turn implies an external deficit. The counterpart of the current account deficit is a reduction in private sector saving associated with the expenditure effects of high real balances.

To defend the nominal exchange rate in the face of the external deficits generated by the expansionary monetary policy, the central bank has to intervene in foreign exchange markets. Thus the external deficits generated by expansionary monetary policy lead to reductions in the central bank's international reserves. If the central bank runs out of foreign exchange, the external deficits associated with the expansionary monetary policy become impossible to finance, and the exchange rate has to be devalued. When this happens, the economy moves to a new equilibrium, in which the domestic currency prices of both the traded good and the nontraded good have increased in proportion to the rise in the money supply.

Two points about devaluation warrant some emphasis. First, we see here the inflationary cost of devaluation; however, it is not the devaluation itself that bears responsibility for the inflation, but rather the expansionary monetary policy that made the devaluation necessary. Second, failure to devalue after a monetary expansion delays much of the inflation and in doing so makes future devaluation and inflation predictable. This expectation of devaluation induces domestic residents to try to protect their wealth by obtaining foreign assets, thereby causing a deterioration of the balance of payments not only on the current account but also on the capital account. We shall see that, although Nigeria's external deficits were primarily the result of current account transactions rather than capital flight, the deficits were aggravated by outflows on the current account when people realized that devaluation was in the offing.

Fiscal Policy and the External Equilibrium

We can quickly summarize the effects of fiscal policy. Consider, for example, an increase in domestic taxes or, equivalently, a reduction in government transfers to the private sector. At given relative prices, these changes reduce private sector demand for both the traded and the nontraded good. If the nominal exchange rate is held fixed, the economy moves to a point at which the domestic price level has fallen, the real exchange rate has depreciated, and the current account has moved into surplus.

Thus governments can use contractionary fiscal policy to eliminate an external deficit, but such a policy does not substitute for an appreciation in the real exchange rate. Real depreciation is required because, if relative prices do not change, the fiscal contraction leads to an excess supply of nontraded goods, which leads, in turn, to unemployment. Real depreciation induces firms in the tradables sector to hire labor that has been released from the nontradables sector, thus establishing equilibrium for domestically produced goods and at the same time increasing the size of the current account surplus generated by the fiscal contraction.

Changes in government spending have effects similar to changes in government taxes, except that one needs to specify whether spending on the nontradable or the tradable has changed. Reductions in spending on the nontradable reduce domestic demand. At the original exchange rate and price of nontraded goods, an excess supply of nontradables emerges. Elimination of this excess supply requires a reduction in the price of nontraded goods, that is, a real-exchange-rate depreciation that coaxes resources from the nontradables sector into the tradables sector. The expansion in output of tradables leads to a trade surplus.

Thus reduced government spending leads to an increase in the trade surplus, even if the spending reduction falls on domestic goods.

The effect, however, is an indirect one that operates through an induced decline in the price of nontraded goods. If relative prices take some time to decline, then the immediate effect of the spending reduction may be to generate an excess supply of domestically produced goods and a transitory period of higher unemployment. Eventually the unemployment goes away, but at the expense of a depreciated real exchange rate.

The government can avoid these effects by concentrating spending reductions, to the extent possible, on internationally traded, as opposed to nontraded, goods. The domestic equilibrium is unchanged, but a current account surplus emerges. There are, however, limits to the wisdom and the feasibility of such a policy. For the government as well as the private sector, traded goods are imperfect substitutes for nontraded goods. Consider the following particularly relevant example. In many developing economies, investment is a very import-intensive activity; such economies simply do not produce many of the required capital goods. During an attempt to eliminate an ongoing fiscal and external deficit, governments are often tempted to cut investment spending, not only because such reductions have a smaller impact on current standards of living but also because investment spending is import-intensive, which means that a given improvement in the current account can be achieved with a smaller required adjustment in the market for domestic goods. Although, as discussed in the first section, there may be good reasons why a government should meet a deterioration in the terms of trade with a reduction in investment spending, a desire to postpone required adjustments in labor and product markets is probably not one of them.

The Terms of Trade in a Monetary Economy

Finally, let us analyze an exogenous change in the terms of trade. Once again, we imagine that an economy that begins in a position of internal and external balance is disturbed by an adverse movement in the terms of trade. At the initial equilibrium prices, the external accounts have now moved into deficit. Reestablishing external balance requires depreciation. On the assumption, however, that government spending does not respond immediately, the short-run domestic equilibrium remains but is now accompanied by external deficits. The domestic counterpart of this external deficit is a domestic fiscal deficit, caused by the loss of government export revenue.

In the first section we discovered several circumstances under which a deterioration in the terms of trade should be met with a transitory period of foreign borrowing. If, however, consumers are as myopic or constrained in capital markets as we have assumed in this section, there are strong grounds for presuming that they will adjust their expenditure insufficiently and therefore that the current account deficit that emerges will be undesirably large. Elimination of the external deficit requires some combination of fiscal contraction, monetary contraction, and nominal exchange rate depreciation. The above discussion of the separate instruments can be applied directly to the problem of eliminating the deficit generated by the terms of trade deterioration.

Case Study: Nigeria

In this section we apply the principles outlined earlier to a discussion of Nigeria's recent economic history, which divides naturally into several subperiods. We begin with a very brief discussion of Nigeria's economic development before the 1973 oil boom. It was during the period between Independence in 1960 and the 1973 oil shock that some of the economy's weaknesses first appeared. We then turn to a discussion of the five-year period following the first of the two major increases in oil prices that rocked the world economy in the 1970s and 1980s. Shortcomings in the response to that price increase were revealed when oil markets began to soften in 1978 and early 1979.

In 1980 the Nigerian authorities were saved by the second round of oil price increases that followed upon the supply disruptions associated with the Iranian revolution and the Iran-Iraq war. Though sharp, this increase in oil prices was more short-lived than the earlier disturbance, and by 1981 oil markets had begun to weaken considerably. They found a plateau during 1982–85, when Nigeria's external position was almost, though not quite, as favorable as it had been during the 1973–79 period. The last stage in the oil cycle began in 1986, when the bottom fell out of the oil market.

We break the period since 1979 into two stages, distinguished not by conditions in the oil market but rather by Nigeria's policy response to those conditions. The first period, 1980–83, was a period of almost lurid fiscal and monetary excess, carried out essentially with no regard for budgetary realities. The legacy of this period continues to haunt attempts to stabilize the Nigerian economy today. The second period, 1984 to the present, was one in which the government reversed those fiscal and monetary excesses—at first tentatively, then more forcefully during Babangida's regime.

Act 1: The Formation of the Oil Economy

During the period leading up to the first oil shock, Nigeria's economic record was quite favorable. If the IMF data are to be believed, Nigeria's economy grew 9 percent a year during the 1950s and about 5.5 percent a year during the first twelve years after Independence—this despite the disruptions caused by the four-year civil war of 1967–70.

Up until about 1960 agriculture dominated the Nigerian economy. Farming of domestic crops was the main occupation, and domestic agriculture was supplemented by a vigorous export-oriented agricultural sector. Nigeria was for many years a dominant producer of cocoa, palm products, and other tropical agricultural products.

Upon Independence in 1960, a new political class, with a new set of priorities, obtained control of the government (see Bienen 1983 and Kirk-Greene and Rimmer 1981 for a discussion of the political attitudes of the Nigerian authorities). There was a strong and understandable desire to see the benefits of development directed toward Nigerians and away from the colonial elite, and development was understood above all to entail industrialization. In practice, these priorities led to the development of a highly interventionist state that used its power to protect local producers by subsidization, protection from foreign competition in commodity markets, and, in the "Nigerianization" program of the 1970s, protection in factor markets.

The interventions had two effects that concern us here. First, protection of urban manufacturing led to the development of an inefficient manufacturing sector that relied highly on imported intermediate goods. The external resources that fueled this sector could come only from the oil sector, for during the 1960s and 1970s, policymakers' neglect of the agricultural sector had led to a dramatic shrinkage of Nigeria's once robust agricultural exports (see table 8-2).

By 1972 production of most major export crops had shrunk dramatically. This was partly because of the ravages of the civil war. It was

Table 8-2. Traditional Exports from Nigeria, 1964–78

(thousands of tons)

Crop	1964–66	1970–72	1976–78
Cocoa beans	218	232	193
Groundnuts	554	179	1
Groundnut oil	95	57	..
Palm kernels	409	213	172
Palm oil	145	10	2
Rubber	71	51	31
Raw cotton	21	17	4
Lumber	594[a]	220[a]	14[a]

.. Negligible.

a. Thousands of cubic meters.

Source: Kirk-Greene and Rimmer (1981).

in part a natural response to the increase in oil wealth during the 1960s, as factors of production were pulled out of the non-oil export sector and put into domestic crop production. But the decline of export agriculture was also caused by a tendency for government commodity boards, ostensibly created to stabilize crop prices, to tax farmers by paying them substantially less than the world price. The effect of this policy was the creation of an economy that was excessively reliant on petroleum, not only to pay for imported consumption goods but also to keep the manufacturing sector running. The risks inherent in this policy would become apparent in the crisis of 1981–84.

The major development in Nigeria during the 1960s was the exploitation of its petroleum deposits. Production began in 1958 and by 1966 had reached 418,000 barrels a day. By 1970 production exceeded 1 million barrels a day and in 1973 slightly more than 2 million barrels a day, roughly equal to the present capacity. Not only was the quantity produced increasing gradually, but so was the price in the period leading up to the first oil shock, and by 1973 petroleum revenues accounted for almost 85 percent of Nigeria's exports, 15 percent of GDP, and roughly 60 percent of federal government revenue.

Until 1972 the Nigerian authorities followed relatively restrained financial policies. There was a bout of wartime deficit finance in the late 1960s, but by 1971 the deficits had vanished. Between 1960 and 1972 consumer price inflation averaged about 5 percent a year, close enough to that of Nigeria's major trading partners to make an exchange rate of $1.40 to the naira sustainable from 1960 to 1972.[10] Relatively minor current account deficits were largely financed by foreign investment, and the government's internal and external indebtedness was low.

Act 2: The First Oil Boom, 1972–78

Petroleum prices, like most commodity prices, had followed a generally rising trend during the late 1960s. Then, following an Arab embargo of oil exports to countries deemed supportive of Israel, the world price of oil tripled almost overnight. As table 8-3 and figure 8-4 indicate, Nigeria's terms of trade increased dramatically in 1974.

The first column of table 8-3 gives the World Bank's measure of the terms of trade, which tripled between 1973 and 1974. The second column shows the U.S. dollar value of Nigeria's exports. To facilitate historical comparisons, the third column gives the value of Nigerian exports in real terms, in which the deflator is the price of U.S. industrial goods.[11] We see that the purchasing power of Nigeria's exports doubled in 1974 to almost 20 billion 1988 dollars.

Table 8-3. Terms of Trade and International Payments, Nigeria, 1970–88

(millions of 1988 dollars)

Year	Terms of Trade (1)	Exports (2)	Exports (3)	Current account (4)	International reserves (5)	Foreign debt (6)
1970	23.4	1,248	3,621	−368	202	567
1971	19.8	1,889	5,303	−406	408	651
1972	18.9	2,184	5,862	−342	355	732
1973	22.3	3,607	8,571	−8	559	1,205
1974	65.3	9,698	19,396	4,987	5,602	1,274
1975	57.7	8,329	15,245	42	5,586	1,143
1976	62.7	10,122	17,684	−357	5,180	906
1977	64.0	12,431	20,475	−1,018	4,232	3,146
1978	57.3	10,508	16,056	−3,785	1,887	5,091
1979	70.7	16,774	22,776	1,372	5,548	6,235
1980	100.0	25,741	30,617	5,104	10,235	8,888
1981	108.7	17,961	19,587	−6,220	3,895	12,039
1982	100.9	12,088	12,924	−7,241	1,613	12,908
1983	96.6	10,309	10,887	−4,337	990	18,586
1984	97.2	11,827	12,192	114	1,462	18,664
1985	89.8	13,369	13,850	2,623	1,667	19,522
1986	44.4	6,599	7,041	371	1,081	24,470
1987	49.1	7,702	8,011	362	1,165	28,714
1988	—	7,419	7,419	−555	651	—

— Not available.

Source: IMF (various issues); World Bank (1989a, 1989b).

To put this disturbance into some sort of perspective, note that the $6 billion increase in the value of Nigeria's exports amounted to about ₦ 4 billion, which was, in turn, more than one-fifth of the 1974 Nigerian GDP. The disturbance was even more significant for the primary recipient of the price increase, the Nigerian government. Table 8-4 shows the impact of the oil price increase on the Nigerian government's budget.

With the increase in the value of its oil taxes, the government's fiscal situation was transformed. Petroleum taxes were about 8 percent of GDP in the 1972/73 fiscal year, rising to 9 percent in 1973/74 and 20 percent in 1974/75. There they remained until 1978. In 1974 the government was simply unable to adjust spending rapidly enough to keep up with the growth in revenue. Some increase in spending occurred, but not enough to prevent the emergence of a large fiscal surplus.

The counterpart of this fiscal surplus was a movement of the economy as a whole into surplus compared with the rest of the world. Table 8-5 and figure 8-5 show that in 1974, Nigeria swung into a surplus on the current account of its international payments. Combined with

Figure 8-4. Nigeria's Terms of Trade, 1966-87

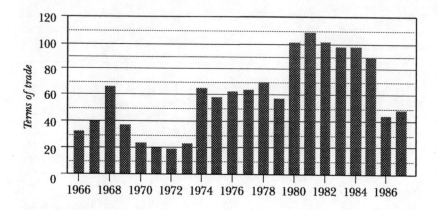

Source: World Bank data.

some net capital inflows, Nigeria ended 1974 with an increase in international reserves of more than $5 billion.

As the end of 1974 approached, the Nigerian government faced all the uncertainties and decisions that were discussed earlier in this essay. The government was unclear whether the change in the terms of trade would be permanent or transitory. It had to decide whether to accumulate more foreign reserves or, instead, spend the higher income. If the income should be spent, was investment or consumption the road to take? If invested, which sectors should receive the resources?

Table 8-4. Oil Receipts and the Fiscal Situation, Nigeria, 1970-1978/79

(percentage of GDP)

Fiscal year	Oil receipts	Spending less other receipts	Fiscal balance	
1970/71	2.20	3.9	−1.6	−119[a]
1971/72	5.60	5.2	0.4	36[a]
1972/73	8.30	9.2	−0.9	−83[a]
1973/74	9.10	7.4	1.7	189[a]
1974/75	20.00	13.3	6.7	1,248[a]
1975/76	20.20	27.0	−6.8	−1,436[a]
1976/77	19.80	26.7	−6.9	−1,870[a]
1977/78	19.10	25.8	−6.7	−2,134[a]
1978/79	13.75	17.3	−3.5	−1,851[a]

a. Millions of nairas.
Source: Pinto (1986).

Table 8-5. International Trade and Payments, Nigeria, 1972–78

(billions of dollars)

Year	Trade balance	Other current account	Current account balance	Net capital movements	Overall balance
1972	0.82	−1.16	−0.34	0.48	0.14
1973	1.89	−1.90	−0.01	0.13	0.12
1974	7.22	−2.32	4.90	0.22	5.12
1975	2.85	−2.80	0.05	0.14	−0.02
1976	2.64	−3.00	−0.36	−0.02	−0.41
1977	2.71	−3.73	−1.02	0.19	−0.95
1978	−1.18	−2.61	−3.79	1.67	−2.34

Source: IMF (various issues).

The answers arrived very quickly. Driven by a political imperative to spend the oil income quickly, the government adjusted expenditure to the new, higher level by 1975. As table 8-4 indicates, by that year the federal budget had moved from surplus to a substantial deficit. This deficit persisted at almost 7 percent of GDP for the next three years. The fiscal authorities chose, implicitly or explicitly, to act as though the improvement in the terms of trade was permanent and to disregard the risk of a future reversal of the current, favorable trends.

The composition of government expenditure, especially in the early years, was fairly heavily weighted toward investment. Current government expenditure grew rapidly, reflecting increases in public sector wages,[12] subsidization of utility prices, and increased spending

Figure 8-5. Current Account, Nigeria, 1966–88

(billions of dollars)

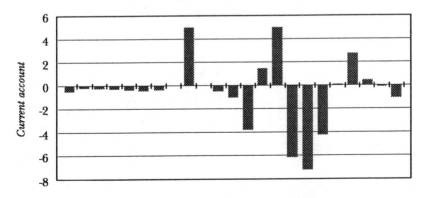

Source: IMF (various issues).

on education, public health, and other social programs. Although current expenditure between 1973 and 1976 rose by a factor of about 3.5, capital expenditure rose by a factor of more than 9. Figure 8-6 shows that real gross investment more than doubled between 1973 and 1977; most, but not all, of this increase was attributable to the public sector.

The response of investment spending is the bright spot of Nigeria's economic management. Saving some fraction of the income gains from a terms of trade improvement is, we argued earlier, a sensible policy when the terms of trade might return to their original level. It is extremely implausible that Nigeria did not have sufficient viable projects with returns higher than the rate of interest on foreign assets. From that perspective, investing domestic savings in domestic capital made sense. But did the Nigerian authorities give themselves enough time to find the right projects and to implement the investments in a reasonably efficient manner? There are strong grounds to suspect that the answer is no. When the magnitude of the petroleum windfall became clear, the military government urged the administra-

Figure 8-6. Gross Investment, Nigeria, 1967–87

(billions of 1980 naira)

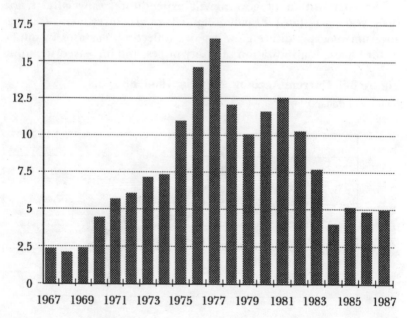

Source: IMF (various issues).

tors simply to scale up expenditure on high-priority sectors such as transportation and education. Without the executive capacity to monitor and execute the rapidly growing public investments, the projects were inevitably marred by unnecessary waste and fraud. A notorious example is the cement scandal of 1976 when, as a result of corrupt practices, more than 400 ships carrying imported cement tied up the harbor at Lagos for many expensive months. Furthermore, the concentration of petroleum wealth in the hands of the government provided a degree of freedom for bureaucratically attractive but uneconomical investments, of which the inevitable steel complex under construction at Udoja is a particularly expensive example.

There are also grounds for questioning the sectoral allocation of the government's investments, which were heavily oriented toward the provision of nontradable services, notably education, health, and transportation. It is not so much that these priorities were demonstrably wrong as that committing the investments so early was incautious. If the oil boom had turned out to be permanent, such an allocation may have been appropriate. But the risk was always present that the oil boom was going to be transitory, in which case planners would regret the absence of investments in the tradables sector, which could have provided an alternative source of export revenue.

Combined with the fiscal response to the oil boom was a strong monetary response. The huge rise in international reserves that occurred in 1974 was not totally sterilized by the monetary authorities. Reserve money almost tripled in 1974, whereas money held by the public roughly doubled. In addition, the fiscal deficits that emerged in the three years after 1974 resulted in rapid monetary growth in those years as well. By the end of 1977 the money supply had risen sixfold from the 1973 level.

Inflation responded as one would expect. Between 1973 and 1978 the consumer price index rose by a factor of 2.7, an average inflation rate of 22 percent a year. With the nominal exchange rate approximately fixed, the real exchange rate appreciated strongly during the period, contributing to the external deficits.

By 1978 these excessively expansionary budgetary and monetary policies were taking their toll on the economy. In 1978 the budget deficit was about 7 percent of GDP for the third year in a row. With private spending relatively robust and with a slight softening of the oil market in 1978, the current account of the balance of payments moved into a substantial deficit, and the government was forced for the first time to obtain loans from foreign banks. More borrowing was projected for 1979.

Before turning to the 1979–83 period, let us briefly summarize and evaluate the policy response to the first oil boom:

- Essentially none of the increased income was saved in the form of foreign assets. The cumulative current account during the five-year period 1974–78 amounted to a deficit of $131 million. This was an incautious policy. A more conservative policy would have been to save some of the increased income in the form of foreign assets, which could easily have replaced export earnings in the wake of a decline in the oil market.

- There was a substantial savings response to the increase in oil income, but the savings were all invested domestically. These domestic investments were positive developments and could have laid the groundwork for higher income in the 1980s, but the evidence suggests that the rapidity with which the public sector investment program expanded lent itself to corruption and expensive mistakes.

- The government adjusted its expenditure to the new, higher level of income with alacrity and within a year of the disturbance was quite overextended. Persistent, large budget deficits emerged and were financed in part by the issuance of money. The inconsistency of the government's fiscal, monetary, and exchange rate policies was becoming increasingly clear by late 1975. Recognition of this inconsistency spurred a sharp depreciation of the parallel-market exchange rate during 1975. The depreciation continued, with occasional interruptions, until 1978 (see figure 8-7).

Act 3: The Second Oil Boom and the Gathering Crisis, 1979–83

In 1978 the Nigerian government faced a difficult economic situation. The external accounts were clearly out of balance: substantial foreign borrowing had been required to finance the current account deficits, and more borrowing was projected for 1979. These external deficits were largely the result of two factors: first, the government's sluggish fiscal response to the weakening oil markets and, second, the accumulated effect on the real exchange rate of rapid monetary growth and the attendant domestic price inflation, unaccompanied by exchange rate depreciation.

The government responded with some measure of fiscal retrenchment. Table 8-4 shows that in 1978/79 the fiscal deficit fell by roughly half, to 3.5 percent of GDP, despite a significant reduction in the value of revenue from the petroleum sector during that year. The excess of domestic spending over the non-oil revenue fell from the 27 percent of GDP it had reached in the previous three years to only 17 percent of GDP in 1978/79. Much of that retrenchment came from reductions in public sector investment (see figure 8-6, which shows a substantial

Figure 8-7. Official and Black Market Exchange Rates, Nigeria, 1969–89
(dollars per naira)

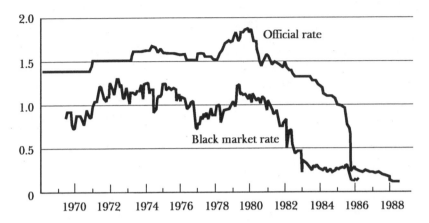

Source: IMF (various issues); *World Currency Yearbook, 1986–87.*

decline in the rate of real investment from the very high levels reached in the mid-1970s). The government did nothing significant, however, about the real exchange-rate appreciation that had occurred during the previous years, and the desirable but somewhat half-hearted fiscal measures of 1978/79 are unlikely to have succeeded if oil markets had remained as weak in 1979 as they were in 1978.

In any event, the Nigerian government was saved from painful adjustment by the (Iranian) bell. In the beginning of the year, the shah of Iran was deposed in an uprising of fundamentalist Muslims. The attendant disruptions in petroleum markets led to a second massive increase in world oil prices, which raised Nigeria's terms of trade by almost 25 percent in 1979 and another 40 percent in 1980. Table 8-3 shows that the increase in the real value of Nigeria's exports between 1978 and 1980 was, in absolute terms, about as large as the increase that occurred between 1972 and 1974. As happened in the earlier period, the current account moved out of the 1978 deficit into a surplus in 1979 and an even larger surplus in 1980. By the end of 1980 Nigerian foreign reserves had reached $10 billion—more than $120 for every man, woman, and child in the country and about 14 percent of the World Bank's estimate of per capita GNP during that year.

Once again, the Nigerian authorities faced the question of how to dispose of this massive infusion of oil wealth. This time, one might have expected a more conservative policy, as the authorities now knew from painful experience that oil prices could fall as well as rise and as they had felt some of the painful consequences of adjusting to such price declines. However, in the years following the second oil shock, the authorities responded with policies that were significantly more incautious and extravagant than were those following the first oil shock.

Table 8-6 provides data on the fiscal accounts during this period. As in 1972–74, the oil price increases led to a vast expansion of government revenue from the petroleum sector, revenue that rose from 14 percent of GDP in 1978/79 (see table 8-4) to 22 percent in 1979 and 23 percent in 1980. The fiscal discipline that was instituted in 1979, however, disappeared during 1980, and although the deficit declined during these two years of the second oil boom, the government remained in deficit during both years. The expansion of government spending during 1980 and 1981 is impressive: in 1980 total expenditure rose by 65 percent, encompassing increases in domestic subsidies, new capital expenditures, and a resumption or acceleration of construction projects that were suspended or slowed during 1978.

If the failure to maintain some measure of fiscal discipline during the two boom years was unwise, the Nigerian authorities' response to the softening of oil markets, which began in the middle of 1981, was disastrous. The decisions taken—or rather not taken—during 1981, 1982, and 1983 are chiefly responsible for the crisis in Nigeria.

We noted that the fiscal restraint instituted during 1978 was relaxed in 1980 and 1981, a relaxation that was accompanied by an increase in oil revenue and an overall decline in the fiscal deficit. In 1981 the oil market softened considerably. Table 8-3 shows that the real value of Nigeria's exports, measured in 1988 U.S. dollars, fell by one-third, from more than $30 billion in 1980 to less than $20 billion in 1981. Table 8-6 relates the fiscal consequences of this decline in oil prices. Revenue from the petroleum sector fell by almost 5 percent of GDP in 1981 and continued to fall during 1982 and 1983.

Table 8-6. Oil Receipts and the Fiscal Situation, Nigeria, 1979–83
(percentage of GDP)

Fiscal year	Oil receipts	Spending less other receipts	Fiscal balance	
1979/80	22.3	24.2	−1.9	−757[a]
1980	23.1	23.4	−0.3	−143[a]
1981	18.5	27.4	−8.9	−4,734[a]
1982	16.7	24.7	−8.0	−4,524[a]
1983	12.0	23.0	−11.0	−6,650[a]

a. Millions of nairas.
Source: Pinto (1986).

The fiscal response to this decline in government resources was negligible. Indeed, during 1981 the non-oil budget expanded significantly, with the excess of domestic spending over non-oil revenue increasing to a historical high of more than 27 percent of GDP. The result was a fiscal deficit in 1981 of almost 9 percent of GDP. This deficit remained about the same in 1982 and increased to 11 percent of GDP in 1983, as small fiscal contractions were overwhelmed by large reductions in the government's petroleum revenue.

The fiscal deficits were accompanied by a generally accommodative monetary policy and, most important, no significant change in the nominal exchange rate. Domestic prices rose 60 percent during 1980–83, responding to lax monetary policy, the inflationary effects of a halfhearted depreciation of the exchange rate, and the lagged effects of the extraordinarily expansive monetary policy pursued in the years just preceding 1980.

The nominal exchange rate was altered insignificantly, compared with the high rate of domestic price inflation, and the real exchange rate therefore appreciated significantly. By 1984 the real effective exchange rate, as measured by the IMF, had appreciated almost 125 percent compared with 1976, when the measures first became available. If anything, this figure probably understates the degree of overvaluation; between 1976 and 1984 the Nigerian economy had accumulated a crushing debt burden, and, as we discussed earlier, the servicing of such a debt burden implies a depreciation of the real exchange rate.[13]

The simple macroeconomic model laid out in the previous section makes a prediction that expansionary fiscal policy, inflationary monetary policy, and deteriorating terms of trade will lead to current account deficits, and table 8-7 shows that current account deficits materialized in this period on a massive scale. During 1981 the current account moved from the $5 billion surplus recorded in 1980 to a deficit of $6 billion. In 1982 the deficit widened to more than $7 billion, and although the deficit shrunk in 1983, it was still clearly excessive.

The fact that the deficits recorded during 1981–83 were excessive is apparent from foreigners' unwillingness to finance them voluntarily. During 1981 the current account and balance of payments deficits were financed entirely from previously accumulated foreign reserves. These reserves therefore fell from more than $10 billion at the end of 1980 to $6 billion at the end of 1981. The lower level of reserves was insufficient to finance the $7 billion current account deficit that emerged during 1982, and foreigners were apparently unwilling to increase their lending to Nigeria at the pace required to finance what the country could not finance by drawing down reserves. The result

Table 8-7. International Trade and Payments, Nigeria, 1979–83
(billions of dollars)

Year	Trade balance	Other current account	Current account balance	Net capital movements	Overall balance
1979	4.07	−2.70	1.37	1.83	3.66
1980	11.11	−6.00	5.10	−0.76	4.69
1981	−0.91	−5.31	−6.22	0.72	−5.50
1982	2.71	0.53	−7.24	1.65	−5.59
1983	−1.08	−3.26	−4.34	1.37	−2.97

Source: IMF (various issues).

was a rapid accumulation of arrears: involuntary extensions of credit
by Nigeria's trading partners, extensions that continued during 1982
and 1983. Estimates of the amount of arrears vary, with the Nigerian
government understandably more reluctant than claimants to grant
the validity of claims, but the accumulation of arrears was by any
calculation large. Foreign exporters claimed obligations amounting to
about $10.5 billion at the end of 1985, whereas importers' records
showed only $7.7 billion (Nigeria 1986). Table 8-8 gives the IMF's
estimates.

Table 8-8 shows that in 1982 and 1983, the height of Nigeria's payments imbalances, arrears were being accumulated at the rate of $2
billion–$3 billion a year, so that a substantial fraction of the payments
imbalances in those years was "financed" by accumulating arrears.
During the entire 1981–87 period, the payments arrears totaled a
staggering $9 billion, roughly one-third of Nigeria's international
debt in 1988.

The authorities responded to the payments imbalances during this
period by imposing increasingly restrictive quantitative controls on

Table 8-8. Arrears in Payments, Nigeria, 1981–87
(millions of dollars)

Year	Unofficial	Official	Total
1981	58	..	58
1982	708	2,843	3,551
1983	883	1,219	2,102
1984	624	424	1,048
1985	221	246	467
1986	..	454	454
1987	..	1,395	1,395
Total	2,494	6,581	9,075

.. Zero or negligible.

Source: IMF (1988). Converted to dollars using dollar/SDR (special drawing rights) in IMF
(various issues).

external payments. Import quotas were applied to an increasingly broad array of goods and services and became more restrictive. The bureaucratic obstacles to obtaining foreign exchange for imported intermediate goods hurt the manufacturing sector badly. As noted above, import substitution policies had fostered the creation of a low value added manufacturing sector that was heavily reliant on inputs that were imported. Like a hothouse flower, this sector could not thrive in the harsh atmosphere of foreign exchange scarcity. Indeed, the whole economy fared poorly during this period. Real GDP, which had been stagnant since 1976, declined by 17 percent between 1980 and 1984, almost 27 percent in per capita terms.

Rationing of foreign exchange, import quotas, and other quantitative restrictions were manifestly unable to contain the imbalances generated by macroeconomic policies so grossly at variance with external conditions. These imbalances materialized in the form of payments arrears, as already discussed, and a huge decline in the naira's value in the only market in which its price was freely determined—the black or parallel market in foreign exchange.[14]

As noted previously, the naira generally depreciated on the black market until some time in 1978 (figure 8-7). It recovered somewhat during that year and much more strongly during 1979 and 1980 as the oil price increased. From early 1979 until the end of 1981, the naira traded at about $1.00. As the oil market softened in 1982, and the inadequacy of the government's response became clear, the black market naira depreciated drastically, until by the end of 1983 its value had fallen to about $0.25. At that point the naira was officially priced well above $1.00, and the black market premium reached almost 350 percent (see figure 8-8 for a plot of the black market premium). This represented a massive vote of no confidence in the government's economic policies. It also resulted in massive transfers from the government to those individuals who were sufficiently lucky or well-connected to receive foreign exchange at the overvalued, official exchange rate (Pinto 1986 estimates the value of these transfers to have been some 10 percent of GDP).

At the end of 1983, the Nigerian economy was in serious disarray. The authorities seemed unwilling or unable to control budgetary and monetary policy, or even to provide a clear accounting of how much was being spent on what. Negotiations with the IMF collapsed when Nigeria refused to agree to the devaluation that the IMF demanded as a condition for balance of payments support. Disappointment with macroeconomic management was compounded by disgust over scandals about particularly egregious examples of administrative malfeasance, and in December 1983, a bloodless military coup led by Major General Buhari wrested control of the government from the civilians.

Figure 8-8. Black Market Premium for Nigerian Naira, 1970–86

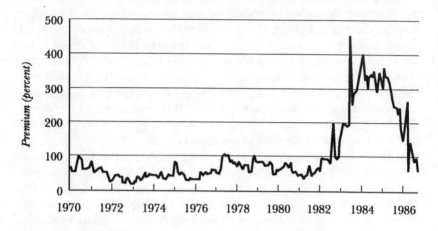

Source: Central Bank of Nigeria data; *World Currency Yearbook, 1986–87.*

The new military government decreed that it would not tolerate "corruption, squandermania, misuse, and abuse of public office for self or group aggrandizement" (*International Currency Analysis 1989,* p. 143). The military government banned political parties, instituted a curfew, and began to grapple with the task of reconstituting Nigeria's crippled economy.

Act 4: Adjustment, 1984 to the Present

In its first two years the military government made substantial progress toward stabilizing the budget and the economy. The government began negotiations aimed at settling trade arrears accumulated during the previous three years, it slowed somewhat the rate of monetary growth, and, most important, it reestablished control over the budget and sharply reduced the fiscal deficit (see table 8-9).

The government sharply reduced expenditure, especially investment expenditure, from 1983 levels. During 1981–83, capital expenditure averaged slightly over ₦ 5 billion a year; in 1984 this was slashed to ₦ 4 billion, and in 1985 investment spending was further reduced to less than ₦ 3.5 billion (Nigeria 1986). Despite a continually weakening oil market, which drastically reduced oil sector revenue, the Nigerian government increased overall taxation from 10.5 percent of GDP in 1984 to roughly 16 percent of GDP in 1986, thus maintaining a fiscal deficit of roughly 2.5 to 4.0 percent of GDP during 1984–86. This

Table 8-9. Federal Budget, Nigeria, 1984–87

(percentage of GDP)

Year	Revenue	Expenditure[a]	Balance
1984	10.5	14.7	−4.2
1985	11.4	13.9	−2.5
1986	15.6	19.1	−3.5
1987	16.0	25.0	−8.9

a. Incudes lending minus repayments.

Source: IMF (various issues).

major shift toward budgetary balance, combined with some inten-
sification of foreign exchange controls, led to a dramatic improvement in the country's external balance.

Moving from deficit into near balance in 1984, the current account
in 1985 registered a surplus of more than $2.6 billion (see table 8-10).
This occurred despite external interest obligations (much of the
"other current account" category in table 8-10) that had by 1985
reached roughly $1.5 billion, roughly 10 percent of exports. This
improvement in external finances was achieved through a drastic
compression of imports, which in turn reflected sharp reductions in
public spending, and through reductions in private spending, as tax
increases and reductions in domestic subsidies reduced private sector
incomes. By 1986 the real value of imports in Nigeria was less than
one-third the 1981 level, and in 1987 real imports amounted to less
than 25 percent of the 1981 level. Indeed, real imports in those years
averaged less than in 1973–74, before income from the first oil boom
was spent.

Thus the Buhari regime must be credited with bringing budgetary
and external accounts toward balance. As a later government was to
argue, however, the Buhari regime's policy was one of "austerity
without structural adjustment" (Nigeria 1986, p. 13). The forceful
measures required to wean the private sector from its reliance on

Table 8-10. International Trade and Payments, Nigeria, 1984–88

(billions of dollars)

Year	Trade balance	Other current account[a]	Current account balance	Net capital movements	Overall balance
1984	2.98	−2.87	0.11	−1.08	−0.97
1985	5.74	−3.12	2.62	−3.87	−1.25
1986	2.54	−2.17	0.37	−1.52	−1.15
1987	3.52	−3.59	−0.07	−2.69	−2.76
1988	2.42	−3.52	−1.10	−3.95	−5.05

a. Incudes external interest obligations.

Source: IMF (various issues).

the government required to wean the private sector from its reliance on the government and the economy as a whole from its reliance on the petroleum sector were not taken. In particular, the government refused to consider exchange rate depreciation, and the real exchange rate continued to appreciate through 1984 and into 1985 (see figure 8-9). Although the real exchange rate remained at this inflated level, there could be little hope of developing a viable non-oil export sector.

The austerity measures that were responsible for the improvement in the current account were also associated with immense reductions in domestic investment, the real value of which after 1983 was lower than in any year since 1971 (see figure 8-6). In short, although the government managed to bring some semblance of balance into the economy's external finances, it did so at the clear expense of prospects for economic growth.

In August 1985 another military coup took place, and Major General Babangida rose to power. Under Babangida economic policy underwent a drastic change of direction. His government sought to diversify the economy from its excessive reliance on the petroleum sector, to achieve fiscal and balance of payments equilibrium, to lay the basis for noninflationary economic growth, and to "lessen the dominance of unproductive investments in the public sector, improve the sector's efficiency, and intensify the growth potential of the private sector" (Nigeria 1986, p. 1).

The Babangida regime's identification of market solutions to Nigeria's economic woes marked a major departure from the approach

Figure 8-9. Exchange Rate Depreciation, Nigeria, 1971–88

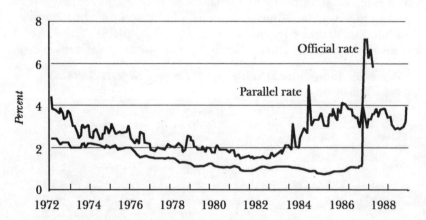

Source: Central Bank of Nigeria data; *World Currency Yearbook, 1986–87.*

of previous governments, military and civilian alike. The earliest, most dramatic, and most fundamental change in policy was the acceptance that the market should determine the exchange rate. In late October 1986 the government abolished foreign exchange licensing for many activities and began to auction foreign exchange, allowing traders to set the price. The first result was a very substantial depreciation. Figure 8-7 shows that the official rate of exchange rapidly fell from $1.00 to roughly $0.25, approximately the black market rate during the previous two years. It stabilized there until late 1988, when it began to decline even further. In July 1989 the naira traded at about $0.14.

This devaluation of the exchange rate had a massive effect on the real exchange rate and therefore on production incentives. We saw that in 1984 the real exchange rate was grossly overvalued, at about double its 1976 value. By the end of 1988 the real effective exchange rate was only 30 percent of its 1976 value and was clearly lower in real terms than it had been at any time in Nigeria's recorded history. Combined with this radical change in production incentives was a substantial liberalization of domestic markets and of the international trading regime. The commodity boards that had so perniciously insulated domestic producers from world prices were abolished as of the end of 1986, interest rates were liberalized and rose in real terms from their persistently negative levels into a range that would reward savers for their thrift, subsidization of petroleum products was ended, and the cumbersome bureaucracy involved in enforcing the import quota machinery was relaxed.

It is too early to tell whether this dramatic change in direction will be successful or even whether it will survive. A hopeful sign exists: the dollar value of nonpetroleum exports rose significantly in 1987. The amounts of nonpetroleum exports remain tiny, however, both compared with petroleum exports and compared with their pre-1980 levels. Former policy mistakes have so eviscerated the non-oil export sector, and the dominance of the state in the economy has become so entrenched, that diversification from oil and reorientation of the economy toward private sector activity will require years of sustained commitment to present policies.

So far, the Nigerian authorities have shown no sign of backing away from their determination to prevent overvaluation by letting market forces determine the exchange rate. The budget deficit widened significantly, however, in 1987; only time will tell whether this reflects temporary factors or a resurgence of past policies.

Conclusion

The theoretical section of this essay lays out a number of arguments why, in the aftermath of an improvement in the terms of trade, authorities ought to take steps to ensure a substantial rate of savings and, at least in the short to medium run, to invest a significant fraction of those savings in the form of foreign assets. One argument for such a policy is that the substantial uncertainty surrounding commodity prices means that changes in the terms of trade may not last as long as expected. The accumulation of foreign assets or viable investments in the export sector provide insurance against unexpected, but possibly adverse, movements in the terms of trade.

A second argument for such a policy is that extremely rapid rates of adjustment and extremely high rates of investment lead to costly mistakes and waste and may foster a confused environment in which fraud is less easily detected and therefore more prevalent. The accumulation of foreign assets can slow the rate of adjustment to a more manageable pace and reduce the incidence of costly miscalculations, bottlenecks, and, perhaps, corruption.

The Nigerian authorities erred, first, in failing to adopt such conservative policies. Foreign assets were accumulated only in the immediate aftermath of the oil price disturbances; spending the revenue as rapidly as it was accruing was physically impossible. Within a year of both disturbances the Nigerian authorities had brought expenditure into line with the higher level of income, and very soon thereafter the public sector and the economy as a whole became seriously overextended. In the first boom especially, much of this expenditure was in the form of investment. But the investments seem to have had a very low rate of return; despite the high rates of investment recorded in the 1970s, real GDP in 1987 remained at about its 1974 level and substantially below that level in per capita terms. Some reasons for this apparent low rate of return on investment may be found in the frenetic environment in which the investment was undertaken. Some may be found in the tendency for governments to invest in projects with high prestige or political payoff, but with little economic rationale.

The second and far more serious mistake was the authorities' failure to respond to the terms of trade declines that followed the end of each boom. The crisis in 1978 was short-lived, because oil prices increased again in 1979 and 1980. But the authorities were not rescued from their mistakes in 1981–83. Adjustment to a deterioration in the terms of trade involves reductions in domestic expenditure. In Nigeria, however, the authorities promoted excessive expenditure both by spending too much themselves and by subsidizing the private sector. Adjustment to a weakening in the terms of trade demands real-exchange-rate *de*preciation, but the authorities promoted real-exchange-rate *ap*preciation by implementing highly inflationary monetary policies and then failing to adjust the nominal exchange rate.

The corrections to policy have managed to bring the Nigerian economy closer to equilibrium in its external payments, but coming as they did years after they were due, they did so only after an enormous foreign debt was accumulated, a debt that bedevils Nigeria's attempts to grow in the 1990s. This legacy of the past decade's policy mistakes is a vivid argument for adopting a cautious approach to disturbances in the terms of trade.

Notes

1. Here we make no attempt to disentangle the separate effects of changes in price and quantity. If commodity markets are competitive, so that price equals marginal cost, then changes in the quantity of exports have (to a first order of approximation) no welfare effects, because the price at which the marginal units are sold exactly equals their marginal cost. Even at the relatively low prices in petroleum markets today, the price of oil is substantially above marginal cost for producers such as Nigeria. Because of these scarcity rents, changes in the quantity of oil exported have large welfare implications.

2. To be more precise, this distance is the first-order approximation of the change in real income caused by a change in the terms of trade. Two second-order considerations make this measure only approximate: the fact that the consumption basket may change in response to the change in relative prices and the fact that the composition of production may change. We discuss changes in the composition of production later.

3. This is a natural assumption for a country like Nigeria, which is so highly specialized in the export of a single, primary commodity. There is, of course, some consumption of petroleum products within Nigeria, but it is a very small fraction of total production.

4. A detailed derivation is not necessary for the purposes of this paper. Interested readers are referred to Gavin (1990), where the model underlying this discussion is laid out in substantially more detail.

5. A fairly large body of literature is available on the impact of changes in the terms of trade on optimal rates of investment and the current account. For recent papers see Brock (1988), Murphy (1989), and Sen and Turnovsky (1989).

6. An early reference is Leland (1968). Zeldes (1989) and Skinner (1988) give evidence on the empirical significance of precautionary savings. Not all utility functions generate a demand for precautionary savings. The precautionary savings motive is intuitively so compelling, however, that we implicitly confine ourselves in this discussion to utility functions that are consistent with precautionary savings.

7. This should be thought of as a composite of all the non-oil traded goods that Nigeria purchases and sells. In particular, it includes exportable agricultural commodities that are produced in Nigeria and that were once such an important part of its foreign trade.

8. This remark is designed only to highlight the fiscal dimension of monetary policy. There is no implication that Nigerian monetary policy is determined only, or even mostly, by the terms of trade. As we will see later, the Nigerian monetary authorities have shown themselves perfectly able to implement very expansionary monetary policy when the terms of trade are highly favorable.

9. There is some evidence that farmers in developing countries do distinguish between permanent and transitory changes in income in the way suggested by the theory (see, for example, Paxson 1989 and Bevan, Collier, and Gunning 1989). At the same time it is well established that, even in industrial economies with well-developed capital markets, consumption is more sensitive to current income than is consistent with simple versions of the permanent income hypothesis.

10. The naira was introduced in January 1973 and was set to equal the value of half a Nigerian pound, the previous currency unit. Before 1973 what I refer to as the naira exchange rate is the naira equivalent of the Nigerian pound exchange rate.

11. This is used as a proxy for the dollar price of Nigerian imports. It is an imperfect proxy because Nigeria also imports from Europe. But movements in the relative price of U.S. and European exports are likely to be minor compared with the oil price changes that dominate the Nigerian terms of trade, so a more perfect measure would not materially affect the analysis.

12. In 1975, the government awarded public sector employees a very large wage increase. This wage increase had major budgetary effects, amounting to almost a quarter of the preceding year's total spending, and contributed substantially to the high inflation Nigeria experienced in the late 1970s (see Bienen 1983).

13. In other respects, 1976 provides a good benchmark against which to evaluate the 1984 real exchange rate. The current account was in balance in 1976, and oil revenues in 1976 and 1984 were, in real terms, roughly comparable (see table 8-3).

14. There are no official sources of information on this market. The data reported in this paper are reported in *World Currency Yearbook*, a standard, if not official, source.

Selected Bibliography

Bevan, David, Paul Collier, and Jan Gunning. 1989. "The Kenyan Coffee Boom of 1976–79." Oxford University, Department of Economics, Oxford, U.K.

Bienen, Henry. 1983. "Oil Revenues and Policy Choice in Nigeria." World Bank Staff Working Paper 592. Washington, D.C.

Brock, Philip L. 1988. "Investment, the Current Account, and the Relative Price of Nontraded Goods in a Small, Open Economy." *Journal of International Economics* 24(3):235–53.

Dixit, Avinash K. 1989. "Intersectoral Capital Reallocation under Price Uncertainty." *Journal of International Economics* 26(3):309–25.

Dornbusch, Rudiger. 1983. "Real Interest Rates, Home Goods, and Optimal External Borrowing." *Journal of Political Economy* 91(1):141–53.

Gavin, Michael. 1988. "Income Effects of Adjustment to a Terms of Trade Disturbance: Asymmetries in the Harberger-Laursen-Metzler Relation?" Columbia University, Department of Economics, New York.

———. 1990. "Structural Adjustment to a Terms of Trade Disturbance: The Role of Relative Prices." *Journal of International Economics* 28(314):217–43.

IMF (International Monetary Fund). 1988. *Balance of Payments Statistics: Yearbook, 1988*. Washington, D.C.

———. Various issues. *International Financial Statistics*. Washington, D.C.

International Currency Analysis, Inc. 1989. *World Currency Yearbook, 1986–87*. New York.

Kirk-Greene, Anthony, and Douglas Rimmer. 1981. *Nigeria since 1970: A Political and Economic Outline*. New York: Africana Publishing Company.

Leland, Hayne E. 1968. "Saving and Uncertainty: The Precautionary Demand for Saving." *Quarterly Journal of Economics* 82(3):465–73.

McDonald, Robert L., and Daniel R. Siegel. 1986. "The Value of Waiting to Invest." *Quarterly Journal of Economics* 101(4):707–27.

Murphy, Robert. 1989. "The Terms of Trade, Investment, and the Current Account." Discussion paper. Boston College, Department of Economics, Boston, Mass.

Mussa, Michael L. 1978. "Dynamic Adjustment in the Heckscher-Ohlin-Samuelson Model." *Journal of Political Economy* 86(5):775–91.

Nigeria, Federal Republic of. 1986. "Information Memorandum." Central Bank of Nigeria and Ministry of Finance, Lagos, November.

Paxson, Christine. 1989. "Transitory Trade Shocks and Saving: The Case of Thailand." Discussion paper. Princeton University, Department of Economics, Princeton, N.J.

Pinto, Brian. 1986. "Nigeria during and after the Oil Boom: A Policy Comparison with Indonesia." World Bank, Country Policy Department, Trade and Adjustment Policy Division, Washington, D.C.

Sen, Partha, and Stephen F. Turnovsky. 1989. "Deterioration of the Terms of Trade and Capital Accumulation: A Reexamination of the Laursen-Metzler Effect." *Journal of International Economics* 26(3):227–70.

Skinner, Jonathan. 1988. "Risky Income, Life Cycle Consumption, and Precautionary Savings." *Journal of Monetary Economics* 22(2):237–55.

World Bank. 1989a. *World Debt Tables: External Debt of Developing Countries*. 1988–89 ed. 2 vols. Washington, D.C.

———. 1989b. *World Tables*. Baltimore, Md.: Johns Hopkins University Press.

Zeldes, Stephen P. 1989. "Optimal Consumption with Stochastic Income: Deviations from Certainty Equivalence." *Quarterly Journal of Economics* 104(2):275–98.

9

Bolivian Trade and Development, 1952–87

Juan-Antonio Morales

BOLIVIA is the most extreme example of the Latin American economic crisis of the 1980s. During 1982–86 the growth rates of GDP were negative every year, and in 1984–85 Bolivia suffered from hyperinflation. Inflation has now been successfully stabilized, but a host of internal and external factors are hindering economic recovery, which is slower than expected. This essay provides an overview of Bolivia's economic policies.

Bolivia is a small, open economy dependent on a few export products and on a small number of large trade partners. The performance of exports and normal access to foreign financing are crucial to Bolivia's welfare. Another characteristic of Bolivia's economy is the size of its public sector. Bolivia's governments have been so overburdened with economic functions that they have on the whole performed poorly. The cost of the public sector and its regulations has unduly affected investment rates and the patterns of foreign trade and indebtedness.

The international debt crisis of the early 1980s put an especially pronounced strain on the Bolivian economy. Exacerbating the effect of increased interest payments on international debt, export earnings collapsed in 1985–86. Internal factors were also involved. To many Bolivian observers the hyperinflation appeared to be more than a transitory monetary disarray. To them it constituted an indictment of the development model Bolivia had followed for the preceding thirty years and the culmination of accumulated economic policy mistakes.

Economic History, 1952–87

Table 9-1 and figure 9-1 depict the main characteristics of the 1957–87 period with regard to growth and overall economic performance.

Table 9-1. Key Indicators of Development, Bolivia, 1953–87

Indicator	1953–61	1962–71	1972–78	1979–81	1982–85	1986–87[a]
Average annual growth rates						
GDP	−0.4	5.9	5.4	0.9	−3.0	−0.8
Population	2.2	2.4	2.6	2.8	2.8	2.8
Per capita GDP	−2.6	3.5	2.7	−1.8	−5.6	−3.5
Consumer prices	56.6	5.1	17.4	32.6	982.7	107.1
Exports	−9.5	11.6	19.5	13.2	−9.1	−14.5
Import capacity[b]	−5.9	5.5	8.2	−4.3	−14.0	4.5
Average ratios						
Investment/GDP	15.8	19.0	16.5	14.0	9.1	7.2
Gross domestic savings/GDP	6.1	11.8	18.4	13.3	10.7	—
Exports/GDP	13.3	19.7	21.9	18.8	15.3	12.9
Exports of tin and natural gas/ merchandise exports	63.5	68.7	56.5	65.9	81.7	73.6
Current account deficit/GDP	—	3.1	2.3	7.8	4.8	10.7
Public external debt/GDP	—	36.1	45.2	63.0	80.0	93.2[c]
Public external debt/exports	—	199.3	194.4	229.5	361.5	516.1[c]

— Not available.
a. Preliminary.
b. Defined as the sum of export receipts and long-term foreign capital inflows deflated by import price index.
c. Value for 1986.

Source: IMF (1987); UDAPE (1987); Afcha and Huarachi (1988); World Bank (1988); Central Bank of Bolivia (various issues).

Figure 9-1. Annual Growth Rates of GDP, Bolivia, 1953–87

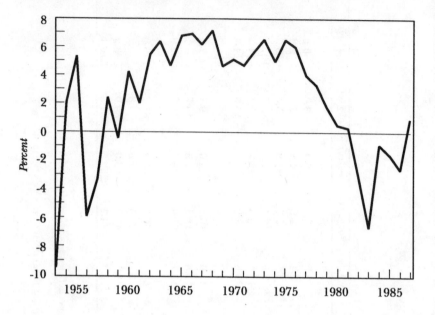

Source: Central Bank of Bolivia (various issues).

The subperiods in table 9-1 are somewhat arbitrary but reveal some dominant patterns. The subperiod 1953–61 is marked by low economic growth rates and high inflation. In 1962 the Bolivian economy initiated a sustained takeoff: high rates of growth of GDP and low inflation rates characterize both the 1962–71 and 1972–78 subperiods. The latter subperiod was also characterized, however, by a rapid accumulation of external debt. The subperiod 1978–81 was defined by extreme political instability and by the beginning of difficulties in servicing the foreign debt. The economic crisis reached its height during 1982–86. During the final subperiod, 1986–87, Bolivia made a successful attempt at stabilization and fought hard to achieve economic recovery.

What made possible the sustained growth during the relatively long period 1962–78? Econometric estimates by Morales (1988) support the view that investment rates, growth in the capacity to import, and political and macroeconomic stability were the main factors behind the GDP growth rates. The capacity to import is given by the sum of export proceeds and foreign capital inflows, computed in constant prices. Ram (1987) finds that export performance in itself was a significative explanatory factor of Bolivian economic growth; however, his results are difficult to replicate.

Table 9-2 shows the main changes in the structure of production between 1952 and 1987. The most salient aspect of the table is the increase in the share of services II in GDP. Services II consists principally of the production of nontradables in foreign trade. Notice that production in the primary sector (agriculture, mining, and hydrocarbons) was reduced as a share of GDP until around 1977. During the crisis years, this share increased somewhat. The manufacturing sector was greatly affected by the crisis of the 1980s, as can be inferred from the strong fall in its share of GDP.

Geography is an important determinant of the pattern of Bolivia's foreign trade. A large share of the population is concentrated in the highlands. The country has no direct access to the sea and only a few waterways free from natural obstacles. Roads and railways are limited because the topography is such that building costs are steep. Thus transportation is very expensive. This implies that exports have to be of high value added per unit of weight.

Bolivia's export base has been heavily dependent on a handful of commodities: tin and other minerals, petroleum, and, more recently, natural gas. In the mid-1970s illegal exports of cocaine and its derivatives made a strong appearance; they have important distorting effects on the legal economy. Table 9-1 shows that exports of tin and, since 1973, of natural gas accounted for more than 55 percent of total (legal) merchandise exports during most of the period. With the onset of the

Table 9-2. Sectoral Composition of GDP, Bolivia, Selected Years, 1952–87

(percent)

Sector	1952	1962	1972	1977	1982	1985[a]	1987[a]
Primary	46.5	39.9	29.1	25.8	35.2	32.2	33.3
Manufacturing	14.2	14.1	14.6	15.9	12.0	9.8	10.8
Services I[b]	4.6	5.4	5.4	5.9	4.0	4.2	3.7
Services II[c]	34.7	40.6	51.0	52.5	46.2	50.7	50.5
Indirect taxes[d]	—	—	—	—	2.6	3.1	1.6
GDP[e]	100.0	100.0	100.0	100.0	100.0	100.0	100.0

— Not available.

Note: Percentages are computed from basic data in real terms.

a. Preliminary.

b. Electricity, gas and water, construction.

c. Commerce, transportation and storage, communications, finance, general government, other services.

d. Included in each sector for 1952, 1962, 1972, 1977.

e. Basic data on GDP are at market prices.

Source: Bolivia (1970); Central Bank of Bolivia (various issues).

crisis in the late 1970s, tin and natural gas made up an even greater percentage of exports. Geographical concentration also increased, as can be observed in table 9-3. Note that in 1985, as much as 56 percent of Bolivia's exports went to Argentina. With this limited export base, Bolivia's vulnerability to international market conditions is not surprising.

Despite the crucial role of exports in the Bolivian economy, their long-run performance has been poor. Between 1952 and 1985 the volume of exports grew at the meager average annual rate of 1.5 percent. Attempts at import substitution were short-lived and had little impact. The Bolivian strategy appears to have been geared more toward terms of trade improvements than to a long-run expansion of the production of tradables. Growth depended to a large extent on improvements in the terms of trade. In 1986, however, the terms of trade took a nosedive (see table 9-4).

During 1952–87, exports and imports made up a relatively high percentage of the national economy. Foreign trade–GDP ratios can be observed in table 9-5. The ratios show a generally stable trend, except over short periods associated with severe disruptions in the economy.

An important feature of Bolivia's development from 1952 onward has been its continued heavy dependence on foreign capital and transfers. During the 1960s the flow of foreign funds took essentially two forms: bilateral or multilateral foreign aid through the official development banks to finance social overhead projects and subsidize small loans to the private sector; and direct foreign investment, heavily concentrated in the hydrocarbons sector. In the 1970s Bolivia gained access to credits from the international commercial banks, as

Table 9-3. Exports from Bolivia, by Destination, Selected Years, 1960–85

(percent)

Destination	1960	1970	1980	1985
Argentina	5.7	4.7	23.7	55.9
Brazil	5.9	0.4	3.5	0.7
Chile	0.4	1.1	4.5	1.6
Peru	0.2	2.7	3.1	1.9
Other LAFTA/LAIA[a] countries	0.0	0.0	1.9	0.6
Total LAFTA/LAIA[a] countries	12.2	8.9	36.7	60.6
Rest of the world	87.8	91.1	63.3	39.4
Total	100.0	100.0	100.0	100.0

a. Latin American Free Trade Association/Latin American Integration Association. The former became the latter in the late 1970s.

Source: Central Bank of Bolivia (various issues).

Table 9-4. Terms of Trade Indexes, Bolivia, 1952–87

(1980 = 100)

Year	Export unit values	Import unit values	Terms of trade
1952	22.9	28.1	81.5
1953	21.5	22.7	94.7
1954	20.3	22.5	90.4
1955	19.0	22.5	84.6
1956	19.5	24.0	81.1
1957	16.9	20.9	80.7
1958	16.4	19.5	83.9
1959	16.7	21.1	79.2
1960	19.9	17.8	111.6
1961	20.5	19.9	103.1
1962	21.1	19.7	107.4
1963	21.1	20.7	102.1
1964	21.8	27.7	78.5
1965	21.6	32.9	65.5
1966	20.7	30.0	69.0
1967	21.3	29.0	73.6
1968	22.0	28.6	76.9
1969	22.4	30.8	72.6
1970	23.2	32.3	72.0
1971	22.5	32.9	68.4
1972	25.2	34.9	72.1
1973	25.5	40.7	62.8
1974	50.7	49.9	101.5
1975	45.5	56.8	80.0
1976	48.3	59.1	81.8
1977	56.7	65.9	86.1
1978	63.1	73.0	86.5
1979	75.0	88.3	84.9
1980	100.0	100.0	100.0
1981	96.7	101.9	94.9
1982	93.3	99.3	94.0
1983	96.2	95.8	100.3
1984	99.1	98.5	100.6
1985[a]	98.8	93.5	105.7
1986[a]	76.3	88.9	85.8
1987[a]	79.3	92.0	86.2

a. Preliminary.

Source: CEPAL (1987, various years).

Table 9-5. Trade as a Percentage of GDP, Bolivia, 1952–87

Year	Exports	Annual average over period	Imports	Annual average over period	Total trade	Annual average over period
1952	17.2		18.6		35.8	
1953	5.9		7.9		13.8	
1954	4.4		5.3		9.6	
1955	4.8	8.1	5.8	9.4	10.6	17.5
1956	13.4		16.0		29.3	
1957	22.5		30.8		53.3	
1958	16.0		25.4		41.4	
1959	20.4		27.1		47.5	
1960	16.2	17.7	23.9	24.6	40.1	42.3
1961	16.4		23.3		39.7	
1962	16.4		24.9		41.4	
1963	17.4		26.5		43.9	
1964	20.7		23.5		44.2	
1965	21.5	18.5	26.6	25.0	48.1	43.4
1966	21.9		26.3		48.2	
1967	22.4		26.0		48.4	
1968	19.7		24.0		43.7	
1969	19.3		23.6		42.9	
1970	20.2	20.7	20.3	24.0	40.5	44.7
1971	17.3		20.0		37.3	
1972	17.2		19.9		37.1	
1973	22.6		23.5		46.0	
1974	28.7		22.2		50.9	
1975	21.3	21.4	26.9	22.5	48.2	43.9
1976	22.5		24.7		47.2	
1977	22.3		25.1		47.3	
1978	18.6		25.3		43.9	
1979	19.3		25.2		44.6	
1980	25.6	21.7	20.2	24.1	45.8	45.8
1981	22.4		21.7		44.1	
1982[a]	21.3		14.8		36.1	
1983[a]	20.1		15.7		35.8	
1984[a]	19.0		12.9		31.9	
1985[a]	16.5	19.9	14.6	15.9	31.1	35.8
1986[a]	14.5		18.1		33.3	
1987[a]	11.3	12.9	19.1	19.0	30.4	31.9

Note: Percentages are derived from national accounts data in current prices for the years 1952–81; percentages for 1982–87 are estimated from balance of payments data.

a. Preliminary estimates.

Source: For 1952–81, Central Bank of Bolivia (various issues); for 1982–87, UDAPE (1987); Afcha and Huarachi (1988).

did other countries in the region. The burden of the heavy indebtedness Bolivia incurred in the 1970s continues to be a major obstacle to economic recovery.

The Revolution of 1952 and Its Aftermath

The revolution of 1952, led by Dr. Víctor Paz-Estenssoro, is the main landmark in Bolivia's recent history. In its aftermath the government nationalized the three largest mining firms and undertook extensive agrarian reforms. Simultaneously, it implemented a policy of import substitution and production diversification. The need to lock in the wealth and income changes of the revolution gave birth to state capitalism, which would prevail until 1985. The political and economic changes of the early 1950s were accompanied by the start of a population movement from the highlands to the eastern lowlands, particularly the Santa Cruz region. The move to the east brought about important shifts in economic and political power.

The period 1952–56 was one of high social mobilization, huge disruptions in production, and inflation that reached 178 percent by 1956. As inflation worsened and foreign exchange and staple foods became scarce, the government gave top priority to stabilization. The stabilization plan, announced by the government in December 1956, indeed ended the high inflation but also led to significant modifications in the development policies of the revolution.

After inflation had stabilized, the government emphasized export-led growth, and the country's dependence on foreign capital inflows increased. Central policies from 1956 to 1964 were the recovery of the tin mines and new investments in the petroleum sector. Policies of import substitution were abandoned, as were all remnants of popular mobilization. There was an inflow of foreign aid, which largely financed physical infrastructure projects. The foreign aid, especially the resources of the Alliance for Progress program (launched by President Kennedy in 1962), had a significant impact on investment rates. These in turn affected GDP growth rates, and beginning in 1962 the economy started to recover.

After twelve years of civilian rule that had started with the revolution of 1952, General René Barrientos led a military coup that deposed President Paz-Estenssoro. Barrientos generally upheld the economic policies implemented after the stabilization program of December 1956. But there were some changes. First, a resurgence of the private sector was made possible through increased inflows of foreign direct investment in the petroleum sector and the return of many Bolivian entrepreneurs who had earlier fled the revolution. Second, substantial credits and grants were made available to the private sector.

The Populist Interlude

Barrientos died in a helicopter crash in 1969 and was succeeded by his civilian vice president, Luis-Adolfo Siles-Salinas. Shortly afterward, General Alfredo Ovando overthrew Siles-Salinas in a military coup. With Ovando and later with General Juan José Torrez, who succeeded Ovando after some confusing coups and countercoups, Bolivia entered an era of open populism. Ovando unwisely nationalized the Bolivian Gulf Oil Corporation and started to build the controversial state-owned tin smelters. Torrez followed an even more populist course, trying to co-opt the labor movement into government. Real wages reached an all-time high. The government also made a determined effort to collect more income taxes, but with relatively little success.

Banzer's Bonanza Years

Torrez lasted less than a year and was deposed in a coup led by the conservative General Hugo Banzer in August 1971. Banzer ruled for seven years, a long time by Bolivian standards. He presided over an era of high economic growth, with an average annual GDP growth rate of 5.4 percent. Two main factors led to the high rates of growth and investment. First, a significant improvement in the terms of trade from 1973 onward caused export prices to double in 1974. Second, Bolivia's access to foreign capital markets increased. In addition, the prolonged period of political stability was undoubtedly a major force behind the economy's good performance. The Banzer boom was temporary, however. It was based on a short upsurge of export prices and high foreign indebtedness. Policymakers did not appreciate the transitory nature of the high prices and favorable interest rates.

The growth rate became smaller after 1978 and turned negative in 1981. This was the result of political uncertainty and reduced efficiency in the use of internal and external resources, which started in the last years of the Banzer regime.

The Years of Political Chaos

Banzer failed in his efforts to build a large political base. The pressures of the Carter administration to restore democracy in Bolivia and the perception of impending economic troubles, whose first symptoms had already appeared by the end of 1977, made Banzer abandon his stated purpose to stay in power until 1980. He called general elections in 1978; however, a clear winner did not emerge, and the elections were annulled. A period of political chaos ensued, with inconclusive elections, interim civilian presidents, and military coups and countercoups. The political turmoil undermined the government's capacity to recognize the economic crisis that was steadily building up and to take appropriate action.[1] Bolivia's fortunes reached a low ebb with the military government of Luis García-Meza in 1980–81, when Bolivia was cut off from international recognition and financial markets.

The Hyperinflation

The military government of the second half of 1982, unable to cope with the deteriorated economy and the growing pressures for a return to democracy, decided to reconvene the congress elected in 1980. Acting as an electoral college, the congress elected as president Hernán Siles-Zuazo, who had received the most votes in the 1980 elections. Siles-Zuazo inherited an economy that was already severely strained. Indeed, the economy had experienced a negative rate of growth in 1982, and the average annual inflation rate in the year preceding Siles's inauguration was already 170 percent. The start of Siles's presidency coincided with the onset of the international debt crisis. One effect of this crisis was that net resource transfers abroad stood at 2.4 percent of GDP in 1982. Siles-Zuazo was completely unable to arbitrate between the demands of rebuilding a crumbling economy and the demands of his electorate, who wanted higher real wages and higher employment and investment in the public sector. In addition, he faced opposition to his policies in a congress that he did not control. His policies and his timid (and sometimes belated) attempts at stabilization, if anything, worsened an already difficult situation. During his presidency, inflation jumped from the hundreds to the thousands: from April 1984 to August 1985, prices increased by a factor of 623, the average increase being 50 percent a month.

Along with the hyperinflation, real per capita GDP declined by some 23 percent between 1982 and 1985. Shortages of food and other essential goods and services were everyday occurrences, strikes and work stoppages were frequent, and several threats to democracy surfaced. The hyperinflation and the economic crisis were as much the result of difficult external conditions, coupled with poor domestic economic design, as of political weakness. Siles-Zuazo was forced to call early elections.

Elections took place in July 1985, and former president Víctor Paz-Estenssoro was elected. Three weeks after his inauguration, he unveiled a package of stabilization measures and policy reforms. The stabilization package halted inflation almost immediately, and the policy reforms set the stage for significant changes in Bolivia's production and foreign trade. For more detailed information about this period of hyperinflation and stabilization, see Sachs (1986, 1987a, 1987b); Morales (1987a, 1987b, 1987c).

In the last quarter of 1985 international tin prices dropped dramatically, and by the end of 1985 the price of tin was half what it had been four months earlier. To compound matters, in the first quarter of 1986 oil prices dropped, which affected the price of Bolivia's other main export, natural gas. In 1986 export prices fell 23 percent, and the decrease in terms of trade was 19 percent. The difficult external conditions continued throughout 1987, hampering the prospects for a strong economic recovery.

The Public Sector

Bolivia's development between 1952 and 1987 cannot be fully understood without examining its public sector. Even after the reforms of 1985, the share of the public sector in total investment is probably the largest of any market economy of the Western Hemisphere (see table 9-6).

Political scientists such as Malloy (1970) view the heavy public sector investment as a manifestation of state capitalism. State capitalism has a number of features. First, and most important, the public sector performs the bulk of capital accumulation, both in social infrastructure and through state enterprises. Second, the government manipulates the system of incentives and penalties to the private sector. Third, there is a large bureaucracy, which frequently pursues its own ends.

Table 9-6. Main Characteristics of the Public Sector, Bolivia, 1958–85

(percent)

Category	1958–61	1961–71	1972–78	1979–81	1982–85
Share of public investment in total investment	42.8	54.7	51.0	58.2	49.9
Share of foreign trade taxes in central government revenues	—	51.4[a]	61.2	60.9	55.4
Consolidated public sector deficit (share of GDP)	—	—	7.9[b]	8.4	17.5

— Not available.

Note: Figures are averages over each period.

a. Over period 1964–71.

b. Over period 1974–78.

Source: Morales (1982); World Bank (1983); IMF (1986); Morales and Sachs (1987).

Fourth, the state often develops a symbiotic relationship with favored segments of the private sector to carry out a particular distributional agenda.

The development plans prepared between 1952 and 1985 contain the philosophy underlying the Bolivian state capitalism model. The most influential development plan was the Socioeconomic Strategy for National Development (SSND), unveiled during General Ovando's regime in 1970. In the SSND the guiding principles of the state capitalism model were clearly spelled out. Investment in sectors defined as strategic was reserved for state enterprises. The SSND included such a restrictive system of incentives and penalties that it hampered the normal development of the private sector. In addition, the SSND emphasized natural-resource-based industrialization, with heavy public investment. The SSND took the position that only that type of industrialization could generate the big surpluses (or profit margins) to give the economy the big push it needed. Although President Banzer abandoned the SSND in 1972, the SSND had a powerful influence on Bolivian policymakers that went well beyond 1972. Its nationalistic approach appealed both to the Bolivian left and to the right-wing officers in the military.

State Enterprises

An examination of the government's role in the economy is incomplete without a discussion of the state enterprises. Since 1952 the export activities of the mining company, Corporación Minera de Bolívia (COMIBOL), and the petroleum company, Yacimientos Petrolíferos Fiscales Bolivianos (YPFB), have provided most of Bolivia's foreign exchange. This has given the two companies a privileged status that is frequently abused by both management and workers. To be fair, however, these crucial export companies have also suffered from the mismanagement of macroeconomic policy, especially from grossly overvalued exchange rates.

From 1962 to 1982 the largest state enterprises generated small surpluses on their current accounts, but these savings were too small to finance their capital expenditures. During the high inflation years of 1982–85, the current account deficits of the consolidated public sector became important for two reasons: the interest servicing of the large foreign debt and the growing employment (and the resultant wage bill) in the public sector.

If the public enterprises' investment record was dismal, their employment policies were little better until recently. Employment in the public enterprises grew at an annual rate of 4.6 percent between 1970 and 1982, a period of strong military presence in government.

The military typically tried to gain popular support through patronage. The return to democracy in 1982 did not reduce the rate of job growth in the most important public enterprises. Overstaffing and completely misaligned prices for the public sector were the main causes of the big deficits of virtually all state enterprises during the crisis years, 1982–85.

Government Financing

One striking fact about government financing in Bolivia is the narrowness of the tax base. Most taxes are related to the performance of the foreign sector: they are either export taxes, import tariffs, or "royalties" on petroleum and mineral products, which are largely exported. Thus, the volume of taxes collected is closely related to what happens in the vulnerable export sector (table 9-6 shows how dependent tax revenues are on foreign trade). Such a narrow tax base can result in punitive tax rates for the few taxpaying activities. Punitive taxation of the mining sector in the past and of the petroleum sector today has long-run costs.

The narrowness of the tax base and the extreme difficulties, political and other, associated with the need to finance growing claims for a more favorable income distribution partly explain the growth of the public sector. During 1952–85 the search for tax revenues became tantamount to a search for investment opportunities for the public sector. Successive governments hoped that they could use the profits generated by public sector investments to pay for more social programs and development projects. The easy access to foreign loans in the 1970s permitted the government to postpone the necessary reforms to broaden the tax base. Had tax reform been carried out in that period, Bolivia could have better withstood the 1982 shock of sudden severance from foreign credits.

Indebted Industrialization and Other Policies

Frieden (1981) defines indebted industrialization as the strategy of rapid growth takeoff based on foreign financing of large-scale public investment projects. (The strategy is similar to the state capitalism model.) For most of the period 1952 to 1985, Bolivian governments followed this strategy. The overall deficits of the consolidated public sector were financed with foreign savings, either aid or loans, and to a lesser extent by the forced savings produced by inflation. During the periods of great disruption, the latter form of financing predominated over the former.

The foreign financing of investments in state-owned enterprises started with the rehabilitation of the state-owned mining enterprise COMIBOL in the early 1960s. In the so-called Triangular Plan, the government obtained credits from the U.S. government, the Inter-American Development Bank, and a consortium of German banks. Two elements were significant in this deal: first, the heavy foreign financing of a state enterprise and, second, the use of an official U.S. loan for a nationalized enterprise. The Triangular Plan to rehabilitate COMIBOL set a precedent for continued use of foreign financing of investment in state-owned firms.

With the growth in world liquidity in the 1970s, the Bolivian government hoped that it could find development funds in the expanding international loan market. With access to large-scale loans from commercial banks, the process of indebted industrialization accelerated. In the second half of the 1970s the capacity of the tin smelters of the Empresa Nacional de Fundiciones (ENAF) was significantly expanded; mills were built by COMIBOL to concentrate low-grade ores as a precursor to the smelting process; a huge polymetallurgic mill was built in Karachipampa, in southern Bolivia; the oil refining installations of the state petroleum company YPFB were increased; and new factories were expanded or built to process agricultural products such as sugar, soya, and milk. Foreign financing made up a substantial proportion of these public investments.

In some cases, the government contracted debts with foreign commercial banks to compensate foreign companies nationalized in 1969 and 1971. It is quite ironic that once more, foreign savings contributed to the expansion of the public sector.

The tin smelting company ENAF and the polymetallurgic smelter Complejo Minero Karachipampa (CMK) exemplify the troubles of public investment financed with foreign indebtedness. The creation of ENAF responded to a long-held Bolivian wish to reduce the transportation costs and dependence on foreign oligopolistic smelting firms for its main export, tin. But of course domestic refining could only make economic sense if the savings in transport and foreign refining costs per unit were greater than the expenditure on domestic smelting per unit of final output. Unfortunately, because of technical problems, related in part to the low metal content of the ores and to poor design and management, smelting costs went well beyond expectations.

The CMK case is even sadder. The project was based on the assumption that a sufficient supply of ores would be available, which turned out not to be the case. An ex post analysis revealed that the strategy of pushing the creation of value added on known mineral deposits at the expense of investing in exploration and development of new mines was misguided.

Public debt also served to finance the undertakings of the private sector. The private sector borrowed heavily abroad, with guarantees by the government. Also, loans contracted directly by the government were intended for and channeled to the private sector. The loans intermediated by the government to the private sector often contained a high subsidy element, and, worse, many of them were never repaid. In addition, many foreign loans to the private sector that were guaranteed by the government went unpaid, and the debt was shifted to the guarantor. The diversion of loans obtained from the government (or guaranteed by the government) from their intended investment uses was common. Thus, we can assume that the foreign debt financed more consumption (and accumulation of assets abroad) than domestic capital formation. Consumption loans had to be repaid by a drop in consumption.

Table 9-7 traces the evolution of Bolivia's external debt, emphasizing the public external debt. By 1982 Bolivia had accumulated a large foreign debt, amounting to 71.2 percent of the GDP. The debt was mostly incurred by the public sector or by the private sector with public guarantees. Given the interest rates in the mid-1970s, a growth strategy based on access to foreign loans was not unreasonable. The problem was not indebtedness per se but, as mentioned earlier, the extremely inefficient use of those external resources. By 1980 Bolivia was already finding it hard to make principal repayments. The severe political problems of that time aggravated the situation. In 1982 the drastic reduction in foreign inflows precipitated a severe domestic crisis. On average, between 1982 and 1985 Bolivia transferred in net terms around 3.5 percent of its GDP to foreign creditors.

The overextension of the public sector in face of the growing financing difficulties once foreign inflows had dried up reached a climax during the crisis years of 1982–85. The appearance of hyperinflation in those years can largely be attributed to this fiscal crisis and the attendant debt problems.

Debt continued to accumulate rapidly, notwithstanding the lack of new commitments and disbursements. In other words, between 1982 and 1985, debt accumulated without new resource inflows; indeed, resource inflows were negative in net terms. The debt growth resulted from arrears and the need to resort to (involuntary) distress financing.

By the end of 1987, after a valiant struggle against inflation, Bolivia had started on the road to economic recovery. Today the country still faces formidable obstacles, however, such as the huge external debt. The overborrowing of the 1970s and, especially, the misuse of foreign credits are important causes of Bolivia's present difficulties.

Table 9-7. External Debt, Bolivia, Selected Years, 1962–86

Debt	1962	1971	1978	1982	1985	1986[a]
Total external debt	—	—	—	3,169.0	4,143.2	4,619.1
Long-term debt (millions of dollars)	—	534.2	1,671.9	2,897.9	3,744.9	4,077.6
Public and publicly guaranteed debt (millions of dollars)	174.0	527.0	1,649.0	2,769.1	3,189.9	3,522.6
Private nonguaranteed debt (millions of dollars)	—	7.2	22.9	128.8	555.0	555.0
Short-term debt (millions of dollars)	—	—	91.5	185.0	347.0	397.0
Public external debt[b] (percentage of GDP)	35.5	42.8	43.7	71.2	109.6	122.2
Public external debt[b] (percentage of exports)	251.0	260.5	233.6	301.5	432.6	516.1
Public external debt service[b]	19.1	31.0	355.0	287.1	242.1	160.8
Interest payments (millions of dollars)	5.5	9.0	84.0	181.0	100.0	86.7
Principal repayments (millions of dollars)	13.6	22.0	271.0	106.1	142.1	74.1
Total debt service (as percentage of exports)[c]	27.6	11.9	49.6	31.3	32.8	23.6
Total debt service (as percentage of GDP)	3.9	2.5	9.4	7.4	6.4	4.3
Memorandum items						
Net resource transfers of public sector (millions of dollars)	—	65.0	17.0	−92.7	−131.9	138.4
Net resource transfers of public sector (as percentage of GDP)	—	5.3	0.5	−2.4	−3.5	3.7
Gross domestic product (GDP; millions of current dollars)[d]	490.2	1,232.5	3,777.2	3,890.7	3,781.5	3,779.5

— Not available.
a. Preliminary.
b. Public and publicly guaranteed debt.
c. Goods and services.
d. Derived from GDP values in current Bolivian pesos divided by a purchasing power parity (PPP) exchange rate.
Source: Inter-American Development Bank (1983) for 1960–78; World Bank (1987) for 1982–86.

Export Policies

Until 1982 the most important and systematic export policy was Bolivia's adherence to the international tin agreements (ITAs). During 1965–80, Bolivia also signed agreements for tungsten and antimony.

Bolivia participated in all the ITAs except the last one signed in 1982, because the government thought that it could ride on the back of the agreement without actually signing it—that is, that it could benefit from the above-equilibrium prices without incurring the costs, just as Brazil was doing.[2]

As a high-cost producer, Bolivia systematically lobbied for a joint policy of high intervention prices. The other countries did not always follow Bolivia's demands for higher prices, because they feared that the upkeep of the buffer stock, the main instrument of price stabilization, would be too costly. More important, they feared that a long-run policy of above-equilibrium prices would backfire. Time proved them right. In the 1970s, in addition to the policy of price support through the ITAs, Bolivia systematically lobbied in the United States to forestall the tin sales of the General Services Administration.

Despite the producers' efforts, the tin market collapsed when the London Metal Exchange ceased its tin operations (see table 9-8 and figure 9-2). Note that although tin prices (in real terms) fluctuated strongly between 1950 and 1987, the trend was upward until 1980. In that year a process of steady decline started that continued until 1985, when the price of tin took a nosedive.

The production and export of tin and other minerals were severely affected by punitive taxes in the 1970s, by the exchange rate policy, and by the decline of the Bolivian tin industry. Few major mines had been opened since the Depression, and the metal content of the ores of the old mines had been decreasing. By 1980 Bolivia had lost its place as a major world tin supplier.

Policies on the other significant Bolivian export, natural gas, were less clear-cut. In 1972 Bolivia signed a twenty-year treaty with Argentina for the sale of natural gas. The natural gas deal included provisions on the quantities to be sold and a fixed price, with rather vague clauses on the procedures for readjustments. Shortly after the treaty was signed, the first oil shock occurred and world energy prices skyrocketed. Bolivia's natural gas exports did not benefit from this increase for quite some time. Until 1980 price increases for natural gas trailed those for petroleum (see figure 9-3).

Only after the second oil shock of 1979 did Bolivia and Argentina agree on important revisions of the unit price of natural gas. After this second shock, natural gas prices have either increased more rapidly or decreased more slowly than petroleum prices. The natural gas nego-

Table 9-8. International Prices of Tin and Natural Gas, Indexes, 1952–87
(1980 = 100)

	Tin		Natural gas	
Year	*In current prices*[a]	*In 1980 prices*[b]	*In current prices*	*In 1980 prices*[b,c]
1952	15.8	58.0	—	—
1953	12.0	45.1	—	—
1954	11.8	45.4	—	—
1955	12.2	46.0	—	—
1956	12.9	47.2	—	—
1957	12.4	44.3	—	—
1958	12.1	42.4	—	—
1959	12.9	45.9	—	—
1960	13.1	45.6	—	—
1961	14.6	50.0	—	—
1962	14.7	49.6	—	—
1963	14.9	51.2	—	—
1964	20.3	68.2	—	—
1965	23.2	77.4	—	—
1966	21.3	68.5	—	—
1967	19.9	63.2	—	—
1968	18.6	59.7	—	—
1969	20.4	62.3	—	—
1970	21.9	62.7	—	—
1971	20.9	56.7	—	—
1972	22.5	56.2	—	—
1973	28.8	62.0	10.6	22.9
1974	48.9	86.5	17.4	30.9
1975	41.0	65.2	25.2	40.1
1976	45.2	71.0	32.3	50.7
1977	64.2	91.6	37.6	53.8
1978	76.9	95.6	45.8	57.0
1979	92.1	101.0	56.2	61.6
1980	100.0	100.0	100.0	100.0
1981	84.4	84.0	141.6	141.6
1982	76.5	78.3	153.4	157.2
1983	77.4	80.3	156.8	162.7
1984	73.2	77.3	136.7	144.4
1985[d]	69.0	73.9	147.1[c]	154.0
1986[d]	38.8	34.3	128.1[c]	113.2
1987[d,e]	41.7	33.1	108.0[c]	85.7

— Not available.

a. Standard, minimum 99.75 percent, settlement price.

b. Current prices deflated by the World Bank Manufacturing Value Added Index.

c. Price adjusted to the austral real exchange rate to take into account Argentine payments in goods and services.

d. Preliminary estimates.

e. June 1987.

Source: World Bank (1986); Central Bank of Bolivia (1987); IMF (1987).

Figure 9-2. Real World Price of Tin, 1950–87

(1980 = 100)

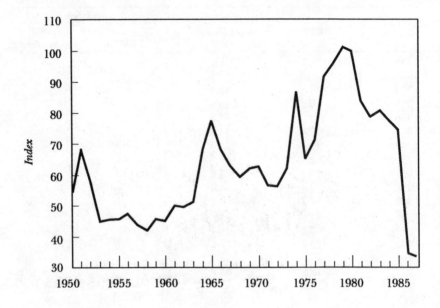

Source: Central Bank of Bolivia (various issues).

tiations in the 1980s were extremely difficult because Argentina had itself found important deposits of this resource, which it had not fully exploited because of its agreement with Bolivia.

The steady fall in energy prices since 1982 has aggravated the problem. Bolivian export volumes and prices have fallen. Moreover, between 1983 and the last quarter of 1987, Argentina made only 40 percent of its payments in dollars, the rest being paid in Argentine goods and services. Because of the frequent overvaluations of the Argentine peso and the austral, the effective price Bolivia received from its natural gas sales to Argentina was substantially smaller than the price indicated by the dollar value. In addition, the frequent delays in the Argentine payments in the 1980s caused liquidity crunches, which had strong repercussions in the domestic economy. In 1974 a far-reaching agreement for sales of natural gas to Brazil was signed, but internal opposition in Bolivia killed the deal.

The promotion of nontraditional exports came relatively late, in 1977. Generous incentives were provided: in addition to tax rebates, there were subsidies at varying rates depending on "embodied value

Figure 9-3. Real World Prices of Natural Gas and Petroleum, 1973–87

(1980 = 100)

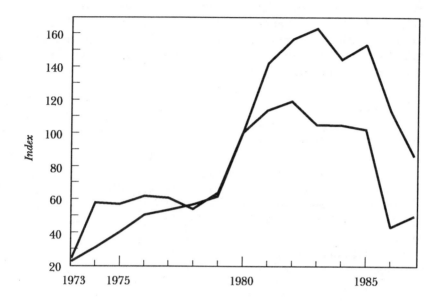

Source: Central Bank of Bolivia (various issues).

added." The concept of embodied value added, used to determine the base for export subsidies, included labor and capital services, as well as all domestic inputs. The base for the benefits was clearly incorrect, discriminated heavily against traditional exports, and was a source of corruption. For instance, Bolivian gold jewelry was priced internationally entirely for its gold content and not for its artistic features, yet it benefited from the highest subsidy. The law promoting nontraditional exports was reformed in 1982, widening the benefits. With the policy reforms of August 1985, which we will discuss later, the varying rates of subsidy (or, more appropriately, tax rebates) were simplified to two rates: 10 percent for nontraditional exports and 5 percent for traditional exports.

In 1966 Bolivia joined the Latin American Free Trade Association, which later became the Latin American Integration Association, and in 1969 it joined the Andean Group. The aim was to promote manufactured exports and, to a lesser extent, agricultural exports. Bolivia's participation in both agreements has been modest despite the government's considerable expectations when it signed the agreements. The scant benefits are mainly explained by Bolivia's initial conditions of extreme industrial underdevelopment and by the uneven quality of the economic policies followed in Bolivia and in the partner countries. Although movements to freer trade may have benefited the country, Bolivia was completely unprepared to follow the joint industrial programming that was the goal of the Andean Group and to adopt a high common external tariff.

Import Policies

Like its export policies, Bolivia's import policies did not have well-defined economic purposes, at least until the policy reforms of August 1985. Domestic industry was protected from competitive imports by import tariffs, quantitative restrictions, and credit subsidies.

The tariff structure had a number of objectives. It was intended to provide fiscal revenues, to substitute for devaluations in the face of transitory balance of payments difficulties, and to provide protection. Tariffs varied depending on whether the items were finished products, intermediate inputs, or capital goods (see table 9-9). The rates on finished goods (especially luxury goods) were frequently determined more by fiscal revenue considerations than by protection, although ultimately this created unintended protection for the domestic production of luxury goods. Many domestic industries were also protected until 1985 by quantitative restrictions on competitive imports, especially by bans. Quotas and import licensing were rarely used.

Both high tariffs and bans were difficult to enforce in practice, given the length of the Bolivian borders, which are sparsely populated, and the extreme administrative weakness of the government. Bolivia's geographical features made control of smuggling difficult.

The import-substituting industries often benefited from two additional forms of subsidy: first, the availability of credit at concessional interest rates, which were negative in real terms on occasion, and, second, preferential government purchases. The effective rate of subsidy was probably very high.

The question then arises as to why Bolivia made so little progress in developing a manufacturing base, especially when compared with other countries of similar market size that fared substantially better. There are three tentative answers to this puzzle:

- The prolonged periods of overvaluation of the Bolivian peso reduced the net effective subsidy rate significantly.
- Macroeconomic and political uncertainty reduced long-term investment. Industrialists were more interested in generating the

Table 9-9. Effective Rates of Protection Yielded by Tariffs, Bolivia about 1982

(percent)

Item	Tariff on intermediate goods[a]	Tariff on finished goods	Effective rate of protection
Products			
Agricultural products	2.0	28.1	31.9
Livestock products	0.0	0.0	−1.2
Forestry products, game, fish	25.8	17.5	17.5
Processed meats	8.3	8.3	80.4
Dairy products	2.0	2.8	2.1
Mills and bakeries	10.0	17.5	65.0
Sugar and sugar products	26.3	41.7	114.5
Other foodstuffs	13.4	19.9	40.0
Beverages	13.3	60.2	88.4
Tobacco[b]	17.6	100.0	195.7
Textiles, clothing, leather, and leather products	38.7	72.2	169.1
Wood and wood products	35.4	62.1	145.8
Paper and paper products	10.8	35.0	76.0
Chemicals	11.7	37.2	64.8
Stone, earth, clay products	16.9	45.6	56.1
Metallic products, machinery and equipment	19.0	45.7	57.4
Others	29.9	43.3	49.9
Other inputs			
Crude petroleum and natural gas	4.0	n.a.	n.a.
Metallic and nonmetallic minerals	11.9	n.a.	n.a.
Petroleum products	4.5	n.a.	n.a.
Basic metals	12.6	n.a.	n.a.
Summary measures[c]			
Weighted mean for all sectors		27.6	44.4
Standard deviation for all sectors		20.1	43.9
Variation coefficient for all sectors		72.7	99.1
Weighted mean for manufacturing sector		47.7	94.1
Standard deviation for manufacturing sector		19.6	44.5
Variation coefficient for manufacturing sector		41.1	47.3

n.a. Not applicable.

a. Intermediate goods imported into the sector.

b. Quantitative restrictions applied in this sector, hence equivalent tariffs have been computed.

c. Weighted by value added at international prices.

Source: National Chamber of Industry (1987).

fast, above-normal profits that the protection structure permitted than in making long-term investments. They seldom reinvested their high profits, because they feared political turmoil and possibly expropriatory measures. The best example of the costs imposed by uncertainty appeared during the hyperinflation years, when, despite the high effective rates of subsidy resulting from such factors as negative real interest rates and foreign exchange controls, investment in the industrial sector was almost nil. Manufacturing value added actually declined a staggering 36 percentage points between 1981 and 1985.

- Excessive protection, especially during the 1970s, may have had high long-run efficiency costs.

Exchange Rate Policies

After the high inflation of the 1950s and until the 1980s, Bolivia maintained a policy of fixed exchange rates. The government's fiscal policies were expansionary, but as long as the fiscal deficits could be financed by borrowing abroad, they had no effect on the exchange rate. Throughout most of the period, the parallel market premiums were very low.[3] One of the main tenets of economic policy was indeed exchange rate stability, and the peso was devalued only twice between 1957 and 1981. Prompted by the debt crisis of 1982, the peso went into free fall until the August 1985 stabilization program.

An overvalued peso has been a permanent feature of Bolivia's economy for the last thirty years. Mild overvaluation hampered the country's export potential in the agricultural and manufacturing sectors more than in the traditional exports, which benefited from high international prices during most of the 1960s and 1970s. The severe overvaluation of the official exchange rate greatly harmed legal exports between 1982 and 1985 by reducing the profitability of the enterprises that produced them. Contraband exports, however, benefited from the favorable parallel market exchange rate and flourished.[4]

Although the evidence supports the notion that overvaluation was present during most of the 1960s and 1970s, the extent of the overvaluation is difficult to assess. The noticeable improvement in the terms of trade from 1960 to 1980 hampers the computation of what should have been the right exchange rate. The real exchange rates shown in table 9-10 indicate what happened, but the numbers are rough and other experts may disagree with the methodology used. Export prices and real exchange rates show a strong negative correlation. The sudden and relatively long-lasting jump in export prices in the 1970s allowed the exchange rate to diverge from the higher long-run value needed for sustained development.

Table 9-10. Real Exchange Rate, Bolivia, 1960–69

(1980 = 100)

Year	Real exchange rate	Year	Real exchange rate	Year	Real exchange rate
1960	171.1	1970	110.5	1980	100.0
1961	155.1	1971	114.2	1981	82.6
1962	142.4	1972	120.1	1982	98.6
1963	142.0	1973	157.3	1983	95.3
1964	131.4	1974	115.7	1984	66.9
1965	134.0	1975	115.4	1985	114.0
1966	128.5	1976	115.7	1986	128.0
1967	112.7	1977	115.6	1987[a]	123.5
1968	108.7	1978	111.4		
1969	112.9	1979	107.2		

Note: Official exchange rates deflated by the ratio of Bolivian consumer prices to U.S. wholesale prices and coverted to index. Exchange ratios and price indexes are annual averages.

a. Preliminary estimate.

Source: IMF (1987), Central Bank of Bolivia (various issues).

More important than a precise computation of real exchange rates is the political economy problem of why no lobby of exporters and other interested groups appeared to push for exchange rate correction. Indeed, the lobbying by tin producers was essentially aimed at decreasing the tax burden on their output and, eventually, on their export sales. They sought to increase their effective exchange rate through reduced taxation rather than devaluation. The other main exporter, the state-owned petroleum company YPFB, made significant profits on its exports of petroleum and natural gas, even during the worst years of overvaluation in the 1980s; therefore, it never lobbied for devaluation. A better strategy for the period would probably have been a more activist exchange rate policy, such as that followed by Indonesia, a country also dependent on resource-based exports.

On the import side, overvaluation was reflected in the relatively high tariffs and the extent of quantitative restrictions. Between 1978 and 1982, except in 1980 when a favorable terms of trade shock occurred, the high tariffs and quantitative restrictions were insufficient to restrain imports and prevent deterioration of the current account of the balance of payments. Trade deficits were financed with increased foreign indebtedness and from foreign exchange reserves.

Overvaluation was also a factor in the huge volume of capital flight between 1976 and 1982. The public's perception that the exchange rate was below equilibrium prompted people to change their pesos into dollars and to deposit their dollar assets abroad. Capital flight accelerated during the military governments of 1980–82 (Ugarteche

1986). With increased awareness of the difficulties Bolivia would face in obtaining new loans and servicing its old loans, speculators and the public increased their assets abroad. The main risks they were hedging against were future peso depreciation and limits on peso convertibility. The continuing capital flight between 1982 and 1985 was almost entirely the result of political uncertainty and macroeconomic instability.

Between 1983 and 1985 exchange rate controls restrained imports more effectively and limited the losses in reserves. The internal costs of the exchange rate controls, however, were huge in terms of efficiency in production and, especially, in the fight against inflation.[5] With the high black market premiums for foreign exchange prevalent at the time, legal exporters often felt penalized, viewing the premium as a tax on their profits. As a consequence, their strategy was frequently aimed at minimizing the burden of this tax. For example, the mining enterprises would accumulate stocks of their output and sell them when the premium was lower. They could finance retention of large stocks because of their access to highly subsidized domestic credit. Less scrupulous exporters would sell abroad and circumvent the exchange rate regulations entirely.

Foreign exchange users in, for example, the manufacturing sector viewed the black market premium as a tax on their inputs and pressed for more access to the already scarce official foreign exchange reserves. Complaints in the press about not having enough foreign exchange to pay for imported inputs were frequent, but although complainants did not have access to all the foreign exchange that they wanted at the official rate, the parallel market could always meet their demands. On the output end, with few exceptions, manufacturers priced their products in dollars, although payable in domestic currency at the black market rate of exchange. Their complaints on the scarcity of foreign exchange at the official exchange rate were actually pleas for more subsidies. Producers' uncertainty about whether foreign exchange would be available at the official rate to purchase imported inputs was one of the main factors reducing production.

In the high-inflation period of 1982–85, exchange rate management was indeed one of the government's most difficult tasks. Because of incomplete, or on some occasions defective, fiscal and monetary policies, the government had to face virtually unsolvable dilemmas. On the one hand, rapid depreciation of the official exchange rate would have increased the inflation rate even more and raised the burden of the foreign debt, as indeed happened. On the other hand, trying to repress inflation with the exchange rate was costly and ultimately ineffective, because black market premiums surged, eventually leading to the needed official exchange rate corrections and to more inflation.

Moreover, the policy of exchange controls led to a high degree of corruption.

The Policy Reforms of August 1985

In August 1985 the newly elected government of Víctor Paz-Estenssoro unveiled a package of extensive policy reforms. The package had two main components that proceeded simultaneously: a stabilization program and a trade liberalization program. The package was followed by a string of other measures collectively known as the New Economic Policy. Liberalization was intended to reinforce stabilization by providing a natural check on domestic price increases, the initial situation being one of disequilibrium in many markets. Liberalization without first achieving stabilization would have probably been impossible, given the pressures on the current account of the balance of payments (see Sachs 1987a for a similar argument).

The core of the stabilization package was a policy of stable and unified exchange rates supported by tight fiscal and monetary policies (see Sachs 1986, 1987a, 1987b; Morales 1987a, 1987b; Morales and Sachs 1987 for a description of the stabilization program and its achievements, and table 9-11 for a summary of the policy reforms). The August 1985 program and subsequent measures complemented exchange rate unification with other far-reaching liberalization measures. All quantitative restrictions on exports and imports were abolished except for those related to imports of sugar.[6] In addition, import tariffs were lowered to a uniform rate of 20 percent except for imports by the petroleum enterprises and imports covered under standing economic integration agreements.

The liberalization of international trade was accompanied by liberalization of domestic markets. Price ceilings have been eliminated in most markets; only petroleum derivatives and a handful of public utilities, most of them state-owned, have regulated prices.

The liberalization of the labor market may be especially relevant to development of the external sector. Job security clauses have been softened, making dismissal of workers easier; wage indexing has been suppressed; and collective bargaining with arbitration by the Ministry of Labor has been greatly weakened, leaving most wages, at least in the private sector, to be set by individual negotiations. The combination of the policy reforms and the collapse of export markets has caused the main export enterprises in both the public and the private sectors to lay off a significant number of employees.

Liberalization of the current account of the balance of payments has proceeded simultaneously with the liberalization of the capital account. No restrictions are imposed on capital inflows and outflows.

Table 9-11. Summary of Main Policy Reforms, Bolivia

Exchange rates	Unified floating exchange rates. Rates determined by auction. Exporters obliged to surrender 100 percent of export proceeds to the central bank.
Foreign trade	All quantitative restrictions on exports and imports lifted. Uniform import tariff rate of 20 percent.
Foreign capital	All restrictions on foreign capital inflows and outflows eliminated. Normalization of relations with multilateral official creditors. Negotiations in Paris Club. Negotiations under way to buy back debt owed to foreign commercial banks with discounts given by secondary market.
Domestic market for goods and services	Price controls eliminated in almost all markets. Price for gasoline and other oil derivatives fixed by government at border prices. Most public utility rates and urban transportation fares fixed by local governments after negotiations with concerned parties. Only a handful of public utility rates set by the central government.
Domestic financial markets	Interest rate ceilings eliminated. Bolivian residents freely allowed to open deposits in foreign currencies in the domestic banking system. All contracts in foreign currencies among residents authorized. Development loans channeled through private banks. Requirements on capital-debt ratios for private banks increased and more ex post supervision of banks portfolio enforced.
Labor market	Job protection clauses in legislation reduced in scope and the principle of marginal market adjustments stated. Wage indexation eliminated.
Fiscal reform	Tax reform enacted with value added tax and wealth taxes as main taxes.
Reorganization of state enterprises	Several mines of state-owned mining enterprise COMIBOL closed and several thousand miners dismissed. Worker dismissals envisaged in the state-owned petroleum company YPFB.
Decentralization	Enterprises of state-owned holding Corporación Boliviana de Fomento ceded to regional development corporations. Assets of the National Transport Company transferred to municipalities.

In addition, the domestic capital market has been completely liberalized by eliminating interest rate ceilings and floors and by permitting the public to open dollar and dollar-indexed demand and time deposit accounts in Bolivian banks. The result is that interest rates have soared, leading Bolivians to repatriate a significant amount of capital—$350 million (or about 8 percent of GDP) in two years. Most of the capital, however, has gone into dollar or dollar-indexed time deposits with very short maturities (thirty to sixty days).

The August 1985 program also called for divestment of certain state-owned enterprises. As a first step toward privatization, the enterprises of the state-owned holding company the Corporación Boliviana de Fomento and a small state-owned public transportation company have been transferred to the regional development corporations and the municipalities. Some other small state-owned enterprises have been dissolved.

It is much too early to give a complete assessment of the accomplishments of the policy reforms. Inflation was rapidly stabilized, however, and in 1987 the country obtained a positive growth rate for the first time in six years. Normalization with official creditors, multilateral and bilateral, has also been achieved, implying significative debt relief and the granting of new loans.

In the first two years after the policy reforms, consumer imports expanded and the current account deficit of the balance of payments rose in both absolute terms and as a percentage of GDP. This growth in imports may, however, be a transitory phenomenon experienced after a process of rapid liberalization.

The reforms have eliminated most policy-induced, anti-export biases, but obstacles of a more structural character remain, including currency overvaluation. The temptation to hold down inflation with overvaluation is a persistent danger (see Dornbusch 1986 for a discussion of this problem in several Latin American countries). Overvaluation is not yet severe, but it is steadily increasing. Also, interest rates are too high and will have to decrease for long-term productive investment to take place. Appropriate disbursement of the foreign loans that Bolivia has contracted may help lower interest rates.

Bolivia must reconstruct its external sector entirely. The collapse of markets for Bolivia's traditional exports (tin and natural gas) and the poor price prospects for most basic commodities that Bolivia could reasonably export in the near future make the situation challenging. In addition, the external debt burden continues to hinge on the country's recovery and growth prospects, compounding the problem of weak markets for exports.

The policy reforms are a step toward recovering previous export levels, but they are insufficient. The structural obstacles to reconstruction of the external sector and achievement of export diversification are indeed formidable. If agricultural exports, including soya and other grains, are to take the place of tin and natural gas, unit transportation costs will have to be lower than current levels. Well-designed investments in the transport infrastructure are a precondition for the resource shifts needed to rehabilitate the export sector. Investment in training workers and managers is also needed, given that the technological content of exports, both agricultural and light manufacturing, is increasing.

Finally, political stability is essential to Bolivia's development, especially for its foreign trade sector. To attract foreign investment, Bolivia must provide not only legal guarantees against expropriation and punitive taxation but also a good social and political environment. In turn, durable political stability will be achieved only if the government finds ways to close the wide gaps in the distribution of income and wealth. This may prove to be a difficult task in view of its current fiscal constraints.

Conclusion

During the last thirty-five years Bolivia has endured two periods of great economic distress, with substantial decreases in the GDP and investment rates and with very high inflation. The first economic crisis occurred in the 1950s during a period of profound social transformation. The second crisis, in the 1980s, followed a long period of sustained growth accompanied by an accumulation of major development problems. It was triggered by an interplay of external shocks and domestic factors. One of the most important internal factors was overborrowing abroad, which was caused by a public sector that was too large, a pattern of resource-based industrialization, and a misuse of investment funds.

Bolivia's development hinges on the performance of its foreign sector. Export earnings that depend on only a handful of basic products are subject to wide fluctuations. For example, more than 50 percent of export proceeds depend on natural gas sales to Argentina.

The jump in export prices and the easy access to foreign debt in the 1970s allowed a substantial discrepancy between the short-run value of the exchange rate and the long-run value needed for sustained growth. The lasting overvaluation impeded the development of a more diversified export basket and a production structure better able to withstand external shocks.

The public sector has had an important role in Bolivia's development as well as its problems. The extraordinary incursion of the public sector in investment is principally explained by the government's

inability to achieve broad taxation in the face of an ambitious redis-
tributive agenda and the continuous reassessment of development
goals. The search for new tax sources became tantamount to the search
for new public investment opportunities. Taxation of a few natural
resources is easier to implement than taxation on a broad base, and
one of the main problems in Bolivia's development has been overtaxa-
tion of the natural resource sector. The state enterprises are also overburdened with their role as the main providers of foreign exchange. In
this role they have been frequent victims of misguided macroeconomic policies that tried to subsidize consumption via the
exchange rate.

The public sector was overextended and weak at the same time. A
good example of the state's weakness is given by the regulations on
foreign trade, many of which stayed on the books and could not be
enforced. For example, high import tariffs were difficult to collect and
only gave rise to more contraband. A similar comment can be made
about the former regime of exchange rate controls. The Bolivian experience clearly shows that a weak state cannot support a heavy burden
of regulations. Most people simply ignore them and, what is worse, the
state and the few who abide by them suffer.

The political instability of some periods took a heavy toll on the
economy. On several occasions, instability impeded timely recognition
of the shocks affecting the economy and thus delayed needed action.
The uncertainty that went with political and macroeconomic instability also imposed heavy costs in terms of production and welfare.
With a high degree of uncertainty, no system of incentives can work
well, and speculation thrives at the expense of productive, long-run
investments.

The policy reforms introduced in August 1985 are promising. The
most immediate and visible outcomes have been the taming of inflation and the introduction of order in the fiscal budget. In the medium
term following the reforms, the results on economic growth are less
encouraging than the results on inflation. But there are already signs
of productivity growth and improvement in resource allocation, which
it is hoped will lead to sustained economic development. Furthermore, the reforms should help in achieving an economy that is more
diversified and open to foreign trade. The problem now is to persist in
the reforms in face of severe obstacles and an increasing impatience in
the public with the still-modest benefits in economic growth.

Notes

1. The attempt at stabilization made by the civilian interim president Lydia
Gueiler stands out as an exception in this chaotic period.

2. The ITAS were agreed on by the main producer and consumer countries, with some important exceptions. The main but not the only instrument for achieving price stabilization was a buffer stock of tin metal. Interventions by the International Tin Council (the governing body of the ITAS), with its buffer stock, and sometimes with the setting of production quotas, helped to achieve producers' price objectives until the third quarter of 1985. After 1981 the ITC sustained prices that were well above long-run market equilibrium prices.

3. The exchange rate was de facto pegged to the dollar during the whole period 1957–82, although some statutory provisions allowed for the possibility of floating and for the rate being fixed in terms of gold.

4. The rapid depreciation of the peso in the parallel market during the period of high inflation led to exports of the most unlikely goods, even of highly perishable goods such as bread, or of those with high transport costs, such as bottled soft drinks. Even tin ores were smuggled out to Peru, which started to appear in the official statistics as a tin producer.

5. The public's belief in the corruption of those persons who either administered the allocation of the rationed foreign exchange or had access to it seems to have been a more important factor than the corruption itself in discrediting the system of controls.

6. Sugar quotas violate the general spirit of the liberalization measures, but given the highly manipulated nature of the international sugar market, Bolivia's regulation of sugar imports has to be viewed as an antidumping measure.

Selected Bibliography

Afcha, Gonzalo, and Gualberto Huarachi. 1988. *El programa económico boliviano: La nueva política económica.* La Paz: Unidad de Análisis de Políticas Económicas.

Bolivia, Ministry of Planning. 1970. *Revista de Planificación.* La Paz.

Central Bank of Bolivia. 1987. *Statistical Bulletin 259.* La Paz.

———. Various issues. *Statistical Bulletin.* La Paz.

CEPAL (United Nations Economic Commission for Latin America). Various years. *Statistical Yearbook for Latin America and the Caribbean.* 1964–85 eds. New York.

———. 1987. *Balance preliminar de la economía.* Santiago, Chile.

Dornbusch, Rudiger. 1986. *Inflation, Exchange Rates, and Stabilization.* Essays in International Finance 165. Princeton, N.J.: Princeton University.

Frieden, Jeffrey A. 1981. "Third World Indebted Industrialization." *International Organization* 35(3):407–31.

IMF (International Monetary Fund). 1986. *Government Finance Statistics.* Vol. 10. Washington, D.C.

———. 1987. *International Financial Statistics Yearbook.* Washington, D.C.

Inter-American Development Bank. 1983. *Economic and Social Progress in Latin America.* Washington, D.C.

Malloy, James. 1970. *Bolivia: The Uncompleted Revolution.* Pittsburgh, Pa.: University of Pittsburgh Press.

Morales, Juan-Antonio. 1982. "The Bolivian External Sector after 1964." In Jerry R. Ladman, ed., *Modern Day Bolivia: Legacy of the Revolution and Prospects for the Future.* Tempe, Ariz.: Arizona State University, Center for Latin American Studies.

————. 1987a. *Precios, salarios y política económica durante la alta inflación boliviana de 1982 a 1985.* La Paz: Instituto Latinoamericano de Investigaciones Sociales.

————. 1987b. *Inflation Stabilization in Bolivia.* Documento de Trabajo 06/87. La Paz: Universidad Católica Boliviana.

————. 1987c. "Estabilización y nueva política económica en Bolivia." *El Trimestre Económico* Special Number (September):179–212.

————. 1988. "Adjustment and Growth in Hyperinflation: The Case of Bolivia." Universidad Católica Boliviana, Department of Economics, La Paz.

Morales, Juan-Antonio, and Jeffrey Sachs. 1987. "The Economic Crisis in Bolivia." National Bureau of Economic Research, La Paz.

National Chamber of Industry. 1987. *Estudio integral del arancel de importaciones.* La Paz.

Ram, Rati. 1987. "Exports and Economic Growth in Developing Countries: Evidence from Time-Series and Cross-Section Data." *Economic Development and Cultural Change* 36(1):51–72.

Sachs, Jeffrey. 1986. "The Bolivian Hyperinflation and Stabilization." Working Paper Series 2073. National Bureau of Economic Research, Cambridge, Mass.

————. 1987a. "International Policy Coordination: The Case of the Developing Country Debt Crisis." Working Paper Series 2287. National Bureau of Economic Research, Cambridge, Mass.

————. 1987b. "The Bolivian Hyperinflation and Stabilization." *American Economic Review, Papers and Proceedings* (May):279–83.

UDAPE (Unidad de Análisis de Política Económica). 1987. *Dossier de información estadística 1980–1987.* La Paz, October.

Ugarteche, Oscar. 1986. *El estado deudor. Economía política de la deuda: Perú y Bolivia 1968–1984.* Lima: Instituto de Estudios Peruanos.

World Bank. 1983. "Bolivia. Structural Constraints and Development Prospects." Report 4194–BO. World Bank, Washington, D.C.

————. 1986. "Commodity Trade and Price Trends." Commodities and Export Projections Department, Development Policy Staff, Washington, D.C.

————. 1987. "Commodity Trade and Price Trends." Commodities and Export Projections Department, Development Policy Staff, Washington, D.C.

————. 1988. *World Debt Tables: External Debt of Developing Countries.* 1987–88 ed. Washington, D.C.

Index